Levinas and Lacan

SUNY Series in Psychoanalysis and Culture
Henry Sussman, Editor

Levinas and Lacan

The Missed Encounter

Sarah Harasym,
Editor

State University of New York Press

Published by
State University of New York Press, Albany

For information, address State University of New York
Press, State University Plaza, Albany, N.Y., 12246

Production by E. Moore
Marketing by Patrick Durocher

Library of Congress Cataloging-in-Publication Data

Levinas and Lacan : the missed encounter / edited by Sarah Harasym.
        p.   cm. — (SUNY series in psychoanalysis and culture)
    Includes bibliographical references and index.
    ISBN 0-7914-3959-3 (alk. paper). — ISBN 0-7914-3960-7
(pbk. : alk. paper)
        1. Lévinas, Emmanuel. 2. Lacan, Jacques, 1901–
3. Psychoanalysis and philosophy—France. I. Harasym, Sarah, 1955–
. II. Series.
B2430.L484L483 1998
194—dc21   97-48472
                                                                        CIP

10 9 8 7 6 5 4 3 2 1

Contents

Acknowledgments

We gratefully acknowledge the kind permission from the following journals, publishers, and authors to reprint, and in some cases translate, the works cited and included in this volume.

To Albin Michel, for permission to translate and reprint Paul-Laurent Assoun's article "Le sujet et l'autre chez Levinas et Lacan," copyright 1996 by Albin Michel. This article first appeared in *Rue Descartes* 7 (1993), pages 123–45.

To Kluwer Academic Publishers, for permission to reprint the following article by Rudi Visker, copyright 1996 by Kluwer Academic Publishers. Reprinted by permission of Kluwer Academic Publishers: Rudi Visker, "Dispossessed: How to Remain Silent 'after' Levinas," *Man and World* 29/2 (1996), pages 119–46. We also would like to thank the editors of *Tijdschrift Voor Filosofie* for permission to print the English version of this essay, "De onteigening. Hoe to zwijgen na Levinas," which initially appeared in *Tijdschrift Voor Filosofie* (Leuven) 57 (1995), pages 631–66.

To Presses Universitaires de France, for permission to translate and reprint Alain Juranville's article, "L'ethique avec la psychanalyse," which originally appeared in *Corps Écrit* 19 (1986), pages 97–111.

To Drucilla Cornell, for permission to edit and print her article "Rethinking the Beyond of the Real." Copyright 1998 by Drucilla Cornell.

As editor, I also would like to acknowledge my indebtedness and gratitude to the authors and translators who have contributed to this collection. I especially wish to thank Denise Merkle and Hans-Dieter Gondek for their continued assistance and support, as well as Laura Thomas.

Introduction

Sarah Harasym

Levinas and Lacan: two proper names that signify two sets of texts, two logics of alterity, two theories of language and subjectivity, two fundamentally different bodies of thought. Ethics and psychoanalysis: two terms that name what historically have been taken as clashing, even mutually exclusive, standpoints. Is a rapprochement between ethics and psychoanalysis possible? If so, on what grounds?

Of course, Levinas's and Lacan's conceptualizations of ethics and psychoanalysis, respectively, differ considerably from traditional ethics and traditional psychoanalysis. Levinas's ethics is an ethics of an inescapable responsibility for the Other that places the human being in a face-to-face position with the Other because of his or her humanity but, also, because of his or her relation to God. Lacan's reworking of Freudian psychoanalysis attempts to establish the epistemological conditions of the science of psychoanalysis. He conceptualizes the structure of desire and reformulates the problem of law and ethics in psychoanalytic theory. Both Lacan and Levinas address the heteronomy of the law and the ethical implications of what has come to be known as the decentered subject. Do these conditions not hint perhaps at possible connections between Lacan and Levinas?

The primary intent of this collection is to begin the task of thinking through what have been up until the writing of these essays anticipated connections and encounters between Levinas and Lacan. I offer next a brief synopsis of the papers contained in the collection to guide the reader through his or her reading.

In seeking to locate a point of orientation for a consideration of Levinas and Lacan, one inevitably encounters the legacy of Hegel. How the influence of Hegel is played out in Levinas's rethinking of the ethical relation and in Lacan's reworking of Freud's thought is the question Tina Chanter addresses in the opening essay of this collection, "Reading Hegel as a Mediating Master: Lacan and Levinas." As Chanter suggests, Hegel's philosophy plays a singularly particular role both for Levinas and Lacan. He is arguably the most profound source for both of them; yet, at the same time, he bears their most potent polemics. Although the central concern of Chanter's paper is to gauge Hegel's role in Levinas's concepts of desire, infinity, and subjectivity and in Lacan's concepts of a decentered subject of the unconscious and in his conceptualization of the imaginary and symbolic orders, Chanter begins by turning back to an examination of the role Descartes plays for both. We discover that Levinas's unpredictable Descartes bears a close resemblance to Lacan's. In fact, both Levinas and Lacan, at least in their early works, favor Descartes's embodied subject, who owes his or her existence to an interruption of being, to Hegel's idealistic subject. With these connections set in place, Chanter turns in the final section of her paper to the work of Luce Irigaray's as representing a point of meeting between ethics and psychoanalysis and between Levinas and Lacan.

In "Cogito and *Séparation*: Levinas and Lacan," Hans-Dieter Gondek attempts a confrontation between Levinas and Lacan, with the goal of clarifying some of their primary concepts more closely and in relation to one another. He systematically discusses Levinas's and Lacan's conceptualizations of the Other, their understanding of the relation to the Cartesian *cogito* as well as of the process of separation in transcendence. He argues that while Levinas shows the relationship to the Other to be a preontological ethical relationship, the "great Other" [*grand Autre*] of Lacan is more representative of the nonpersonal moments of otherness that are revealed by language. Yet, for Lacan also, an ethical relationship is central—the relationship to the unconscious, which *The Four Fundamental Concepts of Psycho-analysis* he comprehends as being "ethically constituted." Indeed, as Gondek's analysis shows, Lacan is closer to the thought of Levinas in this seminar than anywhere else, without there being any indication that he in fact ever read Levinas.

The problematic of the "real" is the topic of the third paper. In "Levinas and Lacan: Facing the Real," Donna Brody charts the modalizations and determinations of an area of "passive sensibility" in Levinas's work, which he calls the *there is*: a horrific "underside" of formless reality, or of "being-in-general," which inhabits, eludes, and haunts the individual existent. This concept, she suggests, can be considered an instance of Lacan's conception of the real [*réel*]. She proceeds to discover those ways in which the real, or the *there is*, traverses and fractures Levinas's own discourse. Although this paper is centrally given over to explicating the infractions of the real within Levinas's discourse, and although certain homologies and differences between the two thinkers are explored, the paper ends by returning the real to Lacan. Brody contends, on the basis of her analysis of the *there is,* that the irrepressible real exceeds and renders ambiguous the very categories and distinctions of Lacan's own encounter with it. She maintains that the immediate accessibility of the real is all-pervasive and cannot be confined to the unmediated access that psychoanalysis reserves for the navel of the dream and for psychosomatic symptoms.

Having come this far in our attempt to establish a link between Levinas and Lacan, the next paper in the collection is one reconstructed from a course Paul-Laurent Assoun gave at *Le Collège international de philosophie* during 1985–87. Assoun's essay is one of the first, if not the first essay, to articulate and assess the differences and proximity between Lacan's and Levinas's theories of subjectivity and alterity. The essay opens with a historic description of the dynamic of Lacan's and Levinas's works. For Assoun, the quarrel over humanism and the debate with post–structuralism provides the topos for constructing a confrontation between these two thinkers. Careful to respect the orientation of each thinker's work, and not to force unfounded parallels between their respective projects, Assoun brings to the fore the central presuppositions that a more detailed analysis would need to systematically work through: suppositions concerning temporality, subjectivity, language, the mirror stage and the *there is,* desire, eros, paternity, the feminine, the law of the Other and, of course, ethics. Assoun warns us that if, in the end, we were to decide that Lacan and Levinas necessarily pass along the same paths, we also would have to acknowledge that they never passed by at the same time, and that this missed encounter, perhaps, is not by chance. If both thinkers can be said to have initiated, in the name of the Other, reformulations in understanding, the stakes, contexts, and contents of their respective claims establish a separation and maintain a distance.

Although in psychoanalytic literature the concept of sublimation is frequently called upon—traditionally the cure is thought in terms of a greater capacity for sublimation and the realm of art and culture is thematized in terms of the sublimation of sexual desire—the lack of a coherent theory of sublimation has remained one of the lacunae in psychoanalytic theory. It should be of no surprise then to discover that Lacan, who attempted to reconceptualise the foundations of psychoanalysis, takes up the task of formulating a theory of sublimation. In *The Ethics of Psychoanalysis,* Lacan defines sublimation as raising an object to the dignity of the thing [*das Ding*].

In his paper "Death and Sublimation in Lacan's Reading of *Antigone,*" Philippe Van Haute offers an interpretation of Lacan's theory of sublimation. Van Haute argues that Lacan's theory of sublimation is indissolubly a theory of the status and meaning of the beautiful and of ethics. He begins his essay with an elucidation of two examples of the beautiful that Lacan employs in Seminar VII, with an explanation of the relation between desire and language and by situating Lacan's insights on sublimation within the context of the decline of an ethics of the sovereign Good. Lacan's tragic ethics should be understood, Van Haute proposes, as Lacan's response to a situation that no longer has anything human about it, and, thus, answers to a world of drives and desires that does not prescribe from out of itself an aim that could be said to give meaning and direction to our lives. With this framework in place, Van Haute then turns to an elucidation of Lacan's reading of *Antigone* and *Oedipus at Colonus.*

The final three papers in the collection, "Ethics with Psychoanalysis," "Rethinking the Beyond of the Real," and "Dis-possessed: How to Remain Silent 'after' Levinas," explicitly address the central issue of ethics and psychoanalysis. Alain Juranville begins his paper "Ethics with Psychoanalysis" with the question of whether we must, with psychoanalysis, go beyond guilt, or whether there is not something irreducibly objective in transgression [*faute*] that would suppose an ascribable Absolute Good? If so, would the affirmation of objective transgression and of the Good not bring us back to the idealism of metaphysical thought? In response to this question, Juranville undertakes a detailed examination of just what can be made of ethics with psychoanalysis in general.

Juranville proposes that ethics requires an objective Good that can be stated in discourse and in relation to which transgression can be determined. The finitude of freedom and the violence of being must be assumed by an absolute freedom that experiences guilt. He proposes that this necessity is precisely what Levinas insisted upon in his ethical critique of Heidegger. For Levinas, the absolute Other, before every possible choice and engagement, makes us responsible for the Other and commands us to substitute ourselves for the victim and renounce being. But, on the other hand, opposing Levinas, Juranville argues, it is necessary that this absolute freedom, which assumes the violence of being and finitude, be able to act according to the Good and choose in full autonomy and without submitting to the Law of the Other. Does psychoanalysis make possible the formulation of this conception of ethics? Situating his analysis within the framework of Lacan's theory of psychoanalysis, Juranville answers in the affirmative. He demonstrates that 1) the Good is conceivable and statable in discourse and, consequently, transgression can be objectively determined, and 2) the Good is realizable, despite irreducible finitude and transgression.

The relation between ethics and psychoanalysis is also the central concern of Drucilla Cornell's paper "Rethinking the Beyond of the Real." Cornell undertakes the difficult task of rethinking the relation between radical alterity (what Lacan calls "the real," or the limit of the symbolic) and what Cornell calls an "ethical relationship." According to Cornell, both Lacan and Levinas, even if for quite different and irreconcilable reasons, argue that the ontological elaboration of the Sovereign Good, attempted by classical ethics, is philosophically unjustifiable, even unethical. This rejection turns Lacan to his Freudian rereading of the inevitability of the imposition of the moral law, whether the moral law is understood as the Ten Commandments or in terms of the Kantian categorical imperatives, two examples Lacan employs in the seminar on the ethics of psychoanalysis. For Levinas, however, the Good, which provides sanctity for the Other, can never be reduced to a set of commandments. The call of the Other is always unique, and how to heed this call cannot be known in advance nor simply through identification with another moral subject. To reduce the Other to a set of definable categories, Cornell argues, would violate her or his alterity. Precisely, because the Good is the good of the Other, it can not be fully actualized.

What is at stake in Cornell's essay is an attempt to reformulate the ethical implications of the beyond of the real through challenging Lacan's formulation of this concept *The Ethics of Psychoanalysis*. She begins with a summary of Lacan's understanding of the relation between the pleasure principle and the beyond of the real. Here, Cornell establishes succinctly how Lacan's elaboration of this relationship only makes sense from within a conceptual foreclosure of the "positive" symbolization of the feminine within sexual difference, a foreclosure not without ethical implications. Drawing on the works of Levinas and Derrida, Cornell then turns toward a reformulation of the concept of the real as the limit of the symbolic. This reformulated concept of the real can be thought without the moral implications of foreclosure.

The collection concludes with Rudi Visker's consideration of Levinas's "uncompromising position" within the contemporary crisis of post–Kantian ethics. His paper is a clarification both of Levinas's concepts of subjectivity and ethical law and of the difference between Levinas's formulations of these concepts and Lyotard's and Lacan's "pagan" formulations, as well as a critique of Levinas. While in the first half of his essay Visker champions Levinas against Lyotard and Lacan in a philosophical debate concerning ethics, in the second half he takes his distance also from Levinas by problematizing the latter's conceptualization of the Good.

Confronted with the face of the Other, the subject, according to Levinas, loses all of its titles. But by the same token, it also reaches its truest and most proper core. As Visker's argument shows, what properly constitutes a subject cannot be understood outside the horizon of this ("initial") dispossession. The horizon, which for Levinas ultimately refers to the Good, has chosen us before we could choose it. In fact, Visker claims, it is because of this prior un-freedom that we can be free at all. But what, he asks, if there were to be more than one "Good" and, hence, more than one "dispossession"? Through an analysis of the concepts of the "face" and of "form," Visker shows not only why Levinas cannot raise this question but also in what sense there is a price to be paid for this omission.

Abbreviations

Lacan's Works

References are given to the French editions first, followed by references to the English editions, whenever the latter is available.

É   *Écrits* (Paris: Seuil, 1966).

E   *Écrits: A Selection*, translated by Alan Sheridan (New York: Norton, 1987).

Sé I   *Les écrits techniques de Freud: Le Séminaire I* (Paris: Seuil, 1988).

SI   *The Seminar of Jacques Lacan: Book I. Freud's Technical Papers*, translated by John Forrester (New York: W.W. Norton & Co., 1988).

Sé II   *Le moi dans la théorie de Freud et dans la technique de la psychanalyse: Lé Seminaire II* (Paris: Seuil, 1978).

S II   *The Seminar of Jacques Lacan: Book II. The Ego in Freud's Theory and in the Technique of Psychoanalysis*, translated by Sylvana Tomaselli (New York: W.W. Norton & Co., 1978).

Sé VII   *L'éthique de psychanalyse: Le Séminaire VII* (Paris: Seuil, 1986).

S VII   *The Seminar of Jacques Lacan: Book VII. The Ethics of Psychoanalysis*, translated by Dennis Porter (New York: W.W. Norton & Co., 1992).

Sé XI   *Les quatre concepts fondamentaux de la psychanalyse: Lé Seminar XI* (Paris: Seuil, 1973).

S XI   *The Four Fundamental Concepts of Psycho-analysis*, translated by Alan Sheridan (New York: W.W. Norton & Co., 1978).

FS   *Feminine Sexuality: Jacques Lacan and the école freudienne*, edited by Juliet Mitchell and Jacqueline Rose, translated by Jacqueline Rose (New York: W.W. Norton & Co., 1985).

Sre   "Some Reflections on the Ego," *International Journal of Psychoanalysis* 34 (1953): 11–17.

Levinas's Works

References are given to the French editions first, followed by references to the English editions. On occasion, only references to either the French or English editions will be made.

AE   *Autrement qu'être ou au delà de l'essence* (The Hague: Martinus Nijhoff, 1974).

CP   *Collected Philosophical Papers* (The Hague: Martinus Nijhoff, 1987).

DE   *De l'existence à l'existant* (Paris: J. Vrin, 1947).

DF   *Difficult Freedom: Essays on Judaism*, translated by Sean Hand (Baltimore: Johns Hopkins University Press, 1990).

DQI   *De Dieu qui vient à l'idée* (Paris: J. Vrin, 1992).

EE   *Existence and Existents*, translated by Alphonso Lingis (The Hague: Martinus Nijhoff, 1978).

EeI   *Éthique et infini* (Paris: Fayard, 1982).

EI   *Ethics and Infinity*, translated by Richard Cohen (Pittsburgh: Duquesne University Press, 1985).

HH   *Humanisme de l'autre homme* (Paris: Fata Morgana, 1972).

OB   *Otherwise than Being or Beyond Essence*, translated by Alphonse Lingis (Dordrecht: Kluwer Academic Publishers, 1991).

PA   "Philosophy and Awakening," *Who Comes After the Subject?*, edited by Eduardo Cadava, Peter Connor, and Jean-Luc Nancy (New York: Routledge, 1991): 206–16.

TA   *Le temps et l'autre* (Mont Pellier: Fata Morgana, 1979).

TeI   *Totalité et infini* (The Hague: Martinus Nijhoff, 1961).

TI   *Totality and Infinity*, translated by Alphonso Lingis (Pittsburgh: Duquesne University Press, 1969).

TO   *Time and Other*, translated by Richard A. Cohen (Pittsburgh: Duquesne University Press, 1987).

TrO   "The Trace of the Other," in *Deconstruction in Context: Literature and Philosophy*, edited by Mark Taylor (Chicago: University of Chicago Press, 1986).

Chapter 1

Reading Hegel as a Mediating Master: Lacan and Levinas

Tina Chanter

The function of a verb does not consist in naming, but in producing language, that is, in bringing forth the seeds of poetry which overwhelm "existents" in their position and their very positivity. . . . Consciousness, position, the present, the "I," are not initially—although they are finally—existents. They are events by which the unnameable verb *to be* turns into substantives.
—Levinas, *De l'existence à l'existant*

What is important is not that the child said the words *Fort/Da*, which, in his mother tongue, amounts to *far/here*—besides, he pronounced them in an approximate fashion. It is rather that here, right from the beginning, we have a first manifestation of language. In this phonematic opposition, the child transcends, brings on to the symbolic plane, the phenomenon of presence and absence. He renders himself master of the thing, precisely insofar as he destroys it.
—Lacan, *Les écrits techniques de Freud: Le Séminaire I*

I begin by quoting the following remarkable passage Levinas writes in *De l'existence à l'existant*:

Since the *discovery of the unconscious*—and this contradiction in terms is evidence of a considerable upheaval—philosophy has been conceiving of the unconscious as another consciousness, failing to recognize the ontological function of the unconscious and its specific relationship with conscious clarity, with sincerity, which separates itself from the obscurity, depth, and ambiguity of the unconscious. The unconscious is interpreted in terms of consciousness, or the reverse. The unconscious appears as a possible, a germ, or as something repressed. In fact, the implicitness referred to in speaking of implicit cognition no longer presents the structure of cognition; the essential event of the world, which is intention and light, no longer means anything here. Consciousness is precisely a sincerity. In taking being-in-the-world as an intention one is above all affirming—and the history of our civilization and our philosophy confirms this—that the world is the field of a consciousness, and the peculiar structure that characterizes consciousness governs and gives meaning to all the infiltrations of the unconscious in the world. It is "before" the world comes about that the unconscious plays its role. (*DE*, 57/*EE*, 38)

As Mikkel Borch-Jacobsen points out, insofar as modern philosophy can be accurately characterized as being the "philosophy of consciousness," the psychoanalytic appeal to an unconscious seems to present philosophy with insurmountable problems.[1] But if, as Levinas suggests in the aforementioned passage, the unconscious has in fact only ever been thought as a modification of consciousness—an imperfect mode of consciousness, where this loss of perfection is recuperable—then the problem is not the apparent incoherence that the unconscious presents to philosophers but rather the failure of psychoanalysis to have taken the unconscious seriously enough. Applied to Lacan, Levinas's suggestion sits strangely, at least at first glance. Are we not told that, in returning to Freud, Lacan stresses precisely the importance of the unconscious?[2] And does not Lacan himself tell us that his account of the mirror stage challenges the Cartesian idea of the subject?: "It is an experience that leads us to oppose any philosophy directly issuing from the *Cogito*" (*É*, 93/*E*, 1). Critics seem to agree that Lacan decenters the subject,[3] that he brings into question its unity, introducing a fragmented, split, or fractured self, and that, as such, the subject is no longer master of its destiny, no longer in control of its self-knowledge. Not only is self-mastery and self-knowledge rendered questionable, but, according to Jacqueline Rose, it is precisely the unconscious that "undermines the subject from any position of certainty, and from any relations of knowledge to his or her psychic processes and history" (*FS*, 29).

What could Levinas mean, then, when he suggests that "[t]he unconscious is interpreted in terms of consciousness, or the reverse"? Is Lacan's conception of the unconscious to be included in this judgement? To the extent that Lacan draws freely upon precisely those philosophers of consciousness—Hegel, Kojève, and Sartre, for example—to whom Levinas objects, it would seem that one could only answer this question in the affirmative. But, as always, things are not quite so simple. To decide in what sense, if at all, Lacan can be accused of not having properly thought through the very implications that a casual perusal of his work might take as its central contribution—namely an elucidation of the meaning of the unconscious—one would need to understand precisely the role Hegel plays for him.

How, then, is the influence of Hegel played out in Lacan's reworking of Freud on the one hand and in Levinas's rethinking of the ethical relation on the other hand? In acknowledging the distinct debts that Lacan and Levinas owe to that master of mediation, Hegel, I will not attempt to reconcile their differences, as if it were still appropriate to stage a confrontation between these two thinkers and engineer an outcome, which develops through a series of negations resulting in a determinate negation and presents a resolution that is attained from the standpoint of a philosopher who presumes to be beyond the conflict that is, in some sense, produced by the very description of their relationship as antagonistic. I will not attempt to present this relationship as if it conformed to a struggle that points beyond itself, passing into a new and higher form of itself, in a movement true to Hegel's *aufheben*. Rather, what I propose, in order to gauge the different roles Hegel plays for Lacan and Levinas, is to turn back first to the father of modern philosophy, the founder of the philosophy of consciousness, the philosopher to whom Husserl and Heidegger, Sartre and Merleau-Ponty, return. Each philosopher seeks—and finds—in Descartes evidence of a different view than his precursor. Levinas's Descartes is the least predictable, the most unrecognized, the most surprising—and, we shall see, the one that in the end bears most resemblance to Lacan's.

There are two, at first sight contradictory, emphases in Levinas's retrieval of Descartes. The first aspect of Cartesian thought that Levinas takes up is one that aligns Descartes with Hegel. Levinas says, "Hegel returns to Descartes in maintaining the positivity of the infinite, but excluding all multiplicity from it; he posits the infinite as the exclusion of every 'other' that might maintain a relation with the infinite and thereby limit it" (*TeI*, 170–71/*TI*, 196). But if Hegel can only conceive of the finite I as subordinate to, and ultimately as absorbed into, the infinite, it is Descartes who maintains the independence of the finite I in relation to the infinite. As Levinas says,

> We recognize in the finitude to which the Hegelian infinite is opposed, and which it encompasses, the finitude of man before the elements, the finitude of man invaded by the *there is*, at each instant traversed by faceless gods against whom labor is pursued in order to realize the security in which the "other" of the elements would be revealed to the same. But the other absolutely other—the Other [*mais l'Autre, absolutement autre—Autrui*]—does not limit the freedom of the same; calling it to responsibility, it founds it and justifies it. The relation with the other as face heals allergy. It is desire, teaching received, and the pacific oppo-

sition of discourse. In returning to the Cartesian notion of infinity, the "idea of infinity" put in the separated being by the infinite, we retain its positivity, its anteriority to every finite thought and every thought of the finite, its exteriority with regard to the finite; here there was the possibility of separated being. (*TeI*, 171/*TI*, 197)

From this passage I want to retain in particular Levinas's notion of the "*there is,*" the pacifism of the relation between the I and the other, the anteriority of the infinite to the finite, and the concept of separation. Let me elaborate on these ideas by turning directly to Descartes.

I: Descartes's Anti-Cartesianism

Descartes has somehow managed to acquire the reputation of the champion of certitude and self-certainty, the quintessential rationalist. But as Kierkegaard points out in the preamble to *Fear and Trembling*, there is another side to Descartes. Not only is Descartes to be venerated, if we follow Kierkegaard, as a humble and honest thinker, but it is precisely his lack of certainty that Kierkegaard contrasts with Hegel's belief in the systematicity of thought and the capacity of the concept. It was the failure of Descartes's self-confidence, Kierkegaard reminds us, that provoked him to write his "Meditations."[4] To point to the lack of confidence in Descartes's ability to know is not the same thing as characterizing him simply as the philosopher of systematic doubt. The importance that Descartes attached to the method of doubt is just as well-known as his desire to know, with certainty, the truth. My point is that neither his desire to know nor his procedure for doubting knowledge put into question the fundamental epistemological framework that his self-questioning assumes. Both his quest for knowledge and his skeptical stance toward that knowledge take place within an unquestioned series of beliefs about the nature of the world and the subject, about the object of knowledge and the subject as knower. In short, we are subjects whose nature it is to know the world—and ourselves—as our object.

But beyond his fundamental approach to human subjectivity as a vehicle for knowing the world, there is another Descartes, one who is not content with the polarized and reified subject–object dichotomy that his own work did so much to install as the linchpin of modern philosophy, and it is this discontented Descartes that preoccupies Levinas.

a) To Take Time

The logic that is an anti-logic, the "logically absurd" movement of the "posteriority of the anterior" (*TeI*, 25/*TI*, 54), dominates the structure of *Total-*

ity and Infinity. It is the retroactive movement of reflection which defines phenomenological thinking and which Levinas seeks to depict as an anti-logic, a paradoxical logic, an illogical logic that is not so far removed from Kierkegaard's logic of the paradox. It is Descartes, and not the existentialists or phenomenologists as such, to whom Levinas appeals most frequently as the thinker to exhibit this movement. Descartes's discovery of the idea of infinity, a discovery that takes place after the *cogito*, but which nevertheless grounds thought, this "revolution in being" (*TeI*, 24–25/*TI*, 54) is what Levinas attends to. He says, "The being infinitely surpassing its own idea in us—God in the Cartesian terminology—subtends the evidence of the *cogito*, according to the third *Meditation.* But the discovery of this metaphysical relation in the *cogito* constitutes chronologically only the second move of the philosopher. That there could be a chronological order distinct from the 'logical' order, that there could be several moments in the progression, that there is a progression—here is separation" (*TeI*, 24–25/*TI*, 54).

And, we might add, here is time. It is the distinction between the order of logic and the temporal order that Levinas asks his readers to focus on in repeatedly drawing our attention to the difference between the order in which Descartes's thought unfolds, the chronological, historical order, and the discovery that the thinking subject makes, which must be registered according to a different order than that of time understood as a sequence of nows parading past the subject who represents them in a linear and continuous fashion.[5] In the temporal order, the *cogito* precedes the idea of an infinite God, but it is the idea of infinity that retroactively provides both the logical and metaphysical foundation for the *cogito*, after the fact. Through reflecting on the *cogito*, on the I think, the I becomes aware of its cause—a cause which, by its very nature—must have existed antecedently to its effect, but which is only attributable by a derivation that postdates the *cogito* (which is nonetheless taken to effect the I, or to bring it into being, to make it appear). Levinas emphasizes the failure of the I to comprehend or encompass the other. And it is to the Cartesian subject that he turns to represent this inadequacy of the I to comprehend or represent the infinite that nonetheless is presented to it by the idea of God that it has—and, the implication is, which must somehow have been formed, or put in the subject. But rather than seeing the inadequacy of the I to match the perfection of God that it understands, albeit it negatively and in contrast to its own imperfection, Levinas sees this lack of adequation between the I and the other not as a failure, but as a positive relation. The inability of the I to anticipate, grasp, control the other also harbors its openness to the other, to learn from the other, and its capacity to be put into question by the other. Equivocal with regard to the identity of—or difference between—the other person [*l'autrui*] and God, Levinas simply suggests that "the distinction between transcendence to the other man and transcendence to God should not be made too quickly" (*PA*, 214).

The passage at the end of Descartes's third meditation is the one to which Levinas most famously and most often appeals,[6] but there is a second insistent reference to the *cogito*, one that makes itself felt in relation to the body, especially in the two texts published in 1947, *Time and the Other* and *Existence and Existents*. This aspect of Levinas's revival of Cartesianism may be less obvious than his repeated and extended references to Descartes's idea of infinity, but it is no less important. If the founding role that the idea of God plays in Descartes's meditations is consonant with his reputation as a systematic philosopher, if God provides the first solid ground for which Descartes searches in his quest to establish the certainty of his knowledge, the role the body plays in his philosophy is more often construed as a problem. It is as if the material, physical, and extended body never quite sits properly with Descartes's rationalist bent. In fact, however, while Levinas does not embrace the dualism of Descartes's metaphysical distinction between thought and extension, he invokes the substantiality of the Cartesian subject (see *DE*, 117/*EE*, 68).

Levinas, always trying to articulate a philosophical path that avoids both the extremes of materialism and the excesses of idealism, favors Descartes's conception of subjectivity over Hegel's ultimately idealist subject. In a passage that might surprise readers who have focused exclusively on the well-known adumbration of Descartes's idea of infinity in relation to the *cogito*, Levinas says in 1947 that "the most profound teaching of the Cartesian *cogito* consists in discovering thought as a substance, that is, as something that is posited" (*DE*, 117/*EE*, 68). What Levinas is particularly concerned to emphasize about the substantiality of the subject is its positionality, which is to be understood not as static, but precisely as taking a position in the sense of positing oneself on the ground. "Through taking position in the anonymous *there is* a subject is affirmed. It is affirmation in the etymological sense of the term, taking a position on solid ground, on a base, fulfilling the conditions, foundation" (*DE*, 139–40/*EE*, 82). The term *"there is"* [*il y a*] signifies the anonymity of existence (*TA*, 26/*TO*, 47), or "existing without existents" (*TA*, 25/*TO*, 46).[7]

II: Existing without Existents

In explicating the *there is,* Levinas often draws upon Maurice Blanchot's depiction of the ego's enchainment to itself.[8] With the term *"there is,"* Levinas names that which escapes the language of objectivity that tries to capture it.[9] "Neither nothingness nor being," it is "the excluded middle" (*EeI*, 47/*EI*, 48), that from which anything like the experience of enjoyment can arise, and into which it subsides.[10] It is unsettling, nonlocalizable, a general uneasiness that Levinas describes as "impersonal" (*EeI*, 46/*EI*, 48), an "anonymous rustling," in which consciousness finds itself "depersonalized" (*EeI*, 47/*EI*, 49). Levinas insists not only upon the impersonality of the "*there is*" but also on the "horror" (*DE*, 100–1/*EE*, 61) that it signifies, thereby distinguishing the "*there is*" from Heidegger's "*es gibt*," which has more positive connotations of "joy" and "abundance" (*EeI*, 46/*EI*, 48).

It is against the background of the impersonal and anonymous "*there is*" that a subject arises, takes a position, and in doing so suspends the *there is* establishing itself in a movement that Levinas says "strictly speaking we cannot give a name to, for it is a pure verb" (*DE*, 140/*EE*, 82). He therefore calls this verbalness of being, this coming into existence by the existent, this upsurge of the subject that resists naming, *hypostasis*, a term that "in the history of philosophy, designated the event by which the act expressed by a verb became a being designated by a substantive" (*DE*, 140–1/*EE*, 82). In the event of taking up a position, in the instant of becoming someone—or perhaps we should say something—Levinas seeks to develop further Heidegger's distinction between *Sein* [*l'être*], in the sense of Being in general, and *Seiendes* [*étant*], with the sense of a being that masters its Being or its existence. In Heidegger's *Being and Time*, the entity that has its being as an issue for it is named *Dasein*.[11] Wanting to catch sight of a way of existing that is not one of mastery, an "existing without existents" [*l'exister sans existant*], Levinas renders Heidegger's ontological difference, we could say, in a way that undermines the ontological significance Heidegger attached to it (*TA*, 24/*TO*, 44). For Levinas, it is inadequate to posit a distinction between Being and beings; he sees the relationship as being one of separation (see *TeI*, 19/*TI*, 48)—it is not merely a matter of conceptually distinguishing the general sense of being from the particular being that exists. Levinas wants to catch sight of the very event by which the existent, or being, takes up its existence. Strangely—or perhaps not so strangely, it may turn out—the term *separation* not only applies to the relationship one has with oneself, but it also will apply to the relation between the I and the other.

It is perhaps not so strange that the term *separation* can apply to the self, both in relation to itself and in its relation to the other, because it is the *cogito*, says Levinas, that "evinces separation" (*TeI*, 24/*TI*, 54). It is not so strange to the extent that the *cogito* makes any relation possible—at least as long as we remain at the level of thought. What interests Levinas is precisely the "doubling back" (*DE*, 27/*EE*, 22) that occurs for the self in the midst of its relationship with the world, a kind of questioning of the very conditions of its intelligibility.

In positing "an existing that occurs without us" (*TA*, 25/*TO*, 45), Levinas seeks to show that "[t]hought has a point of departure. There is not only a consciousness of localization, but a localization of consciousness, which is

not in turn reabsorbed into consciousness, into knowing" (*DE*, 117/*EE*, 68).
One can easily discern the strength of the fundamentally Hegelian insight,
against which Levinas will have to struggle, to maintain that the movement of
thought can be construed as resisting the subsumption of the particular by the
general, or the subordination of the body to the soul—the privilege usually
granted to spirit over matter—or the priority that is generally accorded to gen-
erality and universality over contingency and particularity. Derrida's essay
"Violence and Metaphysics" has made readers of Levinas more sensitive than
we would otherwise have been to the enormity of the task that Levinas sets
himself in his attempt to overcome Hegel and Parmenides, united in their
belief of the priority of unicity, oneness, or the same, over multiplicity, plu-
rality, or difference.[12] Undaunted by the prospect of challenging Hegel, Levinas refuses his post–Cartesian Parmenidean gesture by insisting that one cannot make sense of thought without also attending to the body, and that one
cannot universalize the body to the point of obliterating the particularity of my
hic and *nunc*. "What does sleep consist in?" asks Levinas (*DE*, 119/*EE*, 69).
He answers, "To lie down is precisely to limit existence to a place, a position"
(*DE*, 119/*EE*, 69); and that "the positive relationship with a place which we
maintain in sleep is masked by our relation with things. . . . Sleep reestablishes
a relationship with a place qua base" (*DE*, 119/*EE*, 69–70). Contrasting
Descartes's conception of the I as "something that thinks"—and the "word
thing is here admirably exact" (*DE*, 117/*EE*, 68) adds Levinas—with Hegel's,
which assumes the priority of thinking over that of substance, Levinas says,
"The possibility of sleeping is already seated in the very exercise of thought.
It is not thought and then *here*. It is, qua thought, here, already sheltered from
eternity and universality. This localization does not presuppose space. It is the
very contrary of objectivity. It does not presuppose a thought behind it which
would have to grasp the here, which is an objective *here*—in that dialectic by
which Hegel's *Phenomenology* begins. The localization of consciousness is
not subjective; it is the subjectivization of the subject" (*DE*, 119/*EE*, 69).

Against Hegel's speculative proposition, which asserts the identity
between subject and substance,[13] Levinas insists upon their lack of coincidence. It is the lag, the cleavage, the being out of step with itself, the hesitation in being, the distance that obtains in the relationship that the ego has to
itself that Levinas explores, rather than the simultaneity of subjectivity and
substantiality: "Behind the *cogito*, or rather in the fact that the *cogito* leads
back to 'a thinking thing,' we discern a situation which precedes the scission
of being into an 'inside' and a [sic] 'outside.' Transcendence is not the fundamental movement of the ontological adventure; it is founded in the non-tran-
scendence of position" (*DE*, 172–73/*EE*, 100). Seeing in Husserl—despite all
of the constraints of Husserlian phenomenology that push him in the opposite
direction—a revival or renewal of a psychic energy that will not lend itself

entirely to the seductions of conceptual knowledge to which Hegel was prey, Levinas says, "Contrary to the simple abstraction that moves from 'individual consciousness' to 'consciousness in general,' through an ecstatic or angelic omission of its terrestrial weight and, in the intoxication or idealism of a quasi-magical sublimation—the Husserlian theory of intersubjective reduction describes the astonishing or the traumatising—trauma, not thauma—possibility of sobering up in which the self, faced with the other, is liberated from the self, is awakened from dogmatic slumber" (*PA*, 213–14).

If Husserl allows the other to escape or exceed its constitution by the self, for Hegel—whatever importance otherness has in his philosophy (and Hegel takes it more seriously than most philosophers)—the other is ultimately sublated through a dialectical negation that issues in the absolute. As Levinas occasionally lets his readers know—even if the gesture usually registers the difference between them—Hegel constantly looks over Levinas's shoulder. For Heidegger, a second—if often silent—conversation partner ever present for Levinas, the individuality of beings is subordinated, at least on Levinas's account, to the impersonal question of Being. Here too, then, the other is merely an echo of the same.

Hegel and Heidegger can be seen as representatives of the "rejected alternative," which Derrida describes in a passage that captures the movement of Levinas's text admirably well. Referring to the "unthinkable truth of living experience" that reveals "by philosophy's own light, that philosophy's surface is severely cracked," Derrida goes on to say, "It could doubtless be shown that it is in the nature of Levinas's writing, at its decisive moments, to move along these cracks, masterfully progressing by negations, and by negation against negation. Its proper route is not that of an 'either this . . . or that,' but of a 'neither this . . . nor that.' The poetic force of metaphor is often the trace of this rejected alternative, this wounding of language" (*DE*, 134–35/*EE*, 90). What Derrida's description of Levinas's language brings to light is the way in which, despite its Hegelianism (neither this, nor that), there is a poetry that resists the force of the negative—not because the negative does not accomplish its work in some sense, but because there is another sense, another order that subsists despite its negation.

Hegel's philosophy plays a singularly peculiar role for Levinas, bearing the brunt of his most potent polemics. But it can only do so because Levinas takes it to be so central. That Hegel should bear this contradictory burden should not surprise us; for Heidegger (whose influence on Levinas is far from negligible), Hegel plays a similar role.[14] Hegel both represents for him the highest point of metaphysics and is credited with precipitating its end.

Recall that Levinas says, in the passage I cited at the beginning, "In taking being-in-the-world as an intention one is above all affirming—and the history of our civilization and our philosophy confirms this—that the world is the field of a consciousness, and the peculiar structure that characterizes consciousness governs and gives meaning to all the infiltrations of the unconscious in the world." The phrase "being-in-the-world" alerts us to the fact that Levinas is including Heidegger among those who failed, despite their efforts—and Heidegger's were considerable in this area—to definitively overcome the privilege that, since Descartes, consciousness seems to have maintained for itself—with the support of even those philosophers most eager to overcome it.

III: Lacan and Descartes

"As I have often pointed out, I don't much like hearing that we have *gone beyond* Hegel, the way one hears we have *gone beyond* Descartes. We go beyond everything and always end up in the same place" (*Sé II*, 91/*S II*, 71). Notwithstanding Lacan's dislike of it, it is common to see Lacan heralded as having challenged the Cartesian ideal of self-certainty by presenting the subject not as a unity but as fractured and nonidentical with itself. A closer examination of Lacan's relationship to Descartes and Hegel is called for.[15] We saw that, in 1949, in "The Mirror Stage as Formative of the Function of the I as Revealed in the Psychoanalytic Experience," a paper that revisits the conception of the mirror image he had first articulated at the Marienbad Congress in 1936, Lacan wrote, "It is an experience that leads us to oppose any philosophy directly issuing from the *Cogito*" (*É*, 93/*E*, 1). What is implied by the refusal of a philosophy that "directly" issues from the *cogito*—one that issues indirectly from it, or rather one that questions it in a more originary way? It is striking that two years later, in 1951, commenting on this return to the concept of the "mirror stage," Lacan assigned "a twofold value" to it: "In the first place, it has historical value as it marks a decisive turning point in the mental development of the child. In the second place, it typifies an essential libidinal relationship with the body-image. For these two reasons the phenomenon demonstrates clearly the passing of the individual to a stage where the earliest formation of the ego can be observed" (*Sre*, 14).

What especially interests me about Lacan's observation is that he asserts the importance of the "body-image." It is the work of Paul Schilder, author of *The Image and Appearance of the Human Body*, on which Lacan draws in developing this concept.[16] In particular, it is the phenomenon of the "phantom limb" to which he draws attention, a phenomenon that not only Merleau-Ponty makes a great deal of, but which Descartes, it will be remembered, had already brought to the attention of philosophers.[17] Lacan singles out the relation that the phantom limb phenomenon bears to the experience of a pain that continues in the locale of an amputated limb, although it "can no longer be explained by local irritation." Lacan goes on, "It is as if one caught a glimpse here of the existential relation of a man with his body-image in this relationship with such a narcissistic object as the lack of a limb" (*Sre*, 13).

Turning back to his summary of the "mirror stage," we find Lacan highlighting the "jubilant interest" and "endless ecstasy" of the "infant over eight months at the sight of his own image in a mirror" (*Sre*, 14). Again, Lacan turns to the philosopher—and if there is some question as to whom he refers—himself, or some unidentified (general or singular) philosopher?—this puzzle will soon be clarified. He says, "The purely imaginal play evidenced in such deliberate play with an illusion is fraught with significance for the philosopher" (*Sre*, 14), and he goes on to relate this significance to a comparison of the child and the chimpanzee. Whereas the latter is "certainly quite capable at the same age of detecting the illusion" and "soon loses all interest in it" (*Sre*, 15), the child displays, as we saw, an "endless" and "jubilant" fascination in the illusory image presented in the mirror. Lacan comments wryly, "It would, of course, be paradoxical to draw the conclusion that the animal is the better adjusted to reality of the two!" (*Sre*, 15). Paradoxical—yes, but wrong? To the extent that the mirror offers the child an image of illusory unity, which has a role in strengthening the ego, and to the extent that Lacan suggests that we "reexamine certain notions that are sometimes accepted uncritically, such as the notion that it is psychologically advantageous to have a strong ego" (*Sre*, 16), Lacan does indeed seem to be saying that animals are better adapted to reality than humans. And it is hard not to recognize Sartre's dizzying image of an angst-ridden subject faced with the responsibility of choice, like someone who experiences vertigo on the edge of a precipice, when we read Lacan's description of the ego[18] "in its essential resistance to the elusive process of Becoming, to the variations of Desire. This illusion of unity, in which a human being is always looking forward to self-mastery, entails a constant danger of sliding back again into the chaos from which he started; it hangs over the abyss of a dizzy Assent in which one can perhaps see the very essence of Anxiety" (*Sre*, 15).

The jubilation that the child feels when confronted with his or her mirror image is, Lacan is concerned to point out, due to an "imaginary triumph" (*Sre*, 15). For the child in question is "a babe in arms" or "a child who is holding himself upright by one of those contrivances to help one learn to walk without serious falls" (*Sre*, 15). Thus the child's joy derives from "anticipating a degree of muscular co-ordination which he has not yet actually achieved" (*Sre*, 15). Emphasizing the importance of the "affective value" that the unifying body-image has, Lacan underscores the fact that, unlike the animal, the child is "prematurely born" (*Sre*, 15). Lacan goes on to surmise that it is the "stability" of bodily posture, of which the mirror provides the first image, albeit misleading—enabling the child to anticipate a degree of autonomy that is not yet attainable—"in which the ego finds its starting point" (*Sre*, 15). It is the body-image then, as a coherent and stable image, that provides the child with the makings of the ego.

Lacan begins his 1954–1955 seminar with a lecture that attempts to complicate the usual picture of Descartes, or what he refers to as the dentist's *cogito*—"as *dentists* are very confident about the order of the universe because they think that Mr. Descartes made manifest the laws and the procedures of limpid reason in the *Discourse on Method*. His *I think, therefore, I am*, so essential to the new subjectivity, is not as simple, however, as it would appear to these dentists" (*Sé II*, 14/*S II*, 6). Lacan sets himself the goal of locating consciousness, which Freud begins by equating with the ego but finds himself progressively forced to admit as "unlocalisable" (*Sé II*, 16/*S II*, 8), leaving the problem "unresolved" (*Sé II*, 76/*S II*, 57) so in the end it seems that "the *I* is distinct from the ego" (*Sé II*, 16/*S II*, 8). Lacan suggests that, for Freud, "the reality of the subject" is not in an ego that is the seat of consciousness, but rather that "[i]n the unconscious, excluded from the system of the ego, the subject speaks" (*Sé II*, 77/*S II*, 58).[19]

Lacan proceeds to shed doubt upon the priority that is typically accorded to consciousness,[20] even suggesting that this decentering of the subject from the individual can already be found—"If you take off your dentist's glasses in reading Descartes"—in the "deceiving God" of Cartesianism (*Sé II*, 17/*S II*, 9). This would indicate that, contrary to the popular idea of Cartesianism, as appealing to the transparency of consciousness, there is something left unaccounted for by consciousness, a remnant, or excess that exceeds my reflective act of comprehension, eluding my grasp, so that the reality of subjectivity is not exhausted by consciousness.[21] Rather than regarding ourselves as going beyond Descartes by reinventing "human unity, which that idiot Descartes had cut in two" (*Sé II*, 93/*S II*, 73), Lacan advises us to ask what is at stake when Descartes thinks of "the body as a machine" (*Sé II*, 93/*S II*, 73). Referring to Descartes's *Of Man*, a lesser-known work than the *Discourse on Method*—"dear to dentists"—Lacan suggests that "what Descartes is looking for in man is the clock" (*Sé II*, 74).[22] Lacan's point is not that Descartes was right to construe the body as if it were a machine—"in fact there's every chance that it isn't" (*Sé II*, 93/*S II*, 73), he tells us.[23] What Descartes catches sight of in envisaging the body as a machine, that is, as something that "worked by itself" (*Sé II*, 93/*S II*, 73), is that "it is essential to our being-there, as they say, to know the time" (*Sé II*, 94/*S II*, 74). The "they" to whom Lacan elliptically refers here is obviously the "Heideggerians"—and it is no accident that Heidegger's analysis of inauthentic temporality—the temporality of "the they-self," we might say, employing Heidegger's language—attributes a crucial role to what he calls "clock-time."

To appreciate the value of Descartes's suggestion, let us be clear about the classical conception of the ego that Lacan wants to undercut. He says, "The notion of the ego today draws its self-evidential character from a certain prestige given to consciousness insofar as it is centred on the experience of consciousness, a captivating character, which one must rid oneself of in order to accede to our conception of the subject. . . . The question is—is there an equivalence to be found between these two systems, the system of the ego—about which Freud at one point went so far as to say that it was the only organised thing in the psyche—and the system of the unconscious? Is there opposition like that of a yes and a no, of a reversal, of a pure and simple negation?" (*Sé II*, 77/*S II*, 58–59).

Clearly, the answer, for Lacan, is that there is no such Hegelian negation, since he says the "unconscious has its own dynamic, its own flow, its own paths" (*Sé II*, 148/*S II*, 120). This is an answer that also provides a response to our earlier question regarding whether Levinas's objection to reversibility of consciousness and the unconscious, as if they were both subject to a metaphysics of presence, can be applied to Lacan. Clearly too, this answer tells us why Lacan thinks that "in the end" Hegel "is almost, with respect to Descartes, a bit behind" (*Sé II*, 93/*S II*, 73), for he "completely failed to apprehend [*méconnu*] the importance of . . . the steam engine" (*Sé II*, 94/*S II*, 74). Lacan explains, "In Freud something is talked about, which isn't talked about in Hegel, namely energy," and he goes on to note that "talking of the opposition between consciousness in Hegel's time, and the unconscious in Freud's time" is "like talking about the contradiction between the Parthenon and hydroelectricity, they've got nothing to do with one another. Between Hegel and Freud, there's the advent of the world of the machine" (*Sé II*, 94/*S II*, 74). Levinas and Lacan are in agreement then, in their return to Descartes, and in their championing of Descartes over Hegel, at least in this respect—albeit an unorthodox, and generally unrecognized, Descartes.

Freud "realises that the brain is a dream machine . . . that it is at the most organic and most simple, most immediate and least manageable level, at the most unconscious level, that sense and speech are revealed and blossom forth in their entirety" (*Sé II*, 96/*S II*, 76). What is important for Lacan about the "metaphor of the human body as a machine" (*Sé II*, 96/*S II*, 76) is not only that energy, around which "Freud's whole discussion revolves," "is a notion that can only emerge once there are machines" (*Sé II*, 95/*S II*, 75), but also that the "machine embodies the most radical symbolic activity of man" (*Sé II*, 95/74). Later on, in the same seminar—and there are many intervening steps in between that cannot be followed here—Lacan observes that "the symbolic order is absolutely irreducible to what is commonly called human experience" (*Sé II*, 368/*S II*, 319–20). What I want to emphasize is the extent to which Lacan's reflections on the body as machine bring him to conclusions that overlap with what Levinas recognizes under the heading of the *there is*, in its anonymous and impersonal resistance to the categories of being, logic, language, and time. Let me close this section by simply quoting three brief passages from Lacan that highlight the extent of the correspondence between Levinas's and Lacan's conclusions, which I have only begun to indicate here. Lacan says, "the dream is not in time" (*Sé II*, 184/*S II*, 152); "No doubt something which isn't expressed doesn't exist. But the repressed is always there, insisting, and demanding to be" (*Sé II*, 354/*S II*, 308); "The whole of psychoanalysis is quite rightly founded on the fact that getting something meaningful out of human discourse isn't a matter of logic" (*Sé II*, 352/*S II*, 306).

IV: The Tragedy of Knowing: Conclusion

It is clear enough that Hegel's dialectic has a profound impact on Lacan's conception of the ego. According to Lacan, the ego has "unity, permanence, and substantiality" that "implies an element of inertia, so that the recognition of objects and of the ego itself must be subjected to constant revision in an endless dialectical process" (*Sre*, 12). It is equally clear that Hegel's influence leads Lacan to make certain assumptions about the fundamentally conflictual nature of the relation between egos, whereas Levinas wants to insist that "war presupposes peace" (*TeI*, 174/*TI*, 199)—that the relation between two subjects is originally a pacific one. Lacan says—although one could argue with his interpretation of Hegel, who is in fact more interested in the resolution that does not result in the death of either protagonist, master or slave[24]—"As Hegel's well-known doctrine puts it, the conflict arising from the co-existence of two consciousnesses can only be resolved by the destruction of one of them" (*Sre*, 16).[25]

But Lacan takes his distance from Hegel too, repudiating the priority of theoretical knowledge in much the same way as Levinas. "Everybody is Hegelian without knowing it, we have pushed to an extreme degree the identification of man with his knowledge" (*Sé II*, 93/*S II*, 73). Like Levinas too, Lacan refuses the idea that the principle governing the subject is "assimilable, reducible, symbolisable," that it can be "named" and "grasped"—for Lacan, "it can only be structured" (*Sé II*, 82/*S II*, 63). It would be too simple, then, to dismiss Lacan as "too Hegelian," or even—taking account of Kojève's interpretation of Hegel, so influential in France in the 1940s—"too Kojèvean."[26] To the extent that psychoanalysis refuses the task of normative prescription, Lacan could respond to charges that his preoccupation with a dialectical resolution of the master-slave relationship, his emphasis on aggression, on the differentiation of the self from others, on separation, and so on, is merely the result of how things are. As he says, "after all, it is by our experience of the suffering we relieve in analysis that we are led into the domain of metaphysics."[27] The fact remains, nonetheless, that Lacan throws his lot in with "those who think."[28] Lacan's observations are just as much governed by the theories of the philosophers he takes seriously as they are by the relationships he encounters in clinical settings. He says, "In our view . . . it is novel theories which prepare the ground for new discoveries in science, since such theories not only enable one to understand the facts better, but even make it possible for them to be observed in the first place. The facts are then less likely to be made to fit, in a more or less arbitrary way, into accepted doctrine and there pigeon-holed" (*Sre*, 14). The question becomes then, what would happen to Lacan's theories if we were to apply Levinasian insights to them? How would Levinas's attempt to overcome Hegel fare with psychoanalysis? What would Levinas's face-to-face encounter do for Lacan? What impact would the insistent priority of ethics over ontology that marks Levinas's work make on Lacan? How would Levinas's refusal to reduce the individual to a member of the group—one whose interests are defined by group psychology, or by any other common interest—play itself out for psychoanalysis? While these questions cannot be addressed fully here, I think Luce Irigaray's feminist reformulations of psychoanalysis and ethics is one direction that might be taken in order to pursue them.

Irigaray is, of course, influenced both by Lacan and Levinas. Her work also is steeped in the tradition, whose itinerary has been no more than indicated here, by the names of Descartes, Hegel, Heidegger, and Derrida. Perhaps Irigaray's engagement[29] with the philosophers can best be described in terms of the mechanism of attraction and repulsion. She is both the seducer, and the seduced, the temptress and the tempted, the romancer and the romanced.[30] Irigaray learns from those she mimics, even as she takes her pointed distance from them, pirouetting, more often than not, around the axis of sexual difference. As lover and beloved,[31] it is the middle ground that Irigaray is most interested in occupying—not as an indecisive procrastinator, but as a mediator, as an intermediary, as a messenger. Irigaray can perhaps be seen as the go-between, the cupid who encourages this particular stage of the romance between philosophy and psychoanalysis—the relationship (or lack thereof) between Lacan and Levinas. Could the same be said of Levinas and Lacan as Derrida says of Heidegger and Freud—that they spent all of their time not reading one another?[32]

Levinas's philosophy is infused with the drama of psychoanalysis: the language of trauma, obsession, insomnia, anxiety, boredom, compassion, pain, compensation, tragedy, horror, death, weariness, refusal, evasion, fatigue, suffering, effort, condemnation, withdrawal. The list continues, but we should not conclude from this too readily that he is really "talking about the same thing" as psychoanalysts—or at least that he is talking about it in the same way, for the same reasons, or using it to arrive at the same conclusions.

For one thing, Levinas is just as concerned with egoism, love of life, happiness, independence, plenitude, enjoyment [*jouissance*], bathing in the elements, sensibility, eros, dwelling—much like the ecstasy and jubilation Lacan describes.

First impressions that Levinas and Lacan are in close proximity to one another—both seem fascinated by the absolute alterity of otherness, with ethics, and with language, for example—tend to give way, on closer inspection, to an impasse, a question that can only be answered in silence. An abyss of separation appears to open up between them, a separation that can perhaps be thought of differently according to the place one occupies. One's interest in Levinas may stem from his religiosity (despite his claim that his Judaism does not dictate his philosophy), or one's interest in Lacan, for whom the Freudian corpus takes the place of the Talmud, or it may stem from one's own history, perhaps one's own suffering. Philosophers might prefer Levinas (despite the distance he wants to take from philosophy as it has been traditionally understood, as *theoria*).[33] Others might find Lacan more congenial— or, if he is too sardonic to be congenial, at least he is amusing. Lacan says, "They say Freud isn't a philosopher. I don't mind" (*Sé II*, 117/*S II*, 93)—but clearly he does.

Would the separation between Levinas and Lacan consist of an encounter, a relation without relation—face to face? Or does it consist of a separation that also is a cleaving, a separation that is painful and traumatic, in which one suffers—like the child who must separate from its mother—the necessity of having to be oneself, independent and alone. And how different are these conceptions of subjectivity in the end? Merely a difference of emphasis, perhaps—or is it a question of different histories, preoccupations, influences, nationalities, biographies, lives? And one should not forget the effect that having been a Jewish prisoner of war of the Nazis would have on Levinas. It would be an understatement to say that this experience was formative on the development of a young philosopher who had taken so seriously Heidegger's *Being and Time*. The Shoah, and its relation not only to Heidegger's philosophy but to philosophy as such, called for ethical reflection. That this reflection on ethics took on what might be regarded as an obsessive quality, or that ethics became an obsession for Levinas, should hardly come as a surprise to us, unless we fail completely to see that in the Nazi era humanity itself was at stake.

This relation between Levinas and Lacan is defined, then, not so much by opposition as by confronting in the sense of facing. The question is not who is master and who is slave but rather how to gauge their relationship in a way that avoids subordinating one figure to the other. Is it, then, finally a question of ethics or politics? Not if we fall back on traditional notions of ethics or politics, which amount to choosing sides according to a decision about who is right and who is wrong, whose position is legitimate and whose position is illegitimate. The criteria at work in such a decision appeal ultimately to some preconceived and static notion of force or power, no matter how obvious or obscure its origin or source might be.

How then could Irigaray's work be seen as representing a connection between Levinas and Lacan? I do not mean to suggest that she mediates between them to produce some quasi-Hegelian synthesis (Levinas's ethics + Lacan's psychoanalysis = Irigaray's musings). Irigaray's interest in the role of an intermediary, a role so often demanded of women, is one that affirms the importance of mediation even as it undermines its traditional interpretation, replete with Hegelian overtones.[34] She mediates, we could say, in a Levinasian way, through a relation that leaves in place the terms she nevertheless relates. But the terms do not remain unchanged by the relation—or by Irigaray's intervention.

Irigaray denounces the constraints that cultural expectations impose on women. The fact that women mediate the difficult passages of the lives of others—from womb to world, from young to old; from home to work, from work to home, and so on—demands reflection. Irigaray insists that this mediating role be taken seriously—rather than being taken for granted, as the unthought ground of determinate thought, as the ethical intuitive background against which rational morality flourishes, as Antigone's care of the body, preparing the way for Creon's political order, or, finally, as her "intuitive awareness of what is ethical" (*PhG*, 325/*PS*, 274), as opposed to Creon's consciousness of what is ethical.

Irigaray does not denounce the feminine or the intuitive as such, or the bodily, familial realms that Hegel—or Levinas and Lacan, for that matter—takes women to represent. What she objects to are the ways in which stereotypical ideals of femininity—the role of guardian of the family, for example, have prevented women from being recognized as mediators, the ways in which philosophers have devalued the invaluable passages that women constitute and forge, the homes they make, the nurturance they provide: birth canals, safe houses, battered women's shelters, rape crisis centers.

A mediator, for Irigaray, is one who does not negate by means of opposition but who maintains subtlety and dissonance in an interplay where differences remain more prominent than similarities. Difference—sexual difference as much as, or perhaps more than, any other difference—is to be celebrated, not neutralized. Irigaray often appeals to the contradictory idea of an angelic presence—angels do not exist in the realm of the ordinary world but are figurative representations of divinity, free spirits who move between two worlds—the transcendent and the earthly. They are temporary and fleeting apparitions who appear only to disappear. But they are nonetheless vital for Irigaray, who sees in these intermediary figures who pass between the beyond and the here a function that we, in the modern world, have a tendency to dispense with too easily. It becomes clear that to think through the intermediary role of angelic messengers also requires a rethinking of the separate realms that these messengers both relate and divide. Transcendence and sensibility are both in need of redeployment, not as mutually exclusive opposites but as two poles equally dependent on one another, defined both in terms of and against one another. The mind or the soul, and the body—an example, as Derrida might say, that is not just one example among others.

The function of messengers, who relate two opposites without dissolving their differences from one another, who mediate without negating otherness—an illogical, paradoxical, and magical mode of relating—is both entirely practical and earth bound, and at the same time it is spiritual and otherworldly. Irigaray is not the first to have noticed this, and it is no accident that she turns to ancient mythology and tragedy, to Diotima, Persephone, and Ariadne, each of whom in their different ways enact the role of messenger.

The messenger in Sophocles' *Antigone*, a play to which Irigaray is drawn, is tongue-tied, afraid he will be blamed as being the bearer of bad news. He knows that what he has to say will not please Creon, he understands that Antigone's defiance will not be well received, that for a woman to defy the king's order is out of place. It is as if, as the one who must speak of another's crime, he identifies himself with the doer of the deed. In this case, the doer carries a heavy weight indeed, daughter of Oedipus that she is. By putting into words this event, he breathes life into it, brings it alive, confers reality on what, until that moment, remains a merely abstract possibility for Creon. (One could argue that it remains so; until the death of Antigone, Haemon and Eurydice gives it reality for Creon.) Despite his misgivings, the messenger delivers his message, haltingly, and in fits and starts, but he delivers it nonetheless. He abides by the pragmatic order, observing the constraints of Greek theater, reporting a deed that must occur off-stage, he does what must be done, and he relates his knowledge.

Similarly, those who engage in the talking cure, relieving the moment of suffering, know what has to be done, what is called for. But what, if not suffering, does Levinas's philosophy respond to, in answering to the call of the other? That Levinas and Lacan could be equally accurately described as Hegelian or anti-Hegelian, and that their paths of thought could nevertheless diverge so markedly from one another, presents an irony that would not have been lost on Hegel.[35]

Notes

1. Mikkel Borch-Jacobsen, "The alibis of the subject," *Speculations after Freud: Psychoanalysis, Philosophy and Culture*, edited by Sonu Shamdasani and Michael Münchow (London and New York: Routledge, 1994), pp. 78–96, see especially p. 78.

2. Among those to stress the importance of the concept of the unconscious for Lacan is Jacqueline Rose, "Introduction—II," in *FS*, 27–57.

3. Jonathan Scott Lee, *Jacques Lacan* (Amherst: The University of Massachusetts Press, 1990), p. 22. See also Lacan's statement that "the Freudian discovery has exactly the same implication of decentring as that brought about by the Copernican discovery" (*Sé II*, 16/*S II*, 7).

4. Soren Kierkegaard, *Fear and Trembling* (Harmondsworth, Middlesex: Penguin, 1986).

5. It is no accident that it is Descartes's notion of the instant—along with Malebranche's—as created anew to which Levinas turns in order to emphasize the possibility of genuine novelty, absolute discontinuity, or rupture, rather than a repetition of the same. See *DE*, 128–29/*EE*, 75 and *DE*, 137/*EE*, 80.

6. See *TeI*, 185–87/*TI*, 210–12 and *PA* 206–18, especially p. 215.

7. Also see *TeI*, 142/*TI*, 93 and *TeI*, 197/*TI*, 190.

8. See, for example, Levinas's reference to Blanchot (1942) at *TA*, 37/*TO*, 56.

9. See *DE*, 92–174/*EE*, 57–101; *TA*, 24–38/44–57 and *Eel*, 45–51/*EI*, 47–52.

10. John Llewelyn develops the theme of the "excluded middle," *The Middle Voice of Ecological Conscience: A Chiasmic Reading of Responsibility in the Neighborhood of Levinas, Heidegger, and Others* (New York: St. Martin's Press, 1991), p. 19.

11. Martin Heidegger, *Sein und Zeit* (Tübingen: Max Niemeyer, 1984); *Being and Time*, translated by John Macquarrie and Edward Robinson (Oxford: Basil Blackwell, 1980).

12. Jacques Derrida, *L'écriture et la différence* (Paris: Seuil, 1967); *Writing and Difference*, translated by Alan Bass (Chicago: The University of Chicago Press, 1978). Subsequent references as *ED*.

13. See the preface to G.W.F. Hegel, *Phänomenologie des Geistes,* edited by J. Hoffmeister (Hamburg: Felix Meiner, 1952); *Phenomenology of Spirit,* translated by A.V. Miller (Oxford: Clarendon Press, 1979). Subsequent references as *PhG* and *PS*.

14. Perhaps Hegel, on Heidegger's view, shares the distinction with Nietzsche: Nietzsche is the last metaphysician, but at the same time he foreshadows Heidegger's articulation of a new beginning for philosophy.

15. I am focusing on Seminar II here. For a further discussion of Descartes, see Jacques Lacan, *Sé*, XI.

16. Paul Schilder, *The Image and Appearance of the Human Body* (New York: International University Press, 1978). Lacan says, "We are not unaware of the impor-

tance of Schilder's work on the function of the body-image, and the remarkable accounts he gives of the extent to which it determines the perception of space" (*Sre*, 13). Schilder's work also is an important influence on Maurice Merleau-Ponty, *Phenomenology of Perception*, translated by Colin Smith (London: Routledge & Kegan Paul, 1962).

17. René Descartes, "Meditations on the First Philosophy in which the Existence of God and the Distinction between Mind and Body are Demonstrated," *The Philosophical Works of Descartes*, translated by Elizabeth S. Haldane and G. R. T. Ross (Cambridge: Cambridge University Press, 1979), p. 189.

18. Jean-Paul Sartre, *L'être et le néant* (Paris: Gallimard, 1943), pp. 298–349; *Being and Nothingness*, translated by Hazel Barnes (New York: Washington Square Press, 1966), pp. 340–400.

19. Lacan says, "It seems more and more clear to us that this subject who speaks is beyond the *ego*" (*Sé II*, 207/*S II*, 175).

20. See *Sé II*, 61–62/*S II*, 46 and 74/56.

21. See *Sé II*, 14/*S II*, 6 and 76/58, and 262/224.

22. Lacan notes that "the watch, the reliable watch, has only existed since Huyghens succeeded in making the first perfectly isochronic clock, in 1659" (*Sé II*, 343/*S II*, 298).

23. Among other reasons, the body cannot be a machine because "nothing unexpected comes out of the machine" (*Sé II*, 350/*S II*, 305), and because "[w]ith a machine, whatever doesn't come on time simply falls by the wayside and makes no claims on anything. This is not true for man, the scansion is alive, and whatever doesn't come on time remains in suspense. That is what is involved in repression" (*Sé II*, 308). However, Lacan also says that "the question as to whether it [the machine] is human or not" is not "obviously entirely settled" (*Sé II*, 367/*S II*, 319).

24. Hegel's interest is in the outcome of the master-slave dialectic for those who survive the life-and-death struggle for recognition. In particular, Hegel shows how the relation, which began as a mutual relation between equals—both consciousnesses seek the confirmation of their own idea of themselves as free in the other—turns into a "one-sided and unequal" relation, where one protagonist gains mastery over the other (*PhG*, 191/*PS*, 116).

25. This may be an example of Lacan reading Kojève into Hegel. Kojève says, "To speak of the "origin" of Self-Consciousness is necessarily to speak of a fight to the death for recognition." Alexandre Kojève, *Introduction à la lecture de Hegel* (Paris: Gallimard, 1947), pp. 13–14; *Introduction to the Reading of Hegel*, translated by James H. Nichols Jr. (New York: Basic Books, 1969), pp. 6–7.

26. For a review that reveals the atmosphere generated for French intellectuals by Kojève's and Hyppolite's commentaries on Hegel in the 1940s, see Henri Niel, "L'Interprétation de Hegel" in *Critique* 3, 18 (November 1947): 426–37.

27. *Sre*, 11–17; see especially p. 16.

28. Jacques Lacan, *Sé II*, 14/*S II*, 6.

29. I have in mind here what Margaret Whitford says about the process of "engaging" with Irigaray, "Reading Irigaray in the Nineties," *Engaging with Irigaray: Feminist Philosophy and Modern European Thought*, edited by Carolyn Burke, Naomi Schor, and Margaret Whitford (New York: Columbia University Press, 1994), pp. 15–33; see especially p. 23.

30. Carolyn Burke, "Romancing the Philosophers: Luce Irigaray," *The Minnesota Review* 29. Reprinted in *Seduction and Theory: Feminist Readings on Representation and Rhetoric*, edited by Dianne Hunter (Chicago: The University of Chicago Press, 1989).

31. See *TeI*, 233/*TI*, 256. Also see Luce Irigaray, "The Fecundity of the Caress: A Reading of Levinas, *Totality and Infinity*, 'Phenomenology of Eros,'" translated by Carolyn Burke, in *Face to Face with Levinas*, edited by R. Cohen (Albany, N.Y.: State University of New York Press, 1986), pp. 231–56. Also published in Irigaray, *An Ethic of Sexual Difference*, translated by Carolyn Burke and Gillian Gill (Ithaca, N.Y.: Cornell University Press, 1993), pp. 185–217; see especially p. 188; "Fécondité de la caresse: lecture de Lévinas, *Totalité et infini*, section IV, B "Phénoménologie de l'éros" in *Ethique de la difference sexuelle* (Paris: Minuit, 1984), pp. 173–99, especially p. 175. Originally published in *Exercises de la patience* 5 (spring 1983): 119–37.

32. "Freud and Heidegger, Heidegger and Freud . . . are preoccupied with each other, passing all their time in deciphering each other, in resembling each other, as one ends up by resembling that which is excluded, or, in absolute mourning, whoever has died. They could not read each other—therefore they have spent all their time and exhausted all their forces in doing so." Jacques Derrida, *La Carte postale: de Socrate à Freud et au-delà* (Paris: Aubier-Flammarion, 1980), pp. 379–80; *The Post-card: From Socrates to Freud and Beyond*, translated by Allan Bass (Chicago: The University of Chicago Press, 1987), p. 357.

33. See also Lacan's remarks on *theoria*, *Sé II*, 260/*S II*, 222.

34. See, for example, *PhG*, 328/*PS*, 276.

35. I am grateful to Mary Bloodsworth for reading and responding to this paper with her usual careful attention.

Chapter 2

Cogito and *Séparation*: Lacan/Levinas

Hans-Dieter Gondek

To posit oneself corporeally is to touch an earth, but to do so in such a way that the touching finds itself already conditioned by the position, the foot settles into a real which this very action outlines or constitutes—as though a painter would notice that he is descending from the picture he is painting.

—Emmanuel Levinas

I am not simply that punctiform being located at the geometral point from which the perspective is grasped. No doubt, in the depths of my eye, the picture is painted. The picture, certainly, is in my eye. But I am in the picture.

—Jacques Lacan

How could this *showing* satisfy something, if there is not some appetite of the eye on the part of the person looking? This appetite of the eye . . . is to be sought on a much less elevated plane than might be supposed, namely, in that which is the true function of the organ of the eye, the eye filled with voracity, the evil eye.

—Jacques Lacan

For the presence before a face, my orientation toward the Other, can lose the avidity proper to the gaze only by turning into generosity, incapable of approaching the other with empty hands.

—Emmanuel Levinas

Outline

At first glance the issue of a connection, or even the establishment of a relationship, between Lacan and Levinas hardly seems promising. Levinas is the champion of an ethics of inescapable responsibility for the Other that claims as its central "ethical experience" the face of the Other, and so places the human being in a face-to-face position on account of his or her humanity, but also because of his or her relationship to God. The name *Lacan* stands for an unorthodox "return to Freud," which (though in the practice of psychoanalysis it certainly allows for exceptions) would not think of doing without the *interruption* of reciprocal face-to-face contact—and for good reason. A face-to-face meeting takes place only at the end of the session, when it is time to pay. One could naturally get caught up in the hypothesis that, while the therapeutic act represents a formal inversion of the conditions of the ethical act, it nevertheless serves precisely to recreate the subjective preconditions for the practice of this ethical act. It represents, so to speak, the photographic negative that allows the fundamental film of the ethical to shine through as such, but that cannot adopt the ethical into its own activity, because the subjective preconditions are lacking on the side of at least one of the participants: it is well known that neurotics are precisely those who find it especially difficult to approach the other with an open gaze and with open, but not empty, hands. This formulation is not only highly schematic but also very reminiscent of the well-known Habermasian concept: Where there is a lack of communicative competence, which after all distinguishes modern rationality as a telos of language, therapeutic discourse must come in to remedy the obvious symptoms of a systematically distorted communication.

No, this is not the way to relate Lacan and Levinas. The flaw, however, lies in the assumptions and overly hasty conclusions that one draws from purely physical situations. The presence of the face, that which Levinas also calls an "epiphany," by no means entails that the face is given to the beholder to see and to read like an open blossom or an opened book. Levinas strictly rejects the physiognomic and the plastic, the pictorial and the picturable: "In my analysis the face is not at all a plastic form like a portrait."[1] We will have to ask ourselves how the encounter with the face of the Other is to be understood, what status it has: is it empirical, even if in a special sense, since Levinas has just emphatically rejected as an experience of the Other the sensory presence of the image that is given and can be studied, or is it transcendental—that is, must the face of the Other always already have presented itself to us in such a way as to have spoken that commandment to us: "You shall not kill," "You will not commit murder"?[2] It might even be asked whether the experience of the face of the Other always requires that this be immediately present to the senses—in other words, whether an actual sensory affect must accompany the experience. Levinas's comments on this subject, especially since *Totalité et infini*, are not unambiguous. Once we have gone this far, it also is possible to ask, conversely, whether psychoanalysis, with its elimination of the sensory gaze on each face, does not perhaps represent an outstanding situation for the experience of the epiphany of the face and the experience of transcendence. One thing, in any case, is common to psychoanalysis according to Lacan and to the ethics of the Other according to Levinas: the emphasis on *asymmetry* in the experience of the Other, not only as a description of the starting point, that is, as a condition that is to be sublimated into a higher unity or a balanced reciprocity, but rather as an irreducible and positively valued fundamental condition of any ethical attitude whatsoever toward the Other.

If we then, having gained some confidence, go a step further and ask whether there are not the traces of a rapprochement, of a relation, in the works themselves or even just in the circles of Levinas and Lacan, we will however reach a sobering conclusion. To begin with the names, Levinas does not name Lacan anywhere, nor Lacan Levinas, even though they were born in the same decade (albeit in very different places and in cultures that had little in common) and published the writings with which each of them exerted his greatest influence during the same decade, even though they once published in the same place: Levinas's essay "De l'évasion" and Lacan's discussion of Eugène Minkowski's book *Le temps vécu*—that is, in *Recherches philosophiques*, Volume 5 (1935–36), even though there are individuals with whom both maintained important relationships, who had not an inconsiderable influence on each (I am thinking above all of Maurice Blanchot and Jean Wahl). Levinas's statements on psychoanalysis are ephemeral and strive for distance, although Lacan refers repeatedly to Jewish tradition and stresses the necessity of engaging with theology, his source here being first and foremost the Freud of *Moses and Monotheism*. Yet it is apparent that Levinas's remarks on the issue of psychoanalysis are not hostile in nature; rather, they betray a certain respect as well as a certain fundamental understanding. We may take, for instance, the use of the term *psychoanalysis* in *Totalité et infini*, where it occurs three times. In the first case, he is speaking of an interminable psychoanalysis, a *psychanalyse interminable*, in which the subject may become involved on the basis of the experience that the world of enjoyment, of *jouissance*, does not satisfy the metaphysical claim (*TeI*, 36–37/*TI*, 65). Now "*psychanalyse interminable*" is exactly the term with which the title of Freud's article "Die endliche und die unendliche Analyse" ("Analysis Terminable and Interminable") has been translated, however (in)appropriately. In the second case, where psychoanalysis is mentioned in the context of the "*acte manqué*," the "abortive action," an "unlimited [*illimité*] field of investigation" is attributed to it (*TeI*, 204/*TI*, 228). Is it a coincidence that both times psychoanalysis is mentioned in the text, it or its project is apostrophized as infinite—if not as *infini*, or infinite in the sense of the word that Levinas reserves for the Other and his radical exteriority, then still with related, synonymous terms—terms that perhaps allow us in this way to recognize a relationship, a (limited) synonymity between the two projects, that of Levinas and that of psychoanalysis? There is, however, yet a third case (not listed in the index to the German edition), and here also the reference to psychoanalysis is particularly qualified, this time as *"ininterrompue,"* as "unintermitting" (*TeI*, 60/*TI*, 88).[3] Again this occurs in connection with the possible diagnosis that language is an abortive action—that is to say, when it does not permit the turn toward the Other that for Levinas is made possible only through language. A first supporting clue (and for the present we will not be able to leave the field of clues) is provided by a note to the essay "Leçon talmudique. Sur la justice Leçon talmudique." (1974): "One should set one's mind against the paganism of the expression 'Oedipus complex' on the strength of the lines from Deuteronomy 8:5 (even if they do not appear overly instructive on the surface): 'Know then in your heart that, as a man disciplines his son, the LORD your God disciplines you.' Paternity has the meaning here of a *constitutive category of the sensible and not of its alienation.* On this point at least psychoanalysis confirms the profound crisis of monotheism in contemporary sensibility, a crisis that cannot be traced back to the rejection of some dogmatic statement. It harbours the ultimate secret of anti-Semitism."[4]

On the theme of "fertility" and "paternity" in particular, Alain Juranville has set Lacan and Levinas in relation to one another; he is, to the best of my knowledge, the only one who attempts to bring out a *direct thematic* relationship.[5] The last two chapters of *Lacan et la philosophie* contain a reconstruction of the Lacanian concept of the name of the father and the phallus in Levinasian terms, including the nonontological version of a proof of the existence of God. But the relationship makes its influence felt much earlier still. Juranville takes up precisely the challenge Levinas, as just cited, at least implicitly directs toward psychoanalysis: the psychopathology of an Oedipus complex can only be understood and treated correctly—that is, as a crisis of our time—if the ethical is grasped as that of which the Oedipus complex represents the pathological form. This does not mean the dismissal of the Oedipus complex, but its inscription in a larger frame, in which its universal significance as a neurotic interpretation alone can be acknowledged without difficulty. Freud's error was in wanting to identify the Oedipus complex as a universal *reality* and an unavoidable *condition* of the development of every subject, especially the male subject. According to Juranville, and to Lacan as Juranville understands him (and in some sense according to Levinas), what needs to be demonstrated rather is that there is a *universal* structure of *desire* and a *law* that holds for it (at least in a transcendental sense); from this point alone can the deviant form "Oedipus complex" be thought of and understood as a specific departure and failure. A nonneurotic desire must be conceived of, at least ideally, that does not succumb to the formation of the Oedipus complex; that is, a desire that can be prevented from heading toward the forbidden object, not by the establishment of a rigid superego alone, and that is therefore in principle open to ethical determination.[6]

It would no doubt be going too far were one to see in Levinas's *metaphysical desire* the basis for precisely this revision of the Freudian theory of neuroses with the Oedipus complex at its center. Yet Juranville very soon comes to speak of metaphysical desire in Levinas's sense, although this reference is meant to ensure that a possible misunderstanding is cleared up in good time: the adjective "metaphysical" in Levinas has nothing in common with what Juranville will go on to characterize as *metaphysical discourse*; rather, it designates a desire that is transcendent and aims at the *absolute Other*.[7] The Lacanian theory of desire and its law as a revision of the "neurotic interpretation" of desire according to Freud is undoubtedly his own accomplishment. Still, in this context, Levinas's concept of metaphysical desire and the affirmation of an absolute otherness that manifests itself only ethically via language (in a concept of language that is clearly distinguished from any representative-objective model) and face—in the speaking face—may be quite useful: it is a foil that clarifies by contrast the specific features of the Lacanian theory of desire and otherness.

If, then, in what follows, Lacan is brought into an explicatory relationship with Levinas in this manner—which perhaps grants the appeal of the staged encounter more than it hopes for actual correspondences—this undertaking should not cause us to give up the conjecture (one that can of course only be brought forward with some reservations) that there might also be between Levinas and Lacan (more exactly, from Levinas to Lacan) a line of reception either direct or indirect (that is, mediated through third parties). Once again, to my knowledge, Levinas is never quoted by Lacan, and even Elisabeth Roudinesco, who should know, because she knows everything that concerns the history of psychoanalysis in France, above all in Lacan's circle, never mentions his name.[8]

But Roudinesco does have something else to relate: the Christianizing of psychoanalysis through Lacan. In 1969, a book published by Bela Grunberger and Janine Chasseguet-Smirgel (under the pseudonym André Stéphane) with the title (an infamous one, because it is reminiscent of the books about the Nazi concentration camps and the Gulag Archipelago) *L'univers contestationnaire. Les Nouveaux Chrétiens* (approximately, *The Universe of the Protesters: The New Christians*) exposed the profound anti-Semitism of this movement in an "analysis" of May 1968. But not only this—the book, for the first time in French psychoanalysis, brings the quarrel over the doctrine onto the idea that only affiliation with Judaism can guarantee the correctness of the doctrine, and in this context brands Lacanianism as a Christian deviation from orthodoxy. Roudinesco makes clear that the authors refer to Freud incorrectly: *Moses and Monotheism* is the book in which Freud not only challenges Judaism on the issue of chosenness, but also distances himself from the Judaism of his birth: "Now Freud also defined his own Jewishness in relation to a discovery that he wanted to de-Judaize in order to make it universal. If there were no chosen people, psychoanalysis could become universal, since its object, the unconscious, is universal. Renouncing circumcision, that is, the physical trace of difference, means assuming a symbolic castration according to which there is no superiority or inferiority of one culture in relation to others since all men are subject to the same law despite their differences."[9] Notwithstanding this, the fuss over the symptom, however futile it may be, points back to a schism that, even if it remains anathema in cooperative work, has its specific virulence. The question of the God of psychoanalysis has been posed, and here Lacan—especially in his theory of the Borromean knot,[10] which harks back to the Christian motif of the Trinity—has brought about a shift that cannot be overlooked, and is perhaps even immeasurable. To address it touches on the whole of psychoanalysis and its history, if not on history itself. To leave it out does the same.[11]

The question of the God of psychoanalysis has been posed. This is first of all the question of his necessity—for the practice *and* for the theory of psychoanalysis. It also is true for psychoanalysis, at least according to Lacan, that without the Other, who is *also* God, the relationship of man and woman cannot be thought. But the question also arises whether the God of psychoanalysis is the God of religion, the God of theology, or the God of the philosophers. Or, what is probable, none of the aforementioned and yet somehow all of them. It will be important to differentiate them, to show where the lines of contact can be distinguished, and to trace these in such a way that in them the difference can be recognized that permits contact in the first place.

But let us be cautious. I have suggested the impression that there could be a direct or an indirect reception of Levinas by way of Lacan, which, however, has only expressed itself in hints and traces. It may just as easily prove to be a series of coincidental correspondences, a picking up of something that was in the air. As a rule, researching lines of reception, instances of reception, or even individuals who could have served as intermediaries is futile anyway; it seldom contributes to an understanding of the issue and can at best be useful as a second-rate formulation of the question. Only after the dossier is opened, in other words. With respect to Seminar XI, *The Four Fundamental Concepts of Psycho-analysis*, I would like to indicate and interpret certain correspondences that can be understood in this sense.

The Unconscious and the Other

Seminar XI introduces, as its first fundamental concept, the unconscious. Just as in the already cited essay "La position de l'inconscient," which

Lacan edited for publication at about the time of this seminar, a definition of the unconscious via consciousness is rejected. The Freudian unconscious discloses itself in the concept of the cause,[12] which itself is to be understood (in contrast to the law) as referring to something anticonceptual, undefined. Cause is there where there is a lack; or, "what the unconscious does is to show us the gap through which neurosis recreates a harmony with a real—a real that may well not be determined" (*Sé XI*, 25/*S XI*, 22). Insofar as it is the *nonrealized* that comes into effect in this gap, Lacan feels compelled to introduce a feature into his concept of the unconscious that not only clearly breaks with any image of mechanical causality (of which one may sometimes be reminded in the early Freud, who was likewise trying to characterize the unconscious by a hidden causality), but also makes the unconscious in its "coming" dependent on something that is doubly *beyond being* (that is to say, on this side of being). In other words, it is not just a matter of the nonrealized—that is, of something that has never come into being—that expresses itself, that "speaks" here, but even more, of its need for something that expects it—not in the sense of a concrete expectation that has determined beforehand the being of that which is to come, but rather in the mode of an expectation or a patience that is simply trying to do all it can so that whatever merits the qualification "unconscious" in this sense can come. Lacan identifies this specific event of arrival, for which the analyst should be prepared without trying to have grasped it in advance, as "*trouvaille*"—found material, sudden idea. The situation as a whole—that the nonrealized, for the sake of its *belated* realization,[13] needs the *attend*ance of someone who makes its arrival easier (a midwife instead of the abortionist [*faiseuse d'anges*] to whom Lacan alludes), is summed up by Lacan with a specific emphasis: "The status of the unconscious, which, as I have shown, is so fragile on the ontic plane, is ethical" (*Sé XI*, 34/*S XI*, 33).[14] Also, "The gap of the unconscious may be said to be *pre-ontological*" (*Sé XI*, 31/*S XI*, 29). Finally, the "gap" is described as "ontic" through which the unconscious presents itself for a moment before it immediately closes again in accordance with its pulsating motion.[15]

It is Levinas who diagnoses as a fundamental characteristic of Western philosophy an "ontological imperialism" (*TeI*, 15/*TI*, 44)[16] or a primacy of ontology (*TeI*, 15/*TI*, 45; cf. also *DE*, 103)[17] that reveals itself above all in a subordination of the ethical as a specific but limited region of being and who in the course of a reversal, sets a "primacy of the ethical" (*TeI*, 51/*TI*, 79) in opposition to it. Even if Levinas does not characterize the ethical as pre-ontological,[18] the way is still prepared for this: there is an infinite that cannot be contained in any ontological order, and that *is* the infinite Other in his transcendence. As already mentioned, Levinas also identifies this transcendence (in a departure from the usual use of the term) as a "metaphysics" and can consequently assert, "Ontology presupposes metaphysics" (*TeI*, 18/*TI*, 48).[19]

Lacan postulates a *subject of the unconscious*. On the whole, it is hardly to be expected that such a subject could be brought into relation with a philosophical understanding of subjectivity. Yet we must pay attention to the path by which Lacan goes back to Descartes. The starting point is Freud's *Interpretation of Dreams*, or, more precisely, the passage on "The Forgetting of Dreams" with which the seventh chapter opens. There Freud engages the question of whether the *narration* of the dream distorts its content and how a doubt that the patient notes about certain elements of the reported dream is to be handled. Freud sees in the identified doubt precisely an outstandingly appropriate moment for further work: a doubt stands for a resistance on the part of the patient's ego against the unconscious content that relates to the relevant element of the dream, and it is very well confirmed when the patient, during a repetition of the dream narrative, replaces expressions in the "cloak" of the dream at this point. In this way Freud lets a certainty arise from the connotation of doubt—the certainty that here an *act of unconscious thought* forms the basis.[20] Here is a convergence between the methodologies of Freud and Descartes: The certainty of the *cogito* rests precisely on the fact that such a fundamental and radical doubt as the hyperbolic doubt, which affects even mathematical truths and exposes me to the *genius malignus*, the deceitful god, still lies behind the fact that I am the one who doubts. There is a subject of doubting or (to name the genre to which doubt, in Descartes, belongs) of thought. "In order to understand the Freudian concepts, one must set out on the basis that it is the subject who is called—the subject of Cartesian origin" (*Sé XI*, 47/*S XI*, 47).

But there also is an asymmetry between Freud and Descartes: for Freud—or better, for Freud according to Lacan[21]—the subject is at home with himself (*chez soi*) in the *field of the unconscious*. Lacan stresses the difficulty in which the Cartesian *cogito* stands in the moment of its certainty: it is certain of itself *in the act*, as something acting in this way (thus the specific formulation already in Descartes, in the Second Meditation, "that this proposition: I am, I exist, is necessarily true each time I pronounce it, or that I mentally conceive it"[22])—but no more. Between the act–certainty of the *cogito* and the truth of objective propositions there is, however, a gap that cannot be bridged from the side of the *cogito* alone. It requires the reintroduction of a guarantor of universal truths, for which even a *cogito* that is certain of itself cannot vouch. The Third Meditation brings that (in)famous ontological proof of God, which, from my inborn idea of God as "a substance that is infinite, independent, all-knowing, all-powerful," on the basis of my existence as creature, deduces the sole "cause" of this idea, that is, this infinite substance itself: "For although the idea of substance is within me owing to the fact that I am substance, nevertheless I should not have the idea of an infinite substance—since I am finite—if it had not proceeded from some substance which was veritably infinite."[23]

Lacan has emphatically stressed in Seminar XI that with Descartes's God "it is a question . . . of an infinite being" (*Sé XI*, 204/*S XI*, 225). That cannot be taken for granted. For as the Third Meditation goes on, and then again in the Fifth Meditation, Descartes concerns himself with God under the aspect of his perfection, and in the literature on the ontotheological proof of God's existence this point also stands in first place.[24] Levinas, for his part, radically brackets the ontotheological context in *Totalité et infini* (cf. *Tel*, 19–20/*TI*, 46–49).[25] For him, the *infinite* God of Descartes is, alongside the *Good* "beyond being" in Plato and the *One* in Plotinus, one of the rare instances of an incursion of transcendence into Western philosophy, which is otherwise wedded to ontology.

Already for Levinas the (self-)grounding of the *cogito*—and he, like all modern interpreters, considers it undecidable whether it is to be ascribed to a *deduction* or an *intuition*[26]—is inseparable from the idea of the infinite. One could say that the *cogito* is the event within the self for which the idea of the infinite forms the "pendant" of the other—or, better, conversely: the *cogito* testifies to the separation (*séparation*, a concept to which we will soon turn in more detail) of the self from the other. Levinas also calls this separation "psychism" or "interiority" (*Tel*, 23–29/*TI*, 53–58). One might be tempted to speak here of "individualization," but that would presuppose a superior category that encompasses the self and the other—and it is just this type of category that Levinas is refuting.[27] For this separation Levinas also has ready the term *atheism*, which at first sight seems quite remarkable. Yet this does not stand in opposition to the idea of the infinite as the infinite Other, God. On the contrary, only an infinite God is a transcendent God, and vice versa. Atheism, then, is the break with the "question of being," the break with the potential and the desire to think an existing God. What is required is an "ontological atheism" or an "atheistic de-ontology."[28] Without atheism as interruption of all participation—as participation in a being—there is no receptiveness for the idea of the infinite, no relationship to an *absolute* Other, no metaphysical desire. Bernasconi speaks in this context, taking up an expression of Derrida's, of a "double origin"[29]—a *chronological* one (that is, in the *cogito*), and a *logical* one, in the idea of the infinite. "The cause of being is thought or known by its effect *as though* it were posterior to its effect. . . . The posteriority of the anterior—an inversion logically absurd. . . ." (*Tel*, 25/*TI*, 54[30]).

In "Dieu et la philosophie," an essay first published in 1975, Levinas clarified the relationship of the infinite to the finite, of the infinite Other to the *cogito*. "The difference between the Infinite and the finite is a non-indifference of the Infinite to the finite, and is the secret of subjectivity."[31] The *in* of *infini* here is not to be understood only as a negative prefix, but also as the *in* of inclusion:[32] of the infinite in the finite, the other in the self. That this is a clarification becomes obvious when one looks at the term *infinition* in *Total-*

ité et infini—for this means nothing other than "the astonishing feat of containing more than it is possible to contain," of which subjectivity shows itself to be capable (*TeI*, xv/*TI*, 27).

We will see later that Lacan also offers a version of *infinition*, although it carries the name *infinitisation* and will only become comprehensible once the functions "alienation" and "separation" are introduced. Let us put it aside for the moment. For that matter, we must not indiscriminately list references, correspondences, similarities, and relationships among themes, theses, and methods. If Levinas locates the Cartesian *cogito* in the dependence on the idea of the infinite and thus on a preexisting relationship to God, this may still be relevant for Lacan as a reconstruction of Descartes; in itself, his own grasp of the *cogito* goes in the opposite direction. The Cartesian God is taken by Lacan simply as a contrasting foil in order to clarify the specific intuitions and expectations that are imposed on the analyst in practical psychoanalysis. Characteristic in this regard is the confrontation of specific anxieties: the fear of being deceived by the *genius malignus* versus the fear of deceiving *the analyst*, a fear that, according to Lacan, manifests itself in certain moments of analysis (*Sé XI*, 37/*S XI*, 37; 126/137; 211/233). The concept of a *sujet supposé savoir*, a subject who is *supposed* to know—and it is certainly not only the analyst of whom this is presumed, rather, an "unconscious knowledge" is to be presumed as ultimate motive on the part of the one who undergoes analysis—simply serves, not only to determine the function of the idealization of the analyst, which is inevitable in certain phases of analysis, but also to cut short the thought of any resemblance between the analyst and God in connection with this unavoidable evocation. At one point Lacan even sets the *sujet supposé savoir* and God—that is, a very specific God—in direct relation: "The *subject supposed to know*, God himself, to call him by the name that Pascal gives him, when one describes him through his opposite: not the God of Abraham, Isaac, and Jacob, but the God of the philosophers, the very one who is disturbed out of his latency in all theory. *Theoria*—might that be the place in the world of theo-logy?"[33] In this context a fundamental difference between Lacan and Levinas on the question of the Other needs to be brought out. While "Levinas's thought remains in play—a play of difference and of analogy—between the face of God and the face of my neighbour, between the infinite Other as God and the infinite Other as the other person,"[34] the Other for Lacan is first of all faceless: the Other is *a site*. The Other only obtains a face when someone actually inhabits this place, for instance the mother (*É*, 813) or an "exemplar" of the opposite sex (*É* 849). Only then, for that matter, does it become meaningful to speak of a *real* Other (primarily the mother qua maternity and biological birth), a *symbolic* Other (first of all the father as the dead father, the ancestor), and an *imaginary* Other (the staged Other of fantasy). But first and fundamentally the Other is a site that is required so that the play of signifiers does not remain an empty play, or one running on empty. Lacan assigns it variously articulated determinants that end however in one and the same function.

1. the Other as "the locus of speech and, potentially, the locus of truth," which can be called on, even from the position of the unconscious, and which, latent or not, is always already there (*Sé XI*, 118/*S XI*, 129);
2. the Other as the "site at which speech verifies itself in meeting the exchange of signifiers, the ideals they support, the elementary structures of kinship, the metaphor of the father as principle of separation, the division that is always reopened within the subject in his primary alienation" (*É*, 849);
3. the Other—"the site of the Other, the Other (as) witness, the witness Other than any one of the partners" (*É*, 807);
4. the Other as "the site of the thesaurus of the signifier" (*É*, 806);
5. the Other as discourse of the Other: "The unconscious is the discourse of [*de*] the Other, where one must understand the *de* in the sense of the Latin *de* (as specification of the object): *de Alio in oratione* (to be completed: *tua res agitur*)" (*É*, 814);
6. the Other who "is nothing else than the pure subject of modern game theory" (*É*, 806), "the ostensible site of the pure subject of the signifier" (*É*, 807).

The first three aspects (of the aforementioned list, which is not intended to be complete[35]) are no doubt closely linked: they describe the transcendent Other who can be addressed and to whom one can refer, the irreducible expulsion of the possibility of truth in speaking (not, however, of its factual guarantee). The second point stresses the contractual aspect of this Other, which Lacan elsewhere also calls the "symbolic pact": here the Other merges with the codified and justified symbolic order—the binding laws of exchange, the elementary structures of kinship, the implicit "social contract." The third aspect lays claim to a testimony that cannot be provided by those who are speaking to one another—but even this can be better understood from the perspective of truth than from a religious understanding of "testimony," such as one finds in Levinas.[36] The Other can therefore be understood in Lacan as, at best, a secularized "idea of God," as the depersonalized symbolic function robbed of the attribute of a face,[37] which can be called on for the sake of truth and justice.[38] Can be called on—no less, but also no more. The Other, beyond the fact of holding open the dimension of truth, has no further guaranteeing function in Lacan. This finds expression in formulations and formulas like "there is no Other of the Other"[39] or the "s($\cancel{A}$)"—the "signifier of the lack in the Other that is inherent in its very function of being a thesaurus of the signifier" (*É*, 818).

The Other also proves to be desiring and vulnerable to castration.

Let us come to the other Other, that of the next three aspects. According to number 4, the Other is nothing other than language in the sense of a "synchronic battery of signifiers," which the subject makes use of in the diachronic speech act. Number 5 names the inner otherness of the "unconscious," which is (and this is the barrier that Lacan methodically sets up against any possible "naturalization") in itself nothing other than the external otherness of language and discourse (*"l'inconscient est structuré comme un langage"*—"the unconscious is structured *like* a language/*as* a language," where the second version, to which I myself incline, puts greater emphasis on the methodological element: the unconscious is structured when it is examined *as* a language[40]). As far as the sixth point is concerned, the Other here seems to be established as a complementary function of the subject, even if an overrated and idealized one. The Other in game theory, for instance, is the fictive ideal of one who makes infallible calculations. He is a pure subject of the signifier, in the sense of doing nothing other than fitting in with this signifier, in contrast to the subject of the unconscious, who, being qua drive still bound to *objects* and in this way always referring at least to a *remainder of the real*, is always only an "impure" subject of the signifier. A pure subject of the signifier perhaps only exists in a purely theoretically defined moment—that of the *infinitisation* or infinitization of the subject, when the *ur*-signifier is pure nonsense and does not let any unconscious meaning arise in the subject, but completely abolishes this meaning (*Sé XI*, 227/*S XI*, 252). Only this "case" does not seem to be so eccentric, since Lacan immediately afterward formulates the project of achieving, through formalization, "the mediation of this infinity of the subject with the finiteness of desire" (*Sé XI*, 228/*S XI*, 252). So Lacan too is concerned with the relation between an infinite and a finite, even if in a very different way from Levinas. Here we are dealing, after all, with the infinity of a subject—which, however, can only come into existence in the first place because the subject is called on to realize himself in the *field* of the Other.

The Place and Function of the Cogito and the Other in Lacan and Levinas

Field is a term used frequently by Lacan, seldom by Levinas. I could have added the Lacanian "field of the Other" as yet a further meaning in the list of aspects of otherness, if the field–quality did not form, as it were, the structural element of all of the accentuations of the function of the Other listed here. But before I address the "field of the Other" and the operations of alienation and separation that are to be carried out in it by the subject, it is important first to return once again to the Cartesian *cogito* and to establish the situation of the subject—both Lacan and Levinas offer him a "home," a "*chez soi*." For Levinas, however, this is quite a dubious home, namely one in which the ego, its link *as cogito* with the idea of the infinite dissolved, resides in a realm of the *self*, in which it is free (*TeI*, 7/*TI*, 37). As we know, Levinasian ethics is fundamentally a *critique of freedom* as spontaneity; responsibility for the other is anterior to freedom—I do not even have the freedom to close myself off from this call to responsibility for the other, for thereby the responsibility only increases (which does not mean that it decreases if I heed the call—it always increases). According to Levinas, responsibility does not rest on a freely chosen commitment; rather, I am always already called to this responsibility, called in such a way that my belatedness is unavoidable and I am always already guilty (*AE*, 174ff./*OB*, 136ff.).

We will see later that Lacan also does not understand freedom as the spontaneity of a self-positing subject, but instead assigns it a specific place on the way to realization in the field of the Other. The "home" he himself first offers the subject is already from the outset implicated in an otherness. The site of the subject—and by this is still meant the Cartesian subject, the *hypokeimenon* of that which says *cogito, je pense, I think*—is the complete, total site of the web of signifiers: *there, where it was*, where it has always been, that site is the dream. "*Here, in the field of the dream, you are at home. Wo es war, soll Ich werden.*[41] . . . But the subject is there to rediscover *where it was*—I anticipate—the real" (*Sé XI*, 45/*S XI*, 44–45). The site of the dream is an interval not only in the spatial sense—*between perception and consciousness*—but also in a temporal sense. The diachronic temporality of "where it was"/"I am to become" ["*wo Es war*"/"*soll Ich werden*"] is the temporality of a transition in which something always comes too late: consciousness.

"[The *cogito*] does indeed mark commencement because it is the awakening of an existence that takes charge of its own condition. But this awakening comes from the Other. Before the *cogito* existence dreams itself, as though it remained foreign to itself. It is because it suspects that it is dreaming itself that it awakens. The doubt makes it seek certainty" (*TeI*, 58/*TI*, 86). This certainty, however, is always only that of the *cogito*, never that of where it was and what it was there. For the task that is set by the "becoming there" "where it was" is that of grasping primary process. This is clearly distinguished from the *cogito*: in the dream, no reflexivity, no self-confirmation is possible. "[The subject] may say to himself, *It's only a dream*. But he does not apprehend himself as someone who says to himself, *After all, I am the consciousness of this dream*" (*Sé XI*, 72/*S XI*, 75–76).

The moment of rupture is at the same time the moment of transition: the event of awakening. Lacan relates how he *wakes up* out of a dream, *awoken*

by a knock on the door—to the *belatedness* of this narration is added a doubling, the recital of which demands a diachronic beginning. On the one hand,
the causal event is reconstructed that brings about the awakening out of the
dream (and through the dream) from outside of the dream (here it is the
knocking on the door). On the other hand, that itself is worked into the dream,
which tries to connect to another real (to this, in terms of its temporality,
namely that of a past which from the outset cannot be recalled, an always-
already-lostness, may be ascribed precisely those attributes that Levinas has
grasped in his term *trace*: for that to be the past which has never been the present)—to that traumatic real that is always missed and that constitutes the *ker-
nel* of the unconscious. In awakening I reconstitute my representation around
this perception (the knock); my consciousness reorganizes itself, namely as a
purely representing consciousness. From where *I* now *think*, that is, as a consciousness dependent on the representation, I can no longer come to the "what
I am at that moment—at the moment, so immediately before and so separate,
which is that in which I began to dream under the effect of the knocking which
is, to all appearances, what woke me" (*Sé XI*, 56/*S XI*, 56). With the "emergence of the represented reality," awakening achieves the contours of a
"*béance*," a "gaping" or a "gap" (*Sé XI*, 56/*S XI*, 57) that cannot be closed.

Yet with awakening we are not free of the problem of dream and *cogito*; also, consciousness or the conscious, self-reflexive ego is not out of the
woods. For even representation does not guarantee full transparency and,
above all, it does not reduce the minimal temporal difference. *Between perception and consciousness*—the psychic location of the dream since Freud—
is also an interval between *perception* and *consciousness*. "That which shows
itself must already have been lost in order to be found again by consciousness."[42] To that extent, the *cogito*, the *I think*, as an act of stating, is always
separate from the *I am* as statement: however clearly, physically, and immediately I may feel that I am, while I think and state that I am, that I exist—as
soon as I form a representation of my "I am," I have the problem that I am *and*
that I am in my representation, where the two modes of being need not immediately coincide (as the famous saying of Parmenides goes, which is conven-
tionally translated "for thinking and being are the same"[43]). Lacan also uses
the modifying phrase that one does not find in Descartes: "*De penser, je suis*";
"I think—by virtue of thinking, I am" (*Sé XI*, 36/*S XI*, 35). With the turn
toward *je suis*, a "real" is aimed at but not reached—at least not as a true one.
The problematic whereby the *cogito* may have the *certainty* that proceeds
directly from its act of thought, but not yet the *truth* of itself, does not lie in
the fact that the *cogito*, in the process of its achievement as doubt, has rendered all possible truth invalid. It lies rather in the constitutive split between
thinking and *being*, between myself as *thinking thing*, as *res cogitans*, and
myself as *existing thing*, as *res extensa*. In a certain way, *I am* as a valid mean-

ing for me of *I think* is only guaranteed me *insofar as and as long as* I think. Precisely this is the starting point that renders it necessary for Descartes to dispel the disturbing hypothesis of the *genius malignus*, that is, to return to a God who guarantees metaphysical truths. And Levinas, as we have seen, placed before the *cogito* the relationship toward the infinite itself.

Levinas also has focused specifically on the "evil genius" that is articulated in Descartes, and recognized its proper malignancy in the fact that it denies the affirmative word, and in fact any speech whatsoever, and so releases a *lie* that cannot be refuted because it is not even established verbally in the first place (*TeI*, 63–64/*TI*, 90–92). For the *cogito* as the end and turning point of a process of doubt, of which the highest point consists precisely in the fact of being at the mercy of this evil genius, means that for the moment it achieves itself only as "the thinking subject which denies its evidences" and attains in the *cogito* "the evidence of this work of negation"—thus Levinas (*TeI*, 65–66/*TI*, 93). "Perhaps the *I think*, reduced to this punctuality of being certain only of the absolute doubt concerning all signification, its own included, has a still more fragile status than that in which we were able to attack the *I am lying*"—thus Lacan (*Sé XI*, 129/*S XI*, 140–41). This "movement unto the abyss," this vertigo that carries the subject off with it, can only be halted by the word of the other, for "[i]t is not I, it is the other that can say *yes*" (*TeI*, 66/*TI*, 93). And Levinas concludes this disturbing thought–experiment of a world without the Other, a "world absolutely silent that would not come to us from the word" (*TeI*, 63/*TI*, 90), with the assurance that—and this holds true, in his opinion, for Descartes—"to possess the idea of infinity is to have already welcomed the Other" (*TeI*, 66/*TI*, 93).[44]

In Lacan, the emphasis shifts. "I" am to realize myself in the field of the Other. "I" am, as it were, to go out to him, to break through an interiority or at least the appearance of one, even if it is posed only by the narcissism of the ego.[45] But in a certain way the Other is always already with me, in me—so much in me, with me, that he represents my own "with me," my "at home": the unconscious. The atheism of a break with participation in Levinas, which is at the same time a prerequisite for my being able (having been able) to receive the Other—and this must still be examined more closely with respect to separation—finds its pendant in a formulation of Lacan's that questions especially drastically the guaranteeing function of the Other, but in a certain way also gives it new support: "The true formula of atheism is not *God is dead* . . . the true formula of atheism is *God is unconscious*" (*Sé XI*, 58/*S XI*, 59). We also can see this sentence as an exaggeration of Nietzsche's famous dictum that "we are not rid of God because we still have faith in grammar":[46] that is, that God can exert an especially powerful influence there, in the unconscious.

More important still is that the Other to whom the subject must turn and to whom he must hold for the sake of realization is also understood as *desir-*

ing (I do not dare pose the question here whether this holds only for the Other as site insofar as it is occupied by someone—perhaps father or mother—or whether a desire can also be attributed to the Other as thesaurus of language—perhaps that desire of the Other of which Lacan says that it is the desire for the human being). It also holds true for Lacan that the Other is always already there, if not exactly via the idea of the infinite as one who is welcomed, then still as addressee of my speech and my desire.

This also can be demonstrated precisely in relation to the dream, which Freud recognized as a type of unconscious thought. If Lacan attributes a subject to this unconscious thought (that is, a subject of the unconscious), this means in relation to the dream that "it thinks before it attains certainty" (*Sé XI*, 37/*S XI*, 37). This certainty is for Lacan one that attaches itself to constellations of signifiers—thus the examination of the repetition of the dream narrative and the observation of the changes that are recognizable in it. But what is even more important is that certainty is not in the same place as the expression of the dream. "For the subject of certainty is divided here—it is Freud who has certainty" (*Sé XI*, 47/*S XI*, 46). In other words, the constellation of the subject of the unconscious and his certainty already stands in a relationship to the *Other*, a relationship that already bears the decisive marks of *transference*, as Lacan understands it. For as he will say later in the part of Seminar XI devoted to transference, "The subject is looking for his certainty. And the certainty of the analyst himself concerning the unconscious cannot be derived from the concept of the transference" (*Sé XI*, 118/*S XI*, 129). The analyst is called on to give "ethical witness," that is, in the "moment when he feels he has the courage to judge and to conclude" (*Sé XI*, 40/*S XI*, 40). It is the responsibility of the analyst, in the individual analysis as well as in general, to hold open access to the unconscious, or, because the unconscious invariably closes itself up again (and here again is meant the closing up that occurs in individual analysis as well as the loss of the "unconscious" in the history of psychoanalysis)—Lacan speaks in this context of a "pulsation" (*Sé XI*, 44/*S XI*, 43, 115/125, 131/143, 189/207)—to be by his presence a "witness of this loss" (*Sé* XI, 116/*S XI*, 127) and to enter into "a new alliance."

Lacan differentiates in transference between an affective element and a structural element. It is not that Lacan rejects the understanding of transference as affect; he only thinks it does not go far enough. The aforementioned affect is for him transference love, and it brings in the dimension of *deceit*,[47] which in a conventional understanding of transference is too quickly reduced to the effect of confusion. To speak of confusion presupposes too much: namely, that one has control over access to the truth, to a reality that can be used as a reliable measuring rod. This is not the case. Moreover, the affective element is flanked by the structural element as a necessary condition, and this is nothing other than the analytical situation as a situation of speaking in the presence of the analyst. One could also speak of synchronic organization. In relation to this, transference love forms the diachronic element, that is, as the achievement of a closing of the unconscious—which, as such, is not merely disadvantageous but is rather the necessary condition for interpretation to begin in earnest (*Sé XI*, 119/*S XI*, 131).

"*Transference is the enactment [mise-en-acte] of the reality of the unconscious*" (*Sé XI*, 137/*S XI*, 149). To be noted here is the ethical connotation of "*acte*,"[48] the act which, whether as a sexual or testamentary act, always implicitly or explicitly gives testimony. It is only that the status of testimony, as far as the reality of the unconscious is concerned, lies with the Other—in this case, with the analyst.

Séparation

The whole of Seminar XI contributes to the more exact definition of that which was already clarified in the discussion of the Cartesian *cogito* as the actual problem of subjectivity (as a subjectivity affected by the unconscious): the subject is divided within himself, and this division or rift is one that manifests itself as an effect of language. Lacan distinguishes the subject of stating (which is here correlated with the *I think*) from the subject of the statement (the *I am*, more or less). Now this distinction is also found in linguistics and there serves in the analysis of what Husserl once called "occasional expressions," which, like the personal pronouns, have no actual definable meaning, but have to be filled in each time by the "real." What looks linguistically like a bridging function between speech and reality, sense and existence, always remains in tension for Lacan and never closes itself up. The treatment of the *cogito* has shown that here also a temporal difference is inscribed—a diachrony, as one could say with Levinas. It has not gone unnoticed that the distinction between the subject of stating and the subject of the statement also corresponds to the Levinasian distinction between *dire* and *dit*, between *saying* and *the said*, which at least since *Autrement qu'être* has achieved preeminent methodological value in Levinas.[49] However, to my knowledge, it has not been noticed that Lacan also speaks increasingly of *dire* and *dit*, in formulations which in their tone also are strongly reminiscent of Levinas. To give only one example

> The *saying* of Freud [*le dire de Freud*] follows from the logic that has as its source that which is *said* by the unconscious. Insofar as Freud has discovered this *said*, it ex-ists.

> It is necessary to reconstitute the *saying* of it so that the discourse of analysis can constitute itself (to which I contribute), namely from the experience in which it shows itself to exist.

One cannot translate this saying into truth-terms, for truth is only available *half-said* [*midit*], smoothly cut off, but that there is this pure *half-said* (it may be conjugated on the model of *tu médites, je médis* [*you consider, I insult*]), achieves its sense only from this *saying*.[50]

More could be said concerning the relation between *dire, dit,* and *Dieu*.[51] But I would now like to turn to a result that bears on it indirectly, insofar as it becomes noticeable in a mutual exclusion between *being* [*Sein*] and *sense* [*Sinn*]. The starting point is the necessity that has already been discussed for the subject to realize himself in the field of the Other (that is, above all, but not exclusively, in the field of language). This necessity deepens and widens the division of the subject: "Through the effects of speech, the subject always realizes himself more in the Other, but there he is already pursuing no more than half of himself. He will simply find his desire ever more divided, pulverized, in the circumscribable metonymy of speech. The effects of language are always mixed with the fact, which is the basis of the analytic experience, that the subject is subject only from being subjected to the field of the Other, the subject proceeds from his synchronic subjection in the field of the Other. That is why he must get out, get himself out, and in the *getting-himself-out*, in the end, he will know that the real Other has, just as much as himself, to get himself out, to pull himself free" (*Sé XI*, 172/*S XI*, 188 [translation amended]). The latter point, however, does not let us conclude that there is a reciprocity between the subject and the Other; here Lacan draws a line between circularity and reciprocal relationships (cf. *Sé XI*, 188/*S XI*, 207; *É*, 839). On this point there is no difference between Levinas and Lacan. The aforementioned synchronicity is to be understood in two ways: on the one hand, as a synchronicity of the signifier, and that always means as the structural condition of language itself; if *something* is significant, meaningful, so by the same token *everything* is meaningful—nothing is excluded from *significance*, from *meaning*, so the "encounter" with this *something* as the (fictive) first signifier turns directly back to the subject—in the search for my own significance.[52] On the other hand, it is to be understood in that temporally paradoxical sense of the concept of structure as a methodological cut through time, by which diachronic events can be distinguished even more clearly. Lacan also stresses this peculiar temporality: "The subject is born insofar as the signifier emerges in the field of the Other. But, by this very fact, this subject—which was previously nothing if not a subject coming into being—solidifies into a signifier" (*Sé XI*, 181/*S XI*, 199).[53]

The situation of realization in the field of the Other as subjection to the signifier, as something represented by a signifier for a signifier (*É*, 840), is not without an alternative, although the alternative is more of a seeming alternative: it is called *aphanisis* and denotes a *fading* of the subject, with lethal tendencies (*Sé XI*, 189/*S XI*, 207–8). In the operation denominated *alienation*, the subject in the act of self-establishment must choose between the *sense* produced by the signifier on the one hand and *aphanisis* on the other. This is a choice that is not really a choice in the sense that one can have that on which one decided: the choice of alienation always ends in the need to let something go. If we try to hold on to one thing, the other disappears.

The alternative itself already represents a foreshortening. Lacan clarifies this in the apparent opposition between the subject's *sense* [*Sinn*] and *being* [*Sein*]. If one chooses the being of the subject, precisely that subject disappears who must achieve realization in the field of the Other, of language, and who can achieve sense only there; if one chooses sense, one must be equally prepared for a loss—that of the nonsense that the unconscious represents, the formations of which, we remember, have the status of the non-realized, which cannot be classified as either being or non-being. The lethal tendency of the choice of alienation becomes even clearer in the example *your money or your life*—either I lose both, or I keep a life diminished by the element of money. Lacan traces this back to the fact that the *vel*, the *or*, of alienation functions in the sense of union in set theory and consequently becomes equivalent to an *et (sic et non)* (*É*, 840).

With the return out of alienation the second operation sets in, which Lacan outlines in the context of the realization of the subject in the field of the Other as an "encounter" with the signifier: this is *separation*. In set theory, the function of *intersection* corresponds to it. In an expansive analysis of the meaning of the verb *se parare*, Lacan derives from this verb the meanings "to defend oneself," "to resist," but also "to adorn oneself," "to dress oneself," and finally "to generate oneself." Essentially, however, separation is a response of the subject to the "intimation that the Other makes to him by his discourse." The subject thereby becomes aware of something that in itself is the desire of the Other, but that cannot yet be experienced by the subject as desire, and instead presents itself in all its impenetrable mystery as a lack. The subject experiences himself as exposed to the question: *"He is saying this to me, but what does he want?"* (*Sé XI*, 194/*S XI*, 214; *É*, 843–44). He answers with the production of a lack of his own, the most convenient one being to offer himself as lack, that is, to offer his own disappearance as an active test of what it is that comes from the Other. Lacan sees in this episode between child and adult the seed of that which is called "mental anorexia."[54] Yet this is not a psychological event, nothing that could be understood as disturbed communication, analyzed and cured. It is not only that the experience of the desire of the Other is unavoidable; just as unavoidable is the confrontation with an inner dimension of loss that advises one precisely to bring oneself into play as loss, as disappearance, if perhaps only for lack of something better. The lethal dimension to which Lacan has referred again and again in the entire passage is not an imaginary one: it is death itself. It is death as the *negative quantity* of the libido—the *negative quantity* of which Lacan speaks for the first time in Seminar XI at the introduction of the cause as explanation for the unconscious, and for the second time when he is concerned with making possible "the mediation of this infinity of the subject with the finiteness of desire" (*Sé XI*, 228/*S XI*, 252).

> It is the libido, *qua* pure life instinct, that is to say, immortal life, or irrepressible life, life that has need of no organ, simplified, indestructible life. It is precisely what is subtracted from the living being by virtue of the fact that it is subject to the cycle of sexed reproduction. And it is of this that all the forms of the *objet a* that can be enumerated are the representatives, the equivalents. The *objets a* are merely its representatives, its figures. (*Sé XI*, 180/*S XI*, 198)

The object *a* is the product of separation (in cases where the subject finds something to separate, something that falls off from the body, and not, as in the case mentioned earlier, where the subject must give himself up as lost), and it is Lacan's response to Heidegger. For him death is "signifier and nothing but signifier, for can it be said that there is a being-for-death?" (*Sé XI*, 232/*S XI*, 257). The object *a* embodies *Dasein*, as Lacan notes elsewhere.[55] It embodies it in the "form" of a negative quantity, a "purely topological reality," an "irreal."

Separation would lead back into alienation (and in the case of "mental anorexia" this is what happens), if the (as it were) ceded object did not intervene. For one also can see this ceding, this letting-something-fall-away-from-the-body or letting-something-emerge-from-the-body, as the genesis of the drive. The drive and the object *a* have the same origin. With the object the lethal dimension of loss is covered over without being able to be completely forgotten; every component drive remains, latently, a death drive. In this way, Lacan has brought about the closest possible connection between death and sexual reproduction, without having to pay the full price of a mythologization of the death drive or a biologization of the theory of drives. Not to mention that in this way he also saves Freud's participation in the search for a substance of eternal life from a mistaken interpretation that would expose it to ridicule.[56]

In Levinas, separation is the division of the self from the Other as a precondition for the fact that a relationship between them is never able to reduce the infinite distance, that is to say the transcendence, which is posited by the division. As we have seen, separation for Levinas is closely bound up with the *cogito*: the *cogito* testifies to the division, and with it that atheism of the break with the heathen gods that is the prerequisite for the assumption of the idea of the infinite. But separation also is the precondition for that which Levinas calls "psychism," the "inner life" or "interiority." However, separation must not be confused with segregation or closing off. Rather, "the uniqueness of separation must paradoxically consist in a structure which cannot be reduced to closure. It must be the work of a primordial change, a 'non-allergic' relationship to otherness that lends or inspires density, or the hyperbolic intensity of uniqueness."[57] Separation as "psychism" or "inner life" is "life from . . . ," is "*jouissance*" ("enjoyment" or "bliss") (*TeI*, 82ff./*TI*, 110ff.). The love of life that makes itself known in this ("Life is the *love of life* . . .") is emphatically distinguished from *care* about being. Separation is, as paradoxical as it sounds, a manner of being-with-oneself, that is, in enjoyment as *life from* . . .: "In enjoyment throbs egoist being. Enjoyment separates by engaging in the contents from which it lives. Separation comes to pass as the positive work of this engagement; it does not result from a simple split, like a spatial removal. To be separated is to be at home with oneself. But to be at home with oneself . . . is to live from . . . , to enjoy the elemental" (*TeI*, 120/*TI*, 147). Thus separation is at the same time a relation of openness to the things in the world that are not prematurely reduced to their usefulness for something. By the *elemental* it is meant in fact the elements—air, water, earth—in which the human being moves, in which he or she "bathes," and which the human being enjoys before considering that and how he or she lives from them. This is an enjoyment that is, in its fundamental nature, however, quickly forgotten in favor of a relationship to the world in which instrumentality, in the shape of availability and accessibility, remolds the elemental, or even the nourishing, and removes it from thematic attention. But below the level of *equipment*, the *element* offers itself to enjoyment as the "universal category of the empirical" (*TeI*, 106/*TI*, 132–33). As such, enjoyment lies on the level of sensibility or corporality: it is prereflexive. And the element even precedes the separation of finite and infinite. "To enjoy without utility, in pure loss, gratuitously, without referring to anything else, in pure expenditure—this is the human" (*TeI*, 107/*TI*, 133).

If one thinks Lacan and Levinas together at this point, then enjoyment would be the expression of libido in life, uninfluenced by anything else—it would be dying as enjoyment and enjoyment in dying, yet precisely "in pure consumption," "in pure expenditure," consequently also before the consciousness that would represent in this context the agency of postponement. It would be the successful "mediation" of the infinite and the finite—so successful that it would no longer even be "mediation" but rather the finite *in* the infinite and the infinite *in* the finite (in the sense described earlier by Levinas); that is to say, it would be precisely the *ideal* which rejects mediation as unnecessary, but which in reality is still mediation, because psychism is not so constructed that it could abandon itself fully to this enjoyment. In Lacan it comes down to a splitting of enjoyment into an enjoyment of the Other, or absolute enjoyment, and a phallic enjoyment (Alain Juranville has described the relationship between them well).[58] The phallus itself takes over the function of this *negative quantity* between finite and infinite, but in this function is constantly threatened by and never ensured against the possibility of being made positive, being made into an image, and being confused with an available worldly object. Only such a *phallus* is as much a theoretical fiction as the representation of pure primary process. And so it is true that death is not only imperceptibly present in an absolute enjoyment that enjoys itself as pure expenditure, but also imposes itself, through "*search*," "*desire*," and the "*question*," as the "scandal" of a "*pur rapt*," a "pure rape/rapture," an "abduction," a "break-out" on a subject who strives for the "mediation" of finite and infinite. "My mortality, my sentence of death, my time at the point of death, my death which is not possibility of impossibility, but pure abduction [*pur rapt*], these constitute the absurdity that makes possible my responsibility for the other at no cost."[59] And at the same time this absurdity causes the "access to a meaning in which the after-death cannot be thought of as an extension of the time of before death after death, but in which the after-death has its own motivations."[60] Two things need to be overcome: death as sacred sacrifice to a "*deus obscurus*" but also the fixation, which in Levinas's view is equally pagan, on one's own death as something that cannot be represented (by another). Both are heroisms that lack one thing: the patience to prove oneself through the death of the other, to let the dying of the other be my death.

For psychoanalysis according to Lacan, castration is the site of a "mediation" of finite and infinite, one that has not just comfortably lived out its term, but rather is sought by the subject. More exactly, this is symbolic castration. While Levinas understands the relation to the death of the other as a responsibility in which I am always already placed, for which I therefore do not have to decide and cannot even do so, psychoanalysis articulates this relationship as one of guilt. In "Formulations on the Two Principles of Mental Functioning," Freud completes the narrative of the patient who had dreamed that his father, who had died some time ago, was alive again and did not know that he had already died, with additions that mark the intervention of the patient's wishes into the dream narrative. It is the guilt of the Oedipal death wish for the paternal rival that Freud exposes in this way.[61] Lacan shifts the emphasis of the interpretation: with the father's death has died the one who, according to genealogy, is earlier in line to offer himself to death, and so is able to relieve the subject of the confrontation; if the father is dead, there is no one left in front behind whom the subject can hide.[62] That the "dead father" himself is still in play, and therefore the protection is not to be had apart from contamination by a profound connection with guilt, strengthens the latent neurotic dimension of this constellation. If one looks at the Levinasian concep-

tion of responsibility for the death of the other together with the guilt relationship of paternity (or, more exactly, of sonship), as diagnosed by psychoanalysis, then they appear as reciprocal avoidances. Levinas emphasizes
responsibility that is not to be rejected, that is second to nothing, to the point
of an immeasurability that causes the element of guilt to disappear behind it;
guilt as active, individual becoming guilty can only be thought as a consequence of this measureless responsibility. Psychoanalysis, by contrast, and
this holds especially for the Freudian kind (but also that of Melanie Klein),
makes the Oedipus complex into a universal constellation that has the subject
become guilty on account of his wishes, before being able even to take on an
ethical responsibility for himself, since moral authority only proceeds from
the defeat of the Oedipus complex. In Lacan, however, a loosening of the
sharp opposition becomes evident, since he, unlike Freud, is not trying to universalize the perspective of the theory of neuroses, but rather subordinates it
to the foundation of a nonneurotic "pure" desire.

If the elemental is to precede the division of finite and infinite, the question of the relationship between enjoyment and God also arises. It is answered
by Levinas at best indirectly, in terms of the connection between separation,
psychism, enjoyment, and the infinite. For this reason it is not advisable to
add in here, without qualification, the corresponding chapter from the seminar *Encore*: "*Dieu et la jouissance de ~~La~~ femme*" ("God and the Enjoyment of
~~the~~ Woman"), where the suggestion is nevertheless offered that we understand
"the part of God as being borne by the enjoyment of woman."[63] Here one
would first have to discuss the feminine in Levinas, and that is a tricky matter.[64] In *Totalité et infini*, the feminine is thematized in the context of inhabitation, which in turn is conceived in terms of separation. "And the other
whose presence is discreetly an absence, with which is accomplished the primary hospitable welcome which describes the field of intimacy, is the
Woman. The woman is the condition for recollection, the interiority of the
Home, and inhabitation" (*TeI*, 128/*TI*, 155). Before entering into an analysis
of the position and function of woman in Levinas, his entire social theory
would have to be engaged. Inhabitation, and the tying of woman to the household that goes along with it, is part and parcel of a wide-ranging attempt to
understand *separation* as an *economy*—as a law of the household, if one goes
back to the Greek terms—but also as an employment of material in the interest of a procrastination, a postponement. What is extraordinary about the Levinasian representation is that in its description it does not even mention the
actual acts that separate, the acts of a "division from . . . ," of a sacrifice (the
only "sacrifice" is the one implicit in separation, that of the heathen gods and
of participation); rather, it is formally oriented toward the positivized results:
the history of separation almost as a history of institutions—inhabitation,
household, property, labor, the body subjected to a will, and finally the free-

dom of conception and creation, later the work, commerce, and law. What is extraordinary is that all of this becomes more comprehensible if one understands *separation* in exactly that double sense which Lacan too has proposed for this expression: *division*, but also *generation, self-generation*. We might even consider whether the perspectives of Lacan and Levinas, as far as separation is concerned, do not stand in a complementary relationship. Yet the pursuit of such a hypothesis, even if it does not seem tangential here, should be considered with care; it seems to me that for the present we will get further by proceeding with a contrasting evaluation.

In *Autrement qu'être*, this already reads quite differently. There "*jouissance*" is closely linked with pain (cf. *AE*, 71/*OB*, 55, 80/63–64, 83/66)—in a way that Juranville has also shown to be valid in his reconstruction of Lacan.[65] "[E]njoyment is the singularization of an ego in its coiling back upon itself" (*AE*, 93/*OB*, 73); thus it fulfills the function of *separation*, which in this work no longer plays the organizing role it does in *Totalité et infini*. Also, the linking of *cogito* and *separation* on the one hand, and of the Other as infinite, no longer appears as harmonious as in the 1961 book. In *Autrement qu'être*, Levinas has not only intensified the demand of responsibility into sheer immeasurability, but also exposes to this demand, besides psychism, the body in particular. The consequence is "an incessant alienation of the ego (isolated as inwardness) by the guest entrusted to it. Hospitality, the one-for-the-other in the ego. . . . The animation of a body by a soul only articulates the one-for-the-other of subjectivity" (*AE*, 99/*OB*, 79).[66] In a note to the last sentence, Levinas points out the acuity of the Cartesian move, which consists in not admitting any commonality between the body as source of the sensible and the knowledge of ideas. For Levinas, this proves "the unintelligibility of incarnation, the 'I think' separated from extension, the *cogito* separated from the body. But this impossibility of being together is the trace of the diachrony of the one-for-the-other. That is, it is the trace of *separation* in the form of inwardness, and of the for-the-other in the form of responsibility" (*AE*, 100/*OB*, 79).

Thus in Levinas, too, those terms are paired which are known to us as a pair from Lacan: alienation/separation. Several times "psychism" [*le psychisme*, here translated by Lingis as "psyche"] is defined as "the other in the same, without alienating the same" (*AE*, 143/*OB*, 112, 146/115, 160/125). And on page 75 of *Autrement qu'être* Levinas defends his move against the hermeneutics of suspicion, that among other things calls into question the responsibility of the human being from the point of view of psychoanalysis in the guise of an objective anthropological knowledge. This anthropological knowledge, which assumes that the human being is conditioned, subjected to a *conditio humana*, is, however, irrelevant considering one's neighbor and the demand that has always already been issued to me by him; still, Levinas poses the question, "what would there be if . . .": what would there be if "anything in the world [were to] deliver more immediately, beneath its alienation, its non-alienation, its separation, its holiness?" (*AE*, 76/*OB*, 59).

Actually we should now turn back from Levinas to Lacan. Actually we should now enter anew upon the movement of approach and distantiation, of setting in relation and assuming distance, of drawing together and withdrawing—in a movement that orients itself according to that which Levinas has outlined as the step from *dire* to *dit* and *dédire*, calling back—in order to arrive in this way at a *midire*? Who knows? Nothing has yet been said, and above all far too little about the ethical in Lacan and Levinas.[67]

—Translated by Angela Esterhammer

Notes

1. Levinas, "Philosophie, justice et amour," in *Entre nous. Essais sur le penser-à-l'autre* (Paris: Grasset, 1991), p. 122.

2. For the conversion of the experience of the face into the commandment (which is formulated more ambiguously in the French translation of the Bible and can also be read as a prediction, a prophecy, "You *will* not commit murder") and the "ethical resistance" that makes murder *ethically* impossible, even if it can be committed in fact, cf. *TeI*, 172–74/*TI*, 197–200. Levinas stresses "the very straightforwardness of the face to face, without the intermediary of any image, in one's nudity, that is, in one's destitution and hunger" (174/200). [Quotations from Lacan and Levinas are taken from the English translations listed earlier. Texts that have not been published in English are given in my own translations, translated directly from the French texts whenever these were available.—Tr.] For the question of the status of the experience of the face—empirical or transcendental—cf. Theodore de Boer, "An Ethical Transcendental Philosophy," in *Face to Face with Levinas*, edited by Richard Cohen (Chicago: The University of Chicago Press, 1986), p. 83ff., and Robert Bernasconi, "Rereading *Totality and Infinity*," in *The Question of the Other*, edited by Arleen B. Dallery and Charles E. Scott (Albany, N.Y.: State University of New York Press, 1989), p. 23ff., who takes issue with de Boer.

3. Frustratingly translated in the German edition as *unendlich* 'infinite, unending,' the German translation of *Totalité et infini* by Wolfgang Nikolaus Krewani is thoroughly problematic. For one thing, the translator misses the precision *within* Levinas's terminology (for instance, occasionally tricky distinctions such as between *jouissance* 'enjoyment' and *joie* 'joy,' or *maîtrise, domination,* and *souveraineté,* which may of course all be translated 'mastery,' but which, used next to one another, take on very different connotations—with Krewani this often gets confused). Second, he also seems to have great difficulty with the (translation of) Levinasian syntax and often breaks up his admittedly complex sentence structures into smaller units—not always without the loss of allusiveness. Not to mention the distortion in

tone when, for instance, *production* is universally translated as *Ereignis* 'event,' and the tendency toward euphemization or moderation of extreme images: a "cut into life" where the original has a "*coupure dans la chair vive,*" an "incision in the living flesh" (*TeI*, 48/*TI*, 76).

4. In *L'Herne*, No. 60, *Emmanuel Lévinas* (Paris: L'Herne, 1991), p. 133 (emphasis in original). The final sentence in Levinas's answer to an interviewer's question about his relationship to psychoanalysis and its practice is similar, "One speaks of the man who has 'gone through his Oedipus complex' (*fait son Oedipe*)—who has symbolically killed his father and taken his mother to wife—as of someone who has received first communion." But here too there is a clear difference between a practice and above all the misuse that can be made of it ("I have a great mistrust of the practice of psychoanalysis and its abuses")—apparently what is meant here is an ideologically normative abuse in the doxa of a culturally socialized psychoanalysis and a society permeated by psychoanalytic culture—and the concept of the unconscious, assuming that this unconscious is no longer thought of as a representation or re-presentation, but as something unfolded in a temporal dimension, as Heidegger has explicated it in "The Anaximander Fragment" (Emmanuel Levinas, "Entretien," in *Répondre d'autrui. Emmanuel Lévinas*, edited by Jean-Christophe Aeschlimann [Neuchâtel: La Baconnière, 1989], pp. 13–14). Also worth noting is Levinas's attitude during a conference devoted to the question *La psychanalyse est-elle une histoire juive?* ("Is Psychoanalysis a Jewish History?"). Confessing his embarrassment over his sketchy knowledge of psychoanalysis, Levinas, who himself presented "*Quelques vues talmudiques sur le rêve*" ("Some Talmudic Observations on Dreams"), describes this more specifically: "My embarrassment derives, incidentally, from the fact that I stand completely outside of psychoanalytic research, under whatever forms it is pursued, and that I am neutral toward the battles it brings about, despite the sympathy that the people themselves evoke in me" (*La psychanalyse est-elle une histoire juive?* Colloque de Montpellier, 1980 [Paris: Seuil, 1981], pp. 114–15). [Levinas is *not* speaking of individual or specific people, that is, of particular figures in the enterprise of psychoanalysis, for whom he might feel a particular sympathy.] And in "Réflexions sur la 'technique' phénoménologique," phenomenological method, as far as its openness and general applicability is concerned, is mentioned in a single breath with the "method of mathematical physics according to Galileo and Descartes," "dialectic according to Hegel and especially Marx," and "psychoanalysis according to Freud" (*DE*, 111). When Elisabeth Weber speaks of a "very summary rejection of psychoanalysis" in Levinas (*Verfolgung und Trauma. Zu Emmanuel Lévinas' "Autrement qu'être ou au-delà de l'essence"* [Vienna: Passagen, 1990], p. 180, n. 96), I consider this, apart from the trivial point that he himself does not work psychoanalytically, as at best exaggerated; and the criticism that she raises with reference to an annotation in *Autrement qu'être*, where *an* unconscious is mentioned as a term that is the inverse of consciousness, which Weber takes as a starting point from which to accuse Levinas of the same misunderstanding of psychoanalysis as Habermas, would find no support in the statement I have cited earlier from Levinas on the unconscious. And if Levinas rejects *an* unconscious, defined as the reverse of consciousness, he is not doing anything different from Lacan: cf. *É*, 830 ("La position de l'inconscient").

5. Despite a multitude of references to Lacan, Elisabeth Weber, in *Verfolgung und Trauma*, restricts herself to extracts that are meant to support, clarify, or even correct and complete particular theorems or arguments in Levinas, and in the course of this instrumental usage she reads him in some places simply as a theory of psychosexual development (for example, pp. 182–85; this is no different from the way Alphonso Lingis proceeds, when he similarly, in the context of a *"genetic analysis* of the meaning and the value of the sign of the subject" assumes something of the Lacanian concept of the entrance of the child ("in-fant") into language; cf. *Deathbound Subjectivity* [Bloomington: Indiana University Press, 1989], p. 7, p. 156ff.). In addition, I know of several works that confront Levinas with Freudian psychoanalysis: the basically interesting article "La proximité chez Levinas et le Nebenmensch freudien" (in *L'Herne*, No. 60, *Emmanuel Lévinas*, 431–43) by Monique Schneider (who gets carried away, however, when she tries to infer the Oedipus complex from the "complex of the *Nebenmensch*" [441]), and the study by Noreen O'Connor, "Who suffers?" (in *Re-Reading Levinas*, edited by Robert Bernasconi and Simon Critchley [Bloomington: Indiana University Press, 1991], pp. 229–33), which is not very enlightening because it remains overly general, and which brings the Levinasian understanding of suffering together with François Roustang's theory of psychoses.

6. Cf. Alain Juranville, *Lacan et la Philosophie* (Paris: PUF, 1984), p. 194ff.

7. Ibid., 13n.

8. Elisabeth Roudinesco, *Jacques Lacan & Co.: A History of Psychoanalysis in France, 1925–1985*, translated by Jeffrey Mehlman (Chicago: The University of Chicago Press, 1990).

9. Ibid., p. 592.

10. Cf. Alain Juranville, *Lacan et la Philosophie*, pp. 407–27.

11. Evidence for and valuable reflections on Christianity as an important point of reference for the Lacanian reformulation of Freudian psychoanalysis can be found in an obituary for Lacan by Michel de Certeau, "Lacan: une éthique de la parole," in *Histoire et psychanalyse entre science et fiction* (Paris: Gallimard, 1987), p. 186ff.

12. The French *cause*, from the Latin *causa*, also means the "issue" concerned, especially if it is controversial or in the courts. Lacan will later speak of a *"cause perdue,"* a lost cause/origin as well as a lost case. And in the same context he will urge a "transcendental analysis of cause" (*Sé XI*, 117/*S XI*, 128).

13. It is clear to me that the terms *belated* and *realization*, especially in combination, are problematic here: they play down the extreme temporal circumstances, insofar as they bring to mind a delay rather than the surfacing of something that has not announced itself in advance by even the tiniest signal. In a certain way Levinas provides the conceptual and descriptive tools for a radical thinking of these matters in his "concept" of the *trace* as an immemorial past, which was never present, and of *diachrony* as an irreducible rift in time.

14. Lacan explicitly admits that he must here break with at least the letter of the Freudian text: "If I am formulating here that the status of the unconscious is ethical, and not ontic, it is precisely because Freud himself does not stress it when he gives the unconscious its status" (*Sé XI*, 35/*S XI*, 34).

15. These statements by Lacan receive an interesting treatment by Jacques Rolland, the editor of various texts by Levinas and the author of studies on him, who, in an essay on Blanchot in which he quotes at length from Seminar XI, does not directly relate Lacan and Levinas, yet opens a way to *Totalité et infini* through the mediation of some of Blanchot's remarks. "Pour une approche de la question du neutre," in *Exercices de la patience*, No. 2, *Blanchot* (1981), pp. 13–16.

16. As early as 1936, in the final sentence of his essay *"De l'évasion,"* Levinas outlined the necessity of a conceptual reversal: "Our concern is to emerge from Being on a new path, at the risk of reversing certain concepts that seem most evident to the general understanding and to the wisdom of the nations" (De l'évasion [Montpellier: Fata Morgana, 1982], p. 99). And in the same essay a complaint is already lodged about "ontologisme" as the "fundamental dogma of all our thinking" (96).

17. Here I cannot go into the clear objections that Derrida raised as early as 1964 against Levinas's remarks on the primacy of ontology or a primacy of being over existents (cf. "Violence et métaphysique," in *Revue de métaphysique et de morale* 69 (1964): p. 452ff.; revised version reprinted in *L'écriture et la différence* [Paris: Seuil, 1967], p. 198ff.; English version "Violence and Metaphysics: An Essay on the Thought of Emmanuel Levinas," in *Writing and Difference*, translated by Alan Bass [Chicago: The University of Chicago Press, 1978], p. 136ff.). For the question of whether Derrida's essay on Levinas is to be read as *critique* (as is generally done) or already as the seed of deconstruction, cf. the article by Robert Bernasconi, "Deconstruction and the Possibility of Ethics," in *Deconstruction and Philosophy: The Texts of Jacques Derrida*, edited by John Sallis (Chicago: The University of Chicago Press, 1987), pp. 122–39.

18. The word itself does not appear a single time in *Totalité et infini*; on the other hand, in *Autrement qu'être ou au-delà de l'essence*, there are allusions to the "pre-ontological weight of language" (55/43) and the "irrecuperable pre-ontological past, that of maternity" (99/78).

19. A complication should, however, not be overlooked. In answer to a question by Theo de Boer, Levinas explains "anteriority," which is to be understood as transcendental, as follows: "with the qualification that the ethical comes before ontology. It is more ontological than ontology, more *sublime* than ontology" (*De Dieu qui vient a l'idée* [Paris: Vrin, 1982], p. 143—emphasis in original).

20. Cf. Sigmund Freud, "The Forgetting of Dreams," in *The Interpretation of Dreams, Standard Edition of the Complete Psychological Works*, Vol. 5 (London: Hogarth, 1953), pp. 512–32. Lacan relies above all on the sentence, "That is why in analysing a dream I insist that the whole scale of estimates of certainty shall be abandoned and that the faintest possibility that something of this or that sort may have

occurred in the dream shall be treated as complete certainty" (516). But the whole paragraph is significant. Right at the beginning Freud points out that there is no basis of "intellectual warrant" for doubt and that "there is in general no guarantee of the correctness of our memory" (515). Shortly before, he had still stressed the necessity of treating the apparently arbitrary improvisation of the dream narrative as "Holy Writ" (514). I have investigated the implications that result from this for an understanding of text and textuality in psychoanalysis in my essay "Text und Unbewußtes (Freud, Lacan, Derrida)," in *Parabel. Schriftenreihe der Evangelischen Studienstiftung*, No. 16, *Textwelt* (Gießen, 1993), pp. 86–110.

21. It is not possible here to go into the diverse questions that result from the Lacanian rapprochement of Freud and Descartes. Cf. Bernard Baas and Armand Zaloszyc, *Descartes et les fondements de la psychanalyse* (Paris: Navarin Osiris, 1988), and Guy Le Gaufey, *L'incomplétude du symbolique. De René Descartes à Jacques Lacan* (Paris: E. P. E. L., 1991).

22. René Descartes, *Meditations on First Philosophy*, translated by Elizabeth S. Haldane and G. R. T. Ross, edited by Stanley Tweyman (London: Routledge, 1993), p. 51.

23. Ibid., p. 67.

24. In Dieter Henrich's account of the Cartesian proof of the existence of God the question of the infinite/finite comes in only at the margins (cf. *Der ontologische Gottesbeweis*, 2d ed. [Tübingen: Mohr, 1960], pp. 10–22).

25. Cf. Robert Bernasconi, "The Silent Anarchic World of the Evil Genius," in *The Collegium Phaenomenologicum: The First Ten Years*, edited by John C. Sallis, Guiseppina Moneta, and Jacques Taminiaux (Dordrecht: Kluwer, 1988), pp. 257–72, who clearly identifies the problems that result from Levinas's disregard of the ontotheological context in Descartes (pp. 258–59), and the more positive essay by Jean-François Lavigne, "*L'idée de l'infini: Descartes dans la pensée d'Emmanuel Lévinas*," in *Revue de métaphysique et de morale* 92 (1987): pp. 54–66. In earlier essays Levinas himself had still put the main emphasis on the perfection of God (cf. *DEHH*, 96, 113).

26. The standard for this question has doubtless been set by Jean-Luc Marion in *Sur la théologie blanche de Descartes* (Paris: PUF, 1981).

27. In "*Le temps et l'autre*," a publication that goes back to lectures from 1946–47, Levinas still outlined this act as "hypostasis" (*TA*, 31ff.). In each case the precondition is the emergence out of all forms of sacred participation. Levinas also refers in this context to Lévy-Bruhl.

28. Thus the formulation of John Llewelyn, *The Middle Voice of Ecological Conscience*: (Basingstoke: Macmillan, 1991), p. 55.

29. Robert Bernasconi, "The Silent Anarchic World of the Evil Genius," p. 266.

30. Cf. also, on posteriority, *TeI*, 126/*TI*, 153 and 143/169.

31. Emmanuel Levinas, "God and Philosophy," in *CP*, 162.

32. Ibid., p. 160.

33. "La méprise du sujet supposé savoir," *Scilicet* 1 (1968): p. 39.

34. Jacques Derrida, *"Donner la mort,"* in *L'éthique du don. Jacques Derrida et la pensée du don*, Colloque du Royaumont, décembre 1990, edited by Jean-Michel Rabaté and Michael Wetzel (Paris: Métailié-Transition, 1992), pp. 80–81.

35. For instance, because of its strongly Hegelian cast, the passage from "The agency of the letter in the unconscious" was deliberately omitted in which Lacan brings the "Other" into operation as "the second level of Otherness": "If I have said that the unconscious is the discourse of the Other (with a capital O), it is in order to indicate the beyond in which the recognition of desire is bound up with the desire for recognition" (*É*, 524/*E*, 172).

36. Cf. especially the lecture "Vérité scomme dévoilement et vérité comme témoignage," in *Le Témoignage (Actes du Colloque organisé par le Centre International d'Études Humanistes et par l'Institut d'Études Philosophiques de Rome)* (Paris: Flammarion, 1972), pp. 101–10, which was adopted in extensively revised form under the title *"Subjectivité et infini"* as the fifth chapter of *Autrement qu'être*. Paul Ricoeur provides a comparative examination of the problematic of testimony in Heidegger (conscience), Nabert, and Levinas: "Emmanuel Lévinas. Penseur du Témoignage," in *Répondre d'autrui—Emmanuel Lévinas*, pp. 17–40. Ricoeur stresses "that testimony opposes the certainty of the *representation* that includes self-certainty and the manifestation of all existents" (p. 35). Levinas, for his part, dedicated an essay to Ricoeur that likewise deals with "giving testimony": "Du langage religieux et de la crainte de Dieu," in *L'au-delà du verset. Lectures et discours talmudiques* (Paris: Minuit, 1982), pp. 107–22.

37. One could perhaps speak here of "de-facement." Levinas speaks in several places of *"dé-visage"* (*AE*, 201–2/*OB*, 158–59).

38. A striking statement is found in *Encore*: "The Other, the Other as the site of truth, is the only place, however irreducible, that we can assign to the term divine being—God, to call him by his name" (Jacques Lacan, *Le Séminaire Livre XX: Encore* [Paris: Seuil, 1975], p. 44. The continuation of this passage can be found in note 51).

39. In contrast to Levinas, who can actually assert, "God is not simply the 'first other,' the 'other par excellence,' or the 'absolutely other,' but other than the other [*autre qu'autrui*], other otherwise, other with an alterity prior to the alterity of the other, prior to the ethical bond with another and different from every neighbor" ("God and Philosophy," in *CP*, 165–66).

40. Cf. the essay of mine mentioned in note 20.

41. Emphasis in original. The quotation from Freud is in German in Lacan's text. Lacan repeatedly stressed that the "I *am to* become" ["*soll* Ich werden"] is to be understood in the ethical sense of a command (cf. the representative passage at *É*, 417).

42. Emmanuel Lévinas, "Langage et proximité," in *DE*, 222.

43. For a critique of the translation and a forced new inflection of this sentence, cf. Martin Heidegger, *Einführung in die Metaphysik*, 4th ed. (Tübingen: Niemeyer, 1976), p. 104ff., and "Moira (Parmenides VIII.34–41)," in *Vorträge und Aufsätze*, 4th ed. (Pfullingen: Neske, 1978), p. 223ff. In particular, *to auto*, the "same," is a "riddle" for Heidegger (p. 233).

44. On this "thought–experiment," cf. also the aforementioned article by Robert Bernasconi, "The Silent Anarchic World of the Evil Genius," p. 269.

45. However, this raises the question of whether in Lacan as well we must assume two different conceptions of the "ego," or whether the devaluation of the ego as a misjudging authority, as generally attributed to Lacan, is the whole truth. For the "I" of the "I am to become" can hardly be the "I/ego" of narcissism, at least not (anymore) once it has become what or where it is to become. Alain Juranville, in his essay at the Zürich symposium "Kant/Lacan—ethische Grundfragen," reached the same conclusion beginning from a different background. Cf. Alain Juranville, "Subjekt, Individuum, Ich" in *Ethik und Psychoanalyse. Vom kategorischen Imperativ zum Gesetz des Begehrens: Kant und Lacan*, edited by Hans-Dieter Gondek and Peter Widmer (Frankfurt a.M.: S. Fischer, 1994).

46. *Twilight of the Idols*, in *The Portable Nietzsche*, edited and translated by Walter Kaufmann (Harmondsworth: Penguin, 1976), p. 483.

47. Lacan provides only very modest hints that this "true love" (as, following Freud, he also refers to it) is more than just deceit, voluntary or involuntary. Alain Juranville has made clear that for the sake of the success of the analysis a love must be evoked that is something other than transference love (cf. *Lacan et la Philosophie*, pp. 333–34).

48. Cf. the essay by Alain Juranville in this volume, where the ethical weight of this term is revealed.

49. Simon Critchley refers to it repeatedly in *The Ethics of Deconstruction: Derrida and Levinas*, while also stressing the nonsynchronicity of *énoncé* and *énonciation* (Oxford: Blackwell, 1992), pp. 7, 163f., 167.

50. Jacques Lacan, "L'étourdit," in *Scilicet* 4 (1973): 10 (my emphasis—H.-D. G.). The relationship of *dire* and *dit* is thoroughly thematized in this essay, also with reference to the distinction between stating and statement. The tone is established right from the beginning: "*que le dire reste oublié derrière le dit*" ("that the saying lies forgotten behind the said") (p. 6).

51. For Levinas, "Saying is witness; it is saying without the said, a sign given to the Other." "I can indeed state the meaning borne witness to as a said [that is, Levinas does not equate the distinction between *dire* and *dit* with that of *stating/statement*]. It is an extraordinary word, the only one that does not extinguish or absorb its saying, but it cannot remain a simple word. The word God is an overwhelming seman-

tic event . . ." (*AE*, 192–93/*OB*, 151). This word is "kerygma," whether it is pronounced as "prayer" or as "blasphemy," for "already the Infinite speaks through the witness I bear of it" (*AE*, 193/*OB*, 151). What would Levinas have thought of the following summation of Lacan's (a continuation of the quotation in note 38): "God is actually the place where, if you will permit the pun, *le dieu—le dieur—le dire* arises. It takes nothing for saying to make God [*Pour un rien, le dire ça fait Dieu.*] And as long as something continues to be said, the hypothesis of God will be there." Here, too, a proximity to Nietzsche can be detected (cf. note 46 earlier).

52. It is important to note that signifiers and not signs are being discussed here; between them, even if Gerda Pagel does not see it this way, there is a significant difference. Cf. the article of mine cited in note 20.

53. This temporality appears so important to him here that he immediately repeats once more: "The subject is this emergence which, just before, as subject, was nothing, but which, having scarcely appeared, solidifies into a signifier" (*Sé XI*, 181/*S XI*, 199). Cf. also *É*, 840, where the precarious temporality is stressed even more strongly in "an instant before"/"an instant after."

54. And perhaps also the seed of *sacrifice*. Hence also comes the necessity of breaking with the sacrifice and the "Dieu obscur" who demands it (cf. *Sé XI*, 247/*S XI*, 275). One could perhaps even say that both Lacan and Levinas understand the overcoming of the sacred, especially of the sacred sacrifice, as an essential element of that which is called *revelation*—through which a God who was previously "dark" and "hidden" becomes a God of the face. For the context of this strange reference to sacrifice in the last session of Seminar XI, cf. also my essay, "Das rituelle und das moralische Opfer," *RISS. Zeitschrift für Psychoanalyse* 18 (1991): pp. 52–65.

55. "De la psychanalyse dans ses rapports avec la réalité," *Scilicet* 1 (1968): 59 ("*ce résidu corporel où j'ai suffisamment, je pense, incarné le Dasein, pour l'appeler par le nom qu'il me doit: soit l'objet (a)*"—"this bodily remainder, in which I have sufficiently, I think, incorporated *Dasein*, to call it by the name that it owes to me: the object *a*"). Other points at which *Dasein* similarly appears, also in more or less explicit relation to object *a*, should be added (e.g., *É*, 40: "*Mange ton Dasein*"—"Eat your *Dasein*"; *Sé XI*, 216/*S XI*, 239: "*Pas de* fort *sans* da *et, si l'on peut dire, sans* Dasein"—"There can be no *fort* without *da* and, one might say, without *Dasein*," where the relation to the *fort-da* game is established). Of course this equation contains some problems that need to be treated separately. Thus, Jacques Derrida, Jean-Luc Nancy, and Philippe Lacoue-Labarthe have accused Lacan of an imprecise use of philosophical terminology, among other things of a self-adornment with words from the Heideggerian environment while at the same time continuing to use the traditional term *subject*. *Dasein* is not a simple substitution for the classical subject, therefore it cannot simply be undone. But to clarify such questions an exact and comprehensive examination of the relationships and encounters between Heidegger and Lacan, above all of the stages of reception by Lacan, would be necessary, which, just like the present reading of Lacan with Levinas/Levinas with Lacan, has Descartes as its central point of reference. A preliminary study in this vein is offered by the middle section of

my article "Die Angst als 'das, was nicht täuscht'" in *Psychoanalyse und Philosophie. Lacan in der Diskussion*, edited by Berhard H. F. Taureck (Frankfurt a.m.: Fischer, 1992), pp. 113–19.

56. Cf. Sigmund Freud, *Beyond the Pleasure Principle*, in *Standard Edition of the Complete Psychological Works*, translated by James Strachey, Vol. 18 (London: Hogarth, 1961), p. 44ff.

57. Joseph Libertson, "La Séparation chez Lévinas," *Revue de Métaphysique et de Morale* 86 (1981): p. 437.

58. Cf. *Lacan et la Philosophie*, pp. 387–88.

59. Emmanuel Levinas, "La mort et le temps" (cours: 1975–1976), *L'Herne*, No. 60, *Emmanuel Lévinas* (Paris: L'Herne, 1991), pp. 73–74; since reprinted separately as *La mort et le temps* (Paris: Librarie Générale Francaise, 1992), pp. 132, 135.

60. Ibid., pp. 47, 67.

61. Cf. Sigmund Freud, "Formulations on the Two Principles of Mental Functioning," in *Standard Edition of the Complete Psychological Works*, translated by James Strachey, Vol. 12 (London: Hogarth, 1958), pp. 225–26.

62. Lacan treats this dream in the first part of his (as yet unpublished) seminar on *Le désir et son interprétation*.

63. *Le Séminaire Livre XX: Encore*, 71 ("*la face Dieu*," which can also mean "the face of God"). [This line has also been translated by Jacqueline Rose as follows: "And why not interpret one face of the Other, the God face, as supported by feminine *jouissance?*" Juliet Mitchell and Jacqueline Rose, eds., *Feminine Sexuality: Jacques Lacan and the École Freudienne* (London: Macmillan, 1982), p. 147.—Tr.]

64. Derrida has insisted on the dubiousness of Levinas's conception of femininity in his two essays on Levinas, "Violence et métaphysique" and "En ce moment même dans cet ouvrage me voici," as well as in other references. A close analysis of the feminine in Levinas is provided by Catherine Chalier, *Figures du féminin. Lecture d'Emmanuel Lévinas* (Paris: La nuit surveillée, 1982).

65. On the reciprocal implications of suffering and enjoyment, cf. *Lacan et la Philosophie*, 407.

66. No doubt there is much to be said about the language of *Autrement qu'être*—about the priority of *dire* over *dit*, with the result that every *thematization* immediately betrays the *saying* of that which in this way is taken only as *said*; about the language of the ethical, which can no longer be the language of ontology; about the language theory of Levinas in general, which no longer measures language against the representation of a preexisting objectivity, but understands it as something given, that itself creates objectivity as the only possible relationship between absolutely separated things (this last point is already to be found in *Totalité et infini*). Thus, in any case, the "thematization" of *Autrement qu'être* undertaken here sets itself in the wrong from the

outset. But for reasons of brevity I must content myself with a reference to the already mentioned book by Elisabeth Weber, who in her first section describes the "Method and Writing" of Levinas comprehensively, exactly, and competently (*Verfolgung und Trauma*, p. 45ff.), and to the essay by Thomas Wiemer (the German translator of *Autrement qu'être*), "Das Unsagbare sagen," in *Parabel. Schriftenreihe der Evangelischen Studienstiftung*, No. 12: *Lévinas* (Giessen: 1990), p. 18ff.

67. To mention only two desiderata: Lacan and Levinas both in certain respects assume an approving attitude toward skepticism (moderated also to stoicism), which Lacan describes as an "ethic" (*Sé XI*, 203/*S XI*, 224) and Levinas in *Autrement qu'être* praises at length (*AE*, 210–18/*OB*, 165–71). A further point that is treated by both is the question of the "fear of God": Lacan addresses it in his seminar on psychoses in connection with the "quilting point" [*point de capiton*] and in relation to a reading of Racine's *Athalie* (*Le Séminaire Livre III: Les Psychoses* [Paris: Seuil, 1981], pp. 298–304; Eng. *The Seminar of Jacques Lacan*, Book III, *The Psychoses 1955–1956*, translated by Russell Grigg [New York: Norton, 1993], pp. 263–68); Levinas in an essay dedicated to Ricoeur: "Du langage religieux et de la crainte de Dieu," in *L'au-delà du verset*, 107–22.

[I would like to thank Hans-Dieter Gondek for his exceptionally detailed and helpful comments on drafts of this translation, Sarah Harasym for additional suggestions, and Karen Wirsig for helping to locate and coordinate texts in three languages from several libraries.—Tr.]

Chapter 3

Levinas and Lacan: Facing the Real

Donna Brody

Introduction

Both Hegel and Kojève in their accounts of the importance of language as an intersubjective domain constitutive of self-formation and meaning had already set the scene for a loosening of the idea that linguistic concepts referred to or stood in a one-to-one correspondence with an extralinguistic territoriality. Preempting the beginning of the collapse of ostensive definition, the writings of the structuralists, Lévi-Strauss and Saussure, further disintegrated the distinction between meaning [*Sinn*] and reference [*Bedeutung*]. These thinkers were to have a tremendous impact on Lacan's reworking of Freud. By the 1950s Lacan was developing a theory of language as constitutive of the subject. For if language does not represent reality, the subject, too, is not a fixed reality, not a simple vehicle for the dissemination of transferred concepts, and not, therefore, identifiable extraneously from a position occupied within a system of linguistic significations. This is not to say that Lacan denies the real effraction of biological processes; he does not. But he does contend that they have no self-sufficent meaning, arguing that they are mediated by the (necessarily linguistic) interpretation of the subject. The problem is that this appears to result in a linguistic circle, a form of linguistic idealism, where one cannot, or cannot simply, linguistically form a route from language to a prelinguistic or extralinguistic dimension, that is, there seems no way of (nonlinguistically) establishing the reality of an extralinguistic world. Lacan, however, does not propose that language swallows up or exhausts reality, nor does he exclude the impingement of reality upon the dyad of orders he considers under the terms of the imaginary and the symbolic which are the orders through which the subject understands what constitutes reality. Rather, he cedes a place and an im-mediable meaning to reality. He calls it the real.

The real is, thus, in itself, immune or resistant to interpretations of its significance. It is we who read off a significance and a meaning pertaining to the external world; we who are able to lend a voice, as it were, to its significance. This is the point of Lacan's remark that perhaps we have indeed shut the stars and planets up—at least for now—having reduced them to a linguistic inscription: it seems that Newton's unified field theory has silenced them. The stars and the planets are purely and simply what they are (*Sé II*, 278/*S II*, 238),[1] with no alterity with respect to themselves, unself-differentiated, and the reason they have nothing to say is because they do not have mouths; ergo they cannot speak. That is to say, they are not human; they are not involved in the symbolic order. Nonetheless, the real has an effect. It may contingently interrupt us, thus necessitating a coaptation of our interpretation to accommodate the disturbance, and it is also that to which our interpretations are limited and constrained: the real is the stubbornly recalcitrant materiality that limits Lacan's ability to lift his table with one hand (*Sé II*, 255/*S II*, 219).[2] The real is an upset, a traversal of incoherence and subreption, an irreducible unpredictability that gets in the way of one's handle on the world. Perhaps the handle suddenly breaks off of one's cup of tea. The real is what is left out, missed, or left behind in discursive significations: a remainder. But if these examples seem inconsequential, the implications are not. If the real is a methexis, an inevitable component of our interpretations of it as the comprehensively missed referent of a signified as unimportant as a table or a tea cup, then it is also that incomprehensible exterior that subsists within any pyschical appointment with an object. Entering into the conditions of the self-constitution comprised through both the ego-identifications of the imaginary and the collusive unconscious laws of the symbolic, it is not merely a material collection of hazards but an inevitable flexure of the mental sphere and just as traumatically ungraspable. Ergo the real encompasses everything, it is All, indistinguishably sussurating across and between all categorial emprise.

In itself without fracture, the real is nonetheless an unknowable fissure between—and in a difficult sense "within"—the orders of the symbolic and the imaginary. "Remember this," Lacan sternly reminds his interlocuter, "regarding externality and internality—this distinction makes no sense at all on the level of the real. The real is without fissure . . . we have no means of apprehending this real—on any level and not only on that of knowledge— except via the go-between of the symbolic" (*Sé II*, 122/*S II*, 97). In any phenomenon, thus, there is a point that cannot be grasped: for both Freud and Lacan the particularly acute revelation of this is oneiric. The real is a navel or fault line between itself and the symbolic, nor is it possible to take up a relation to it without this being an object relation. In this sense it is "at the seam where the imaginary joins the real" (*Sé II*, 122/*S II*, 98). Lacan also suggests that a psychosomatic reaction is an especially intense example of the way the real enters into discourse. "It's a relation to something that always lies on the edge of our conceptual elaborations which we are always thinking about, which we sometimes speak of, and which, strictly speaking, we can't grasp, and which is nonetheless there" (*Sé II*, 120–21/*S II*, 96).

It is within this introductory context serving as a preamble to the dramatic role of the real that the following suggestive commentary given by Lacan, on the first part of Freud's case study on Irma's dream, should be tympanically cast:

> The first leads to the apparition of the terrifying anxiety-provoking image, to this real Medusa's head, to the revelation of something which properly speaking is unnameable, the back of this throat, the complex, the unlocatable form, which also makes it into the primitive object *par excellence*, the abyss of the feminine organ from which all life emerges, this gulf of the mouth, in which everything is swallowed up, and no less the image of death in which everything comes to an end. . . . Hence there's this anxiety-provoking apparition of an image which summarizes what we can call the revelation of that which is least penetrable in the real, of the real lacking any possible mediation, of the ultimate real, of the essential object which isn't an object any longer, but this something faced with which all words cease and all categories fail, the object of anxiety *par excellence*. (*Sé II*, 196/*S II*, 164)

We will follow the real as it is incarnated in an alternative discourse. This discourse is that of Emmanuel Levinas; on the face of it, far removed from pyschoanalytic thought, a discipline even overtly detested by Levinas.[3] Not that Levinas in some happy homology talks of something called the real. But he does chart the function and phenonemal modalizations of something he calls the *there is* [*il y a*]. And, I will claim, the impersonal zone of the *there is* uncannily exemplifies and operates as a virtually exact coordinate of Lacan's conception of the real. The point is not to push a deep comparison on the level of mere description—for example, as will become apparent, the *there is* sounds the keynotes of Lacan's phantasmagoric description of Irma's dream: it is the primordial object of anxiety *par excellence*, a gaping abyss engendering life, a type of death, that in the face of which all categories flounder and fail—but to demonstrate the real in action as it actually eclipses, permeates, evades, and conditions the encounter with it. I shall show how Levinas interrupts himself by way of the failure to secure a purchase on the slippery surface of the *there is*. I shall claim that the model of the Same and the Other is fractured and stressed by the Medusa's head[4] of the *there is* to the point of impossibility. At once discovered by Levinas as a precondition for the accessibility of the Same to the Other, and, conversely, the possibility for the proximity of the Other to the Same, the *there is* renders impossible this structural integrity even as it sets it to work.

Finally I will return the real to Lacan through Levinas's reading of how the real can be accessed by the subject. I will suggest that the real is no mere "in itself" but divided from itself, that is, "for us," unreservedly, and not only with respect to the extremes of psychosis to which Lacan tends to want to reserve it.

I

In commentaries upon Levinas the way in which the *there is* has been thematized by Levinas as an essential coupling jointure between the Same and the Other has been overlooked and disregarded. This raises the question right away of whether indeed the *there is* is in fact indispensable to the signifying structure of the Same and the Other. To respond to this question I will first delineate the structure of the Same and the Other.

The model of the Same and the Other—often substituted for sister distinctions such as that between the finite and the infinite, the subject and subjectivity, or in the linguistic register of the 1974 text *Otherwise Than Being*, the Said [*le dit*] and the Saying [*le dire*]—is itself a shorthand terminology that gives the impression of a Manichean distinction. The notion of the Same is paratactical: gathered under its aegis is what Levinas understands by "ontology," collecting together a number of philosophical "discoveries" he takes as the constitutive conditions of being and consciousness. Primarily this is through his readings of the descriptions of the givenness, structure, and constitution of phenomena offered jointly by Husserl and Heidegger, and especially Husserl's further development of Brentano's thesis of intentional consciousness. According to Levinas, Western philosophy has nearly always been an "ontology," obsessed with the question, "What is?"

The terror for Levinas is the triumph of an impersonal reason or logos grounding the imperialism of the Same in its pretensions to exhaust all meaning. The core of his concern is exposed in his often desultory and allusive remarks: the multiplicity of unique individuals are "bits of dust" and "forgettable moments" (*AE*, 164/*OB*, 104) collected by a Hegelian mind where all that counts is their absorption in the System. Or acts of Husserlian intellection that reduce the Other to the transitivity of comprehending and a "signifying intention"[5]—expanded by Heidegger as the intellection of being in general inseparable from the appearing [*apérité*] of being, comprehension, and the essence of truth resting on the opening of Being. Always and everywhere the violence is to have reduced the Other to an impersonal element, to a mode of understanding, to the Same: a form of identity thinking. Levinas takes it as necessary and inevitable that all forms of comportment in the world are beholden to the meaning bestowing and constituting movement of conscious- ness. In this sense, the Same is always and ultimately an "egology" or a self- relation; all *esse* is *interesse* (*AE*, 15/*OB*, 4). It now becomes clear that when Levinas asks if there can be disinterestedness concern for another, the answer will entail an ethical dimension that signifies in a way that is altogether oth- erwise than, or beyond being.

Levinas's sphere of the Same is also remarkably convergent with Lacan's field of the imaginary: both are the domains of object relations, mean- ing, integrity and identity. The Other in Levinas, as a fundamentally inacces- sible signifying dimension, might be construed as congruent with Lacan's Big Other. Lacan distinguishes between two "others"; one with a big "O" and the second with a small "o"—the sphere of specular ego identifications, the sym- metrical world of egos. But on the other side of the other side of this mirror- ing process is the Big Other or the (unconscious) "subject." The distinction corresponds to his distinction between speech and the organized system of language. Whereas language returns one to the objectified other, speech is addressed to the "true" subjects or Others "on the other side of the wall of lan- guage" (*Sé II*, 285/*S II*, 244). Subjectivity—and Lacan's formulations of inter- subjectivity later become absorbed in the account of the Symbolic Other— elides representation for representation is the sphere of meaning belonging to the Imaginary. In this way, the speaking subject is a signification *manqué*, doomed to failure in finding an adequate self-expression or grasp of the Other: the signifer is a signifier only for another subject—but it is the "unconscious subject [who is] essentially the subject who speaks" (*Sé II*, 207/*S II*, 175). We also may formulate the impasse in terms of a distinction between the subject who speaks or utters [*le sujet de l'énoncé*] and the resulting constative utter- ance [*le sujet de l'énonciation*], where the former slides behind the wall of language characteristic of the latter. There is no signifier, then, that can *rep- resent* the subject. There is, as it were, a fault line separating the speaking act from the spoken fact: an Other—the unconscious—which is a "relation of fundamental alterity" (*Sé II*, 276/*S II*, 236). In this way language is funda- mentally ambiguous, "as much there to found us in the Other as to drastically prevent us from understanding him" (*Sé II*, 286/*S II*, 244). Yet, for Levinas, insofar as the Other—itself figured in relation to the symbolic Laws circulat- ing around the Name-of-the-Father (the phallus that would be *per impossible* the signifier of completion)—*constitutes* the subject as *spaltung*, it would nonetheless fall under the heading of the Same. Correlatively, the absolutely Other in Levinas does not exercise a colonizing power over the Same. This might lead one to think that the real would or could include the divine or God in Levinas, yet it is highly doubtful that Lacan would endorse and covertly underwrite the exteriority to the signifying system that this move would imply.

The Father figure of the Western philosophical tradition Levinas frequently invokes, Parmenides, and whose name he often uses metonymically for the tradition itself, is alive and well: Parmenides cannot conceive of alterity other than relative to being [*to mé on*]. Such an alterity could only be thought of as "not-being." Levinas never does imagine it is possible to kill Parmenides off in the sense that alterity is *thinkable* outside of being. Rather, Levinas argues that alterity is altogether otherwise than being and correlatively *unthinkable*.[6] Accordingly, the central gesture is exclusionary: the Other or the face is situated altogether beyond time, as anarchial, immemorial, hyperoriginal or exorbitantly prior; a protolocution preceding but leaving a trace of itself in all modes of the Same. This is the moment of the Levinasian moment of "inspiration."[7] Before choice or assumption, on the "hither-side" of all spontaneity of thought, the face is the secret "animation"[8] of being; the "first" word or expressive dimension of otherness through which all exchanges of signs, all meaning ontologically regionalized, must first pass through. The levels of the Other and the Same, then, are not alternative orders of discourse—the one is undeclinably punctured by the Other. The Other leaves a trace within any epos, any manifestation of a logos, and any modality of dioptrics or representation that would pretend to saturate and arrogate all meaning to itself. The Same is always already "open" to the Other, "already heard," (*AE*, 67/*OB*, 138) revealed in and through and despite the thematizing occlusions of being. At the same time Levinas can maintain an absolute disjunction between the two: an "excluded middle" (*AE*, 13/*OB*, 29) or nonspace [*nonlieu*].

One problem that this vertical model comprising an asymmetrical relation [*rapport sans rapport*] (*TeI*, 329/*TI*, 295) between the separated terms of the Same and the Other does not have is that of negotiating a *passage* between the two. However, to avoid the Nietzschean critique that the Other amounts to an "idle hypothesis,"[9] Levinas must save the Other from the vacuity of a *via negativa*. To save the phenomena he documents intermediary and "semi-phenomenological" experiences that could be considered the elaboration of a model of *curvature*, falling under and articulating his enigmatic umbrella terms of "passivity," "sensibility," "vulnerability," and "proximity." These moments occupy the fault line between the Same and the Other. "Sensibility" he tells us, for example, is the immediacy of a phenomenal affectivity that has as its source not a prereflective *lebenswelt* but a *nonphenomenon*.[10] Having sketched the structure of the Same and the Other let us now return to the problem of whether or not the *there is* is indispensable to it.

It is certainly possible to provide a narrative account of the Same and the Other that does not regard the *there is* as a necessary factor. This involves situating the *there is* in one or both of two ways, first as introduced by Levinas as fundamental to his critical response to Heidegger. Here one would be required to argue for why a reading of the *there is* could or should be limited to its role in Levinas's disengagement with Heidegger when it is by no means restricted to this function in Levinas's works. Second, the *there is* could be construed as an illustrative example and one of a number of quasi-phenomenological accounts designed to show how the Same is "open" to or affected by either an impersonal otherness [*autre*][11] or to the otherness of another person [*Autrui*]; the divine spark of alterity [*illeity*]. The problem with this is that it fails to explain the persistence with which Levinas reiterates the modality of the *there is,* whereas other cameo phenomenological profiles are developed beyond themselves or else are not taken up again at length. Yet the character of the *there is* is neither developed further nor left behind—Levinas is still concerned with it in the closing pages of *Otherwise Than Being.* An additional problem concerns the diremptive ambiguity of the *there is*: although it is an impersonal otherness rather than the divine trace carried through the Other both occupy an anarchial or untimely nonspace [*nonlieu*], that is, both are irrefusably affective yet exiled from recognition or apprehension by the knowing subject. But this makes it impossible to distinguish between the order of the (ethical) Other and the (unethical) *there is,* as I shall show.

II

This section specifies the various determinations Levinas gives to the *there is* in *Existence and Existents,* a set of studies begun before and continued during the war whilst captive, and the 1948 essay "Reality and Its Shadow." These determinations, underwriting and making possible the substantive and procedural status of the *there is* in later works, can accordingly be classified into descriptive and functional callibrations.

1. The primary functional determination of the *there is* is to account for the ontological conditions for the possibility of a particular existent. Levinas parallels Heidegger's distinction between Being and beings, calling the former the *there is,* "being-in-general" or a "dark background" (*DE,* 98/*EE,* 57) from which a particular being comes to be, emerging into its proper sphere of temporality and consciousness. Elsewhere Levinas will call this the "fathomless depth of the element" (*TeI,* 170/*TI,* 158), the indefinite, the *aperion,* and "prime matter absolutely undetermined" (*TeI,*

170/*TI*, 159).[12] Here Levinas both follows Heidegger's analysis of Dasein in *Being and Time*[13] whilst breaking being-in-general off from any form of intellection. Although the *there is* comprises an ontological source of a particular being, Levinas distinguishes it absolutely from determinate identifications dependent upon the temporally ex-static consciousness of particular beings. This categorial division between existence and an existent precludes the *there is* from time, situating the individual being as cognitively divorced from but constitutionally continuous with its "dark background."

2. Having exluded being-in-general from time, which is the privilege of the distinct existent, Levinas consistently proceeds to characterize it as a "dead time," a "meanwhile," an "interval" of stoppage or a "nothing-interval" (*DE*, 105/*EE*, 64). However, because the particular existent is not detachable from this dark background, Levinas can confirm the traumatic inhabitation of "dead time" in the midst of the timely *reconnoitres* of consciousness. It allows him to argue, *contra* Heidegger, that an unrecollectable element of being is death, "the uncertainty of time's continuation and something like a death doubling the impulse of life" (*CP*, 11). The claim is that life is always already dead or dying and that this is ontologically constitutive. The *there is* is the threat of the impossibility of possibility, an interruption of *Seinkönnen* and taking up one's projects within a determinable world. "In *dying* the horizon of the future is given, but the future as the promise of a new interval is refused; one is in the interval, forever an interval. . . . it is as though death were never dead enough [*comme si mort n'était jamais mort*]" (*CP*, 11). Illustratively, it is no accident that Levinas populates the zone of the *there is* prosopopoeically with ghosts, phantoms, and spectres: structurally, the "living-dead."

3. What evidence do we have that the *there is* is in fact nonisolable from the particular existent? As a "dark background" or being-in-general immune from all intellection, is it not a *via negativa*, something about which we can know nothing, not even that it *is* an ontological precondition for a being to be? It is here that Levinas turns to phenomenology, for he must show that the *there is* makes a difference to being and is in some way accessible. The primary phenomenological experience that yields onto the *there is* is that of insomnia (*DE*, 109–13/*EE*, 65–67); a term often used depositionally for the *there is* itself, as is the "meanwhile." Insomnia, the inability to sleep at night, is the surface phenomenal domain that is then extended and delimited into a phenomenologically inaccessible depth. Levinas describes a superlatively nightly night (*DE*, 94–96/*EE*, 58–59), an absolutely unknowable black hole in the midst of that night that is the familiar counterpart of the day. The affective dimension of this hypernocturnality takes the form of an impersonal vigilence, as if one is being watched by the night itself. As inde-

terminable and unavailable to critical inspection one is filled with the sense of an indefinite threat, menace, foreboding, anxiety, and horror. Insomnia thus comprises a threshold limit-experience opening onto the phantas-magoric and ghastly *there is*, comparable to Lacan's similar oneric condition. For example, commenting on another of Freud's case studies, the dream of the wolfman, Lacan locates "a sort of ultimate experience, confronted by the apprehension of the ultimate real. . . . Enigmatic image apropos of which Freud evokes the navel of the dream, this abysmal relation to what is most unknown . . . in which the real is apprehended beyond all mediation, be it imaginary or symbolic" (*Sé II*, 209/*S II*, 176–77). Levinas's descriptions of the double night similarly sutures the *there is* to a disclosive experience, insomnia, to which it is nonetheless interpretively resistant.

4. The idea that the *there is*, although beyond conscious retrievability, nonetheless extrudes into a particular consciousness, is intensified kinaesthetically. The *there is*, while mute and announcing nothing, does so from an unidentifiable source of implacable noise: it rumbles, whines, buzzes, creaks, and rustles. The phenomenological analyses are designed to provide evidence that the structuration of consciousness is constitutionally continuous with the *there is* such that definitionally a particular existent becomes a terrazo—inlaid with chips of the "meanwhile." Paralleling Lacan's description of the real as transgressing the distinction between an "inside" and an "outside," the impenetrable exteriority of the *there is* is at once an impenetrable interiority; "For *there is* transcends inwardness as well as exteriority" [*L'il y a transcende en effet l'intériorité comme l'extériorité*] (*Sé II*, 94/*S II*, 57).

5. In addition to the experience of insomnia Levinas also analyzes such experiences as indolence, fatigue, and effort. These constitute semiphenomenological modes of continuity between "being-in-general" and the conscious life of the particular existent. These descriptions are exemplary in bringing together and explicitly combining the functional and phenomenological determinations of the *there is*, recapitulating the point that the *there is*, far from an irrelevant ontological backdrop, insists within the experiences of a particular being. These moments comprise both a split between and a stitch across from existence to an existent. Their precise existential status is operant through the impossibility of inscribing a midway zone between the two; for example effort is "still on the hither-side" [*qu'il est en deca*] (*DE*, 45/*EE*, 31) but "takes on the instance, breaking and tying back together the thread of time" (*DE*, 48/*EE*, 33). Fatigue "is this time-lag" (*DE*, 45/*EE*, 31) and indolence "is an impossibility of beginning, or, if one prefers, it is the effecting of beginning."[14] Indolence, effort, and fatigue elide the drawing of a boundary that would otherwise separate being-in-general and the individual existent.

6. The paradoxical character of the instant, the uspurge of the existent into time is to take a position in the anonymous *there is*, to suspend it, Levinas tells us. He calls this affirmation of the subject the "hypostasis" (*DE*, 99/*EE*, 57–58). A significant portion of *Existence and Existents* is devoted to describing the nature of consciousness as positionality or commensurate with a certain temporal localization. The important point concerning us here, however, is that the hypostatic "suspension" of the *there is* does not thereby abolish it. Rather, Levinas's description of the nature of consciousness demarcates a necessary reification or exclusion of the informative excess of the *there is* from apprehension. "Consciousness implies presence, position-before-itself, that is, mundaneness, the fact of being-given, and exposure to the grasp, hold, comprehension, appropriation."[15]

To summarize, Levinas presents a notion of consciousness that is inherently unable to access its own constitutive caesura or evacuation by the dead time of the dispossessing and deindividuating *there is*. We might even go so far as to say that the subject is a psychosis, and Levinas not adventitiously remarks that insomnia and its counterparts are "limit-states" proximal to certain paradoxes of madness (*DE*, 97/*EE*, 60). Because the individual existent is not separable from the *there is* this horror is at once a horror of *oneself*. Completing this preliminary terratology Levinas diabolically hints that we ourselves, without knowledge or undertaking, are unwittingly sealed over in a contract to the profanity of the *there is*. Remembering that the sphere of consciousness is that of the Same, the framework is set up as early as this short work for Levinas to confuse together the Same, or what it is to be, with a "counter-nature, a monstrosity, what is disturbing and foreign of itself" (*CP*, 181).

Being is caught in a double bind: not only does the *there is* provide an ineluctably unknowable *metaphysical* account of evil in being, but it also is an inescapable *immanence* within being: an in-carnation. That unravellable knot becomes the decisive groundwork upon which Levinas will proceed to claim, with all the resources that this knot opens up, that the absurdity and senselessness of the *there is* is necessary for Goodness. Already, he has provisionally demonstrated that there is *good reason* for the necessity of a transcending ethical dimension. And that good reason, ultimately, is a part of the definition of being itself. "There is an ambiguity of sense and non-sense in being, sense turning into non-sense" (AE, 254/*OB*, 163).

III

This section explores how Levinas justifies the necessity of the *there is* for Goodness. The central thought is that the *there is* comprises a thresh-

old that functionally "opens" being to the alterity of the Other. Phenomenologically, the accessibility of the Other strikes being into an awareness
of its ineliminable conspiracy with the senseless *there is*, understood as a
consciousness of being in bad conscience, "the ego is awakened to the condition of the soul that calls upon God" (*CP*, 181). Not only does Levinas's
argument hinge upon the imprecision and obscurity of the notions of
"opening" and "awakening" but, even if we allow the argument to go
through despite that opacity, the *there is*, if it can transform the alterity of
the Other into the negativity of being's self-recognition as essentially bad
conscience and needful of the goodness of the Other, cashes out to the
transformation of alterity to immanence: the otherness of the Other enters
into the constitution of the Same as the precondition for this negative self-
awareness.

The form of this argument hinges on two essays, which should be read
together; Levinas's 1982 essay, "Useless Suffering," and his 1984 essay, "Bad
Conscience and the Inexorable." Here, to sketch out the skeletal parametres of
the argument of the first essay, he maintains that the passive suffering one
undergoes in the face of the senseless horror of the *there is* constitutes an im-
mediable bond with the useless suffering of another. The crucial move is that
this becomes fear *for* the Other, a move apparently obliged by the thought that
the alterity of senseless suffering is subjoined to—or perhaps interrupted by—
ethical alterity, such that the suffering of another is at once a "half-opening"
onto the transcending summons to responsibility. Playing on the French word
mal, which means both "hurt" and "suffering," Levinas runs together the passivity of suffering with the passivity of ethical responsibility. "Is not the evil
of suffering, extreme passivity, impotence, abandonment and solitude—also
the unassumable and thus the possibility of a half-opening, and, more precisely, the possibility that wherever a moan, a cry, a groan, or a sigh happen
there is an original call for aid."[16] In short, the justification for the absurd
senselessness of the *there is* lies in its role such that the fear and horror of evil
is tied up with fear for the injustices suffered by the Other, "the very phenomenon of suffering in its uselessness is, in principle, the pain of the
Other."[17] Levinas does not take the notion of a "half-opening" seriously
enough. How does any of this work? And does this not justify the absurdity
of the *there is* through the back door, namely by exalting it into a moral phenomenon? Additionally, for senseless suffering to be given a meaning through
being ethically persecuted by it requires suffering *in statu*—but is this suffering metaphysically irreducible, or an avoidable eventuality of the actions of
one being with respect to another?

The backbone articulating these transmutations can be found in the
logically antecedant essay, "Bad Conscience and the Inexorable." Intensifying the dysphoric division of the *there is* as both phenomenal and nonphe-

nomenal, Levinas begins the essay with a distinction between the intentional structure of consciousness "at the basis of all consciousness whether theoretical or nontheoretical" and, in a neatly paradoxical formulation since it is difficult to determine where the one begins and the other ends, "non-intentional consciousness."[18] The meaning of the latter is "nonreflective" rather than "preflective" and Levinas—marking a break with the phenomenological tradition—complains that this meaning is liable to be forgotton by reflective consciousness in its haste to consider it a still nonexplicit knowledge or a confused representation awaiting clarification. Of course, this break has been anticipated all along given the halfway house status of the *there is* and other modalizations of "sensibility." And Levinas proceeds to point out the modality of nonintentional consciousness. It is "pure passivity," without aim, nameless. The tension hinges on the slippage of the word "passivity." It operates as a midway slipstream between intentional and nonintentional consciousness. Henceforth, "passivity" constitutes an inexplicable merging of the Same and the Other; indeed, a relationship between terms that, far from separated, are now related and furthermore alterity is produced as a moment *immanent* within being: the nonintentional contact with the Other becomes, precisely, an intentional moment *of* being as it is struck into awareness of its sorry state. Levinas insists upon this. The passivity of nonintentional consciousness calls into question the position in being affirmed by intentional thought. It is "being as bad conscience, being in question,"[19] the necessity of responding to one's very right to be in fear for the Other. The positivity of the Good is the experience of bad-conscience: the two are logically equiprimordial.

Yet the notion of "passivity" shelters an immanence Levinas wishes to debar from the absolutely Other. And Levinas disasterously joins alterity and being together in the ambiguity of the French word *la conscience*, which conveniently means both "consciousness" and "conscience," even as he imagines this amplifies rather than undermines his notion of ultrapassivity, and as if this word circumvents the necessity for an account of how the one automatically coincides with the other. The Other becomes not so much an interruption of being as always already endogeneous to it. Recalling the felicitous ambiguity of the word *mal*, employed in "Useless Suffering," Levinas exacerbates the disaster by combining this ambiguity with that of *la conscience*. Consciousness is at once conscience, at once to suffer the absurdity of senseless suffering and "fear that comes to me from the face of the Other."[20] The very egoity of being is inseparable from its constitutive alternation between the *there is* and a receptivity to the Other that, sliding along the unbroken thread from nonintentionality to an "awakening" or intentional cognizance, becomes itself an immanent, constitutive, mediable, and inerradicable moment of a being's self-understanding.

IV

Whilst the preceding section discovered the *there is* as a semipermeable membrane between the Same and the Other, without a marked difference from either term, it reduced the Other to the Same. To avoid that disaster, Levinas concentrates on the inviolable singularity of the *there is* in an attempt to avoid sinking the Other in the Same. The *there is* is coincident neither with the Same nor with the Other. It already has been suggested that it will become difficult to distinguish the *there is* from its constitutive role in the operations of reflective consciousness. Levinas already has discovered the phenomenological modalizations of the *there is* that creep into experience as anxiety and horror, and he has already discovered that this horror in the face of that subjection is preconditional for the acknowledgement of being in bad-conscience. Hence it is imperative that he both sustain the transgressive function of the *there is* that allows the Other to be accessible to the Same while preserving the distinctness of the *there is* from either.

Although the *there is* connectively brings together the Other and the Same, insofar as Levinas sustains a radical distinction between these two terms, it is not reducible to either. Affirming the midway status and singularity of the *there is*, Levinas situates it between the Same and the Other in *Otherwise Than Being*, claiming that the two are separated by the "meanwhile," and furthermore that the "meanwhile" is not abolished, transcended, or nullified by ethical responsibility (*AE*, 221/141). It remains. Although we have negotiated the *there is* in terms of an insufferable installation within being, it is of course not coextensive with the whole of what makes being tick; on the contrary, far from saturating being, it resists the anamnesis of the present and representation. The question then arises: If the *there is* is characterized as the monsterous and nonintegratable, then how does Levinas characterize being's temporal and knowledgeable comportment? The answer consists of a precarious distinction between the description of consciousness as "imperturable essence, equal and indifferent to all responsibility" (*AE*, 254/*OB*, 168), that is, it is the domain of equality and neutrality, neither intrinsically responsible nor irresponsible, and the "turning," "as in insomnia" of this indifference into "monotony, anonymity, insignificance, into an incessant buzzing that nothing can now stop and which absorbs all signification, even that of which this bustling about is a modality" (*AE*, 254/*OB*, 168). A wobbly distinction, for as being insomniacally turns over in its skin pulsating between its modality as insouciant essence and insurmountable buzzing, where the former collapses or is forever on the edge of collapse into the swallowing up of significance characteristic of the latter, this intrication remains doggedly resistant to discrimination. It is not all certain that this wrenching over of being into its underside could be either knowable or preventable, nor, therefore, whether or to what extent the operations of consciousness periphrastically express the aphotic miasma of the *there is*. That is, it is not at all clear that one could disentangle the neutrality of essence from the infiltrative monstrosity of the *there is*. This thought is confirmed in "Reality and its Shadow" where Levinas writes that the subject is powerless to leave its dark parentage behind; rather, the dead interval out of which it arises extends "to the light itself, to thought, to inner life" (*CP*, 7).

But as being wriggles around between intentional consciousness and the impenetrable exteriority of insomnia, this intermixture allows Levinas the use and profit of the ambiguity to emphasize the constitutional aspect of the *there is*, as "being-in-general," to align it with the Same in spite of—or because of—the tenebrously thin demarcation drawn above between the neutrality of the one and the anonymity of the other. Insomnia is disturbed by the Other in its *sameness* [*inquiée du coeur de son egalité*] (*CP*, 156) writes Levinas. Further still, intentional consciousness is "a modality or modification of *insomnia*" (*CP*, 155). The difference between intentional consciousness and nonintentional consciousness, between sensibility and its nonphenomenal source, becomes attentuated to the point of convergency, providing oblique confirmation of the thought that the operations of consciousness cannot be immune from information either by the *there is* or by the Other. God also enters the fray as Levinas tells us, somewhat obscurely, "God is . . . other than the other [*autre qu'autrui*], other otherwise, other with an alterity prior to the alterity of the other, prior to the ethical bond with another and different from every neighbour, transcendent to the point of absence, to the point of a possible confusion with the stirring of the *there is*" (*CP*, 165–66). Even if God is definitionally discriminable from the *there is*, is He structurally or phenomenologically distinguishable?

It is just as important that Levinas keep the *there is* apart from the signifying dimension of the face if he is both to avoid inextricably ensnaring the one in the other and if he is to avoid blurring the disjunction between the Same and the Other. *Yet because the* there is *acts as a conduit opening the Same to the Other and because the untimely "meanwhile" consorts with the equally untimely an-archiality of the face, Levinas fails to keep the two apart.* Indeed, he sometimes resolves the one into the other. In "Phenomenon and Enigma" he writes that the face is an "insinuation . . . breaking up like the bubbles of the earth [*bulles de la terre*], which Banquo speaks of at the beginning of MacBeth" (*CP*, 70). The face. But he also uses the same expression in *Existence and Existents*, "where being insinuates itself even in nothingness, like bubbles of the earth" (*DE*, 101/*EE*, 62). The *there is*. The "bubbles of the earth is a simile that describes an insinuation or interruption by both the face *and* the *there is*, as "being-in-general." It is impossible to keep the two apart. In "God and Philosophy" Levinas even conflates the two by categorizing insomnia (a modality of the *there is*) with infinity (the atemporal designation of the face) (*CP*, 156). Nor is this this substitutive transposition of terms *aufheben* or transcended in ethical responsibility as if the confusion could be left behind in some sense. On the contrary, it is necessary for being's "awakening" to or recognition of its bad conscience as well as providing the condition for it in terms both of an egoic superintendance and as the corridor extending to the Other. Though the *there is* taps into the Other, the wakefulness, the anonymous vigilence of the *there is* or insomnia, must remain the "wakefulness in awakening [*la veillée de l'éveil*]" (*CP*, 156).

In *Otherwise Than Being* Levinas introduces the necessity of the *there is* once again in terms of articulating the model of the Same and the Other. The distinction is between the "subject"—the Same—and "subjectivity"—an otherness that fractures the integrity of the Same through "substituting" the Other for me, in a kind of psychic gestation or maternity: the "other-in-the-same." Smuggling a moment of alterity into the midst of the unconcerned "atheist" integrity of the subject, Levinas explains subjectivity as a transfer or substitution for the Other; an undeclinable attachment already made, irreversibly past, prior to all recall, and structurally homologous with the notion of a "Metaphysical Desire" that both proceeds from and goes unto the Other. The account of subjectivity, problematic though it is, can be seen as Levinas's answer to the question of how it is that we are not simply deaf to the appeal of the Other. But even here he reintroduces the necessity of the transitional function of the *there is*.

Between the subject and subjectivity—an impossible space excluded by the notion of the *nonlieu* or "excluded middle"—the nodule of the *there is* is required to "bring out" subjectivity: "The *there is* is all the weight that alterity weighs supported by a subjectivity that does not found it. . . . In this overflowing of sense by nonsense, the sensibility, the self [*le Soi*], is first brought out, in its bottomless passivity, as pure sensible point, a dis-interestedness, or subversion of essence" (*AE*, 256/*OB*, 164). Again, "Behind the anonymous rustling of the *there is* subjectivity reaches passivity without any assumption" (*AE*, 255/*OB*, 164). To reach and produce the bottomless passivity of this pure undergoing where the self is substituted for the Other "the excessive or disheartening hubbub and encumberment of the *there is* is needed" (*AE*, 255/*OB*, 164). Separating the Same from the Other, whilst moving in this space in order to bring them together, the *there is* toes the line between them, spreading out on both sides at once yet commensurate with neither. Either the terms of the Same and the Other are no longer wholly distinct—a catastrophe—or else they are separated both the one from the other and each from the *there is* in a propagation of disheartening separations. A catastrophe.

V

In this final section I follow through the implications of the notion that to be a being is necessarily to be entangled with the evil *there is* to the point of the impossibility of discriminating between freedom from and bondage to it. One wonders what it is that guarantees the evil of the *there is* in its function of yeilding onto the alterity of goodness. How could one trust the fundamentally irresponsible *there is* to this effect? Here Levinas relinquishes his hold on that very certainty, which would otherwise negate or sublate the evil of the *there is* by making it an ethical step on the way to the Other. Two new but interwoven thoughts are introduced. First, nothing obliges the *there is* to open onto the alterity of the Other. Second, he argues that the Good requires not only the fact that the birthright of being is the irresponsible *there is*, but that this very irresponsibility may seduce a being into refusing the Other. The problem with this, consistent as it is with Levinas's insistence that the Other is fragile, ungraspable, and an "authority" rather than a "force,"[21] is that once the *there is* has become unknowably meshed with the consciousness of a being, it is no longer possible for a being to know whether or not temptation to irresponsibility has already taken place. In another sense it has always already taken place: to be a being is already to have been suffused by and produced from the *there is*. It becomes impossible for a being to rely on its "good intentions" and this hopeless entanglement with the *there is* makes it equally impossible to cede to the Other a redemptive space that does not beg the question, once more, of how that could be possible or what good it could do.

If the subject is illimitably pervaded by the implacable murmur of the *there is*, making it impossible to localize consciousness as a penumbral exteriority to it, or, inversely, to regionalize the *there is* as wholly otherwise than being—either way would constitute a self-negation—then being is wedded at its inmost point of possibility to the ghastly absurdity of the *there is*. Being cannot be defined independently of its involvement with the malignant *there is*. With unassailable implications. Nor does Levinas wish to contest that always already consummated marriage, for without this disequilibrium of differential identity he could not defeasibly argue that being has good reason to suffer its constitutional inequity, its pangs of conscience, and to expiate for the Other in his or her senseless suffering. He endorses his commitment to what may be considered a veritable nosography of being. "This way for the subject to find itself again in essence, whereas essence, as assembled, should have made possible the present and freedom, is *not a harmonious and inoffensive participation*. It is the incessant buzzing that fills each silence. . . . A rumbling intolerable to a subject that faces itself as a subject, and assembles essence before itself as object" (*AE*, 254/*OB*, 163). The subject finds itself intolerable and its self-conception—a virtual delusion or self-dissimulation—is premised upon the repression of its point of discomfort through representational thought, object-relations, and imaginary projections afforded by the comfort blanket of the present and freedom that inevitably relocute the consorting nullity of the *there is*. We necessarily misrecognize ourselves; a misrecognition signalled by an insomnia that refuses integration into some sure piece of knowledge. Registered here is the documentation of evil in being itself; an evil that poisons the thematizing ego in its very essence. And Levinas goes this far. Commenting on Nemo's interpretation of anxiety in Heidegger in "Transcendence and Evil," Levinas identifies the "original insomnia of being" with "the cutting point at the heart of evil. Sickness, evil in being, aging, corruptible flesh, perishing and rotting . . ." (*CP*, 179).

It follows that if the evil in being conditions the consciousness that on the one hand would cover up the fault and on the other hand would express it, then being cannot be either a self-sufficiency or, what is the same thing, resistant to the corruptive rottonness of its own constitution. But Levinas deepens even this ambiguity, for nothing guarantees the economic necessity of the *there is* in its function as a midway play in the exchange of the Same for the Other. Although it is clear that the incarnation of the subject cannot be unequivocally separated from the insignia of the *there is*, this strange contract between existence or "being-in-general" and the particular existent does not inevitably transgress the separation between the Same and the Other. It is not dominated by that incline and, if it were, although the *there is* would not be abolished thereby, it would at least be certain that it forms a stage on the way to the Other and could be justified ethically. Yet Levinas has insisted that the *there is*, far from a nascent moment of goodness in disguise, is the cutting edge of evil and irresponsibility.

In the 1968 essay, "Humanism and An-archy," it turns out that a being cannot be "possessed" by the command to ethical responsibility for the neighbor *unless* it is risky and under threat; the threat of a certain sort of refusal, a refusal denied to the knowing subject since the advent of the Other is anarchically prior to choice, assumption, or will. The refusal is resultant upon or concommitant with the subversion of being by its own passive entanglement with the *there is*. In a claim that not only stresses the requirement of the sirenic possibility of refusal as a precondition for the Good to become an equivocal or enigmatically undecideable "perhaps," but also runs together the very egoity of being with the evil of the *there is*—moreover the basis for the separateness of the Same from the Other—Levinas writes that possession by the Good "needs the temptation of the facility to make a break, the erotic attraction of irresponsibility. . . . Thus there is, in the midst of submission to the Good, the seduction of irresponsibility, the probability of egoism in the subject. . . . This temptation to separate oneself from the Good is the very incarnation of the subject" (*CP*, 137). The important point concerns the modality of the word "temptation." Since the *there is* is also "prior" to and unavailable to cognition, being appears somewhat unfree to decline the temptation of irresponsibility, indeed, has always already failed to resist it in the sense that irresponsibility coincides with the incarnation of the subject or, at best, cannot be distilled out of it as an externality. And, if it could, being voids itself utterly. Thus, the *there is* becomes capable of withholding the Same from the Other even as it also has the facility to function as a keystone in the midst of the two spans. Anxious that this has not been too powerful and dangerous a thought, Levinas quickly retracts it. "Seductive and facile evil is perhaps incapable of breaking the passivity of the pre-liminary, pre-historical subjection, annihilating the hither-side" (*CP*, 137). And perhaps it is quite capable—after all, the Good "needs the temptation of the facility to make a break . . ." and that break is surely a real possibility if it is not to stand as a casuistic conceit.

We are left with a shrunken Levinasian universe as the refinements of the models that held it together fall away to disclose a bare cosmological war between Good and Evil. In the midst of concretion we are in abstraction, and the individual, the subject, the ipseity of the person Levinas has been so concerned to preserve and refigure with ethical respect becomes an impersonal moment of the system: self-deceiving, ultimately powerless and irrelevant bits of dust collected around the spring-heeled skeleton of the *there is* and forming the beads of sweat on the brow of the Good. Levinas, having gone this far, realizes he has gone much too far. Good and Evil are now definitionally mutually dependent, reciprocally meaningful, and antagonistic: a classic binary opposition. To escape this logic Levinas actually exacerbates it by ontotheologically situating Evil, and as if this is not a foregone conclusion by definition, as a lower value than the Good, as egoism or evil (*CP*, 137), deriving its value parasitically from the Good, and hence intensifying the reciprocity that he is so anxious to deny. Thus, having rehabilitated the axiological bipolarity of Good and Evil, Levinas, in a rare moment of pulpit fervor, denounces it. "But Evil claims to be the contemporary, the equal, the twin of the Good. This is an irrefutable lie, a Luciferian lie. It is the very egoism of the ego [*l'egoïsm même du Moi*] that posits itself as its own origin, an uncreated, sovereign principle, a prince" (*CP*, 138). Being cannot shrug off its spontaneity and freedom, cannot elide the slide of its ego into the evil of the *there is*, "something inhuman and monstrous" (*CP*, 11), cannot but passively await the Other to alexipharmically dispossess it of its identity—perhaps!

Conclusion

The *there is* is structurally coextensive with Lacan's notion of a Borromean knot, linking yet a foreclosed element in the order of the Same and the

Other as it is in the order of the imaginary and the symbolic. Linking and fore-closing, this real, this *there is*, unravels and traumatizes those very distinctions that it sets to work; resisting them and insisting within them. Whilst the *there is* can be thematized as a necessary precondition for the possibility of the accessibility of the Other to the Same it ambiguates that relation to the point of impossibility: the very terms of the relation are absolved from absolute separation, on the one hand, and a preponderance of separations are produced, on the other hand. The *there is*, while relating the Same to the Other, is not reducible to either of these terms. The Platonic model is formally repeated: to account for the relationship between the Good and the changing phenomenal world, Plato on occasion invokes a daemonic intermediary, halfway between mortal and immortal, half-god and half-man, whose function is "[to] interpret and convey messages to the gods from men and to men from the gods. . . . Being of an intermediate nature, a spirit bridges the gap between them, and prevents the universe from falling into two separate halves."[22] The *there is* functions similarly but is prey to the same devastating critique Aristotle leveled at Plato, commonly known as the "third man" argument. This also can be formally brought to bear upon Levinas. To show how the *there is* is connected on either side, to the Same and to the Other, requires further intermediary moments in order to explain the identity and difference between them: these moments then require further moments to explain *their* relationship to yet distinctness from the moments they mediate, and so on ad infinitum. Even if we change the idiom to Levinasese, the "unrelating relation" is replicated ad infinitum. The way out of this is to demonstrate that the *there is* is other than both the Same and the Other, other than absolutely, a *tertium quid*, and not with respect to some relative term, but in that case the *there is* cannot relate the one to the other and is an effective redundancy. Or, it is not radically other than either term, in which case the Same and the Other are not radically other than one another and, moreover, the problems of the "third man" arise. With which other/Other are we faced?

It is within the context of the dramatic role of the *there is*, following and exemplifying the impossible instransigencies and traversals of the real, that the following suggestive commentary given by Lacan, summing up the horror at the navel of Irma's dream, should be tympanically cast:

> Having got the patient to open her mouth—that is precisely what's at stake in reality, that she doesn't open her mouth—what he sees in there, these turbinate bones covered with a whitish membrane, is a horrendous sight. The mouth has all the equivalences in terms of significations, all the condensations you want. Everything blends in and becomes associated in this image, from the mouth to the female sexual organ, by way of the nose—just before or just after this, Freud has his turbinate bones operated on, by Fliess or by someone else. There's a horrendous dis-

covery here, that of the flesh one has never seen, the foundation of things, the other side of the head, of the face, the secretory glands *par excellence*, the flesh from which everything exudes, at the very heart of the mystery, the flesh in as much as it is suffering, is formless, in as much as its form in itself is something which provokes anxiety. Spectre of anxiety, identification of anxiety, the final revelation of *you are this— You are this, which is so far from you, this which is the ultimate formlessness. (Sé II*, 186/*S II*, 154–55)

But let us now cast this summing up back into Lacan. What status can be accorded to this description of the horror at the navel of Irma's dream? In the introduction we saw that Lacan's real prevented him from being caught in a form of linguistic circle. The real traverses the distinction between "internality" and "externality" because there can be no metalanguage that would apprehend the real as a *Ding-an-sich* or as it is "in itself," beyond or outside of our linguistic appraisals. Nonetheless, Lacan specifies two nonlinguistic modes of disclosure: the navel of the dream and the psychosomatic "relation" to the real as "an absolute other" beyond all subjectivity (*Sé II*, 209/*S II*, 177).

If we were to reflect the composition of the *there is* back onto Lacan's notion of the real, concentrating on its aspect as an intramundane alterity, an anamorphotic point within and exceeding the structuration of the subject, then it becomes apparent that Levinas radicalizes the intrusion of the real as an emergent hypotyposis of conscious awareness. This is because Levinas does not reserve an umediated access to the real to the "privileged" experiences of either the navel of a dream or the objectless relation to it of the psychomatic symptom. In the "limit-states" introduced in *Existence and Existents*, "proximal to certain paradoxes of madness" comprising that of insomnia, effort, fatigue, and indolence, he does not consider these experiences under the heading of the *extra*ordinary; rather these are pitched at the level of what we could call the psychopathology of everyday life. One is always sutured to and separated from the "dark background" of the real. Both thinkers characterize that "background" as formlessness, the undetermined as such, and as the ultimate anxiety in the face of a zone that bypasses the possibility of apprehending it by way of object-relations. Just as the contingency of the real plays its part in the object of desire, so—faced with the absence of all objects—the anxiety is at once that in face of the removal or absence of desire, the breakdown of the barrier separating the real from "reality."

In Lacan it is the "barrier" separating the real from the symbolic that prevents psychosis. Is there not a psychotic moment by means of which the real remains exactly as it is within the symbolic, on its own terms, even as it is also rendered through linguistic mediation as "reality"? This is partly what Lacan means when he says that the Other does not exist: it is the unintended "by-product"—a radically uncontrollable contingency of the way our actions "turn out," as it were, and which would not turn out in the same way if the turnout was teleologically aimed at in advance, rather like performatively altering a situation by the attempt to address it "as it is." The address changes the state of affairs, and the message returns in its effective rather than intended meaning. The Other decides on the situation of our agency for us. The Other, then, is always already a little piece of the real. The only way not to be deceived by the dissimulations in relation to the symbolic is to short-circuit the symbolically mediated relation to it by occupying the psychotic position. But when Lacan characterizes the unmediated apprehension of the real as "an essential alien [*dissemblable*], who is neither the supplement, nor the complement [*semblable*], who is the very image of dislocation, of the essential tearing apart of the subject" (*Sé II*, 207/*S II*, 177), the mouthless real is determined not neutrally but as the inverse negative of the imaginary image of completion and integrity and the back of the beyond of the symbolic: death, senselessness, a dissolution of the subject. The question arises: Is this the real speaking through its own mouth, or is this a "speaking for" the real? If it is the former, then the real can no longer be marginalized as, for instance, when Lacan declares that "[e]ach person's drama . . . is of an entirely different order from these appraisals to the real . . . nothing that is effective in the domain of the subject emerges out of it" (*Sé II*, 255–56/*S II*, 219). If this is a "speaking for" the real, as the photographic negative of the symbolic and the imaginary, then the navel of the dream and the psychosomatic relations are not apprehensions of the real "beyond all mediation, be it imaginary or symbolic" (*Sé II*, 209/*S II*, 177) after all.

More acutely, the dreamer or the psychosomatic sufferer is not for all that permanently outside of the domains of the symbolic and the imaginary. To what extent does the unmediated "apprehension" of the horror of the real enter into the signifying structures of the symbolic and the imaginary? Is the horror an inverse designation supplied by the meaningfulness of these registers? In that case we are still within a linguistic circle. Or is the horror the *real real*, neither conditioned nor conditioning the subject at the point of immediate apprehension? In which case, the real determines the symbolic and the imaginary as other than themselves, that is, the real *is* effective in the emergence of the domain of the subject. And the "fissureless" real is fractured with an alterity with respect to itself. At the moments where Lacan *might* admit more about the real he *must* say more if the foregoing analysis is correct. With which other/Other are we faced?

Notes

1. For an excellent introduction to Lacan and especially the real concretely explained through popular culture, see Slavoj Žižek, *Looking Awry: An Introduction*

through Popular Culture to Jacques Lacan (Cambridge and London: Massachusetts Institute of Technology, 1991) and "Which Subject of the Real?" in *The Sublime Object of Ideology* (London and New York: Verso, 1989).

2. Also see Lacan's disccussion of *tuché* in *Sé XI*, 53–62/*S XI*, 53–64.

3. Levinas's fundamental objection to psychoanalysis concerns what he takes to be a model of explanation that is infinitely regressive. See *TeI*, 320–21/*TI*, 202.

4. See Sigmund Freud, "Medusa's Head," in *Freud: Collected Papers* V, edited by James Strachey (London: Hogarth Press, 1971), pp. 320–21 and 202.

5. Emmanuel Levinas, "L'ontologie est-elle fondamentale?" in *Entre Nous: Essais sur le penser-à-l'autre* (Paris: Betrnard Grasset, 1991), p. 14; "Is Ontology Fundamental?" *Philosophy Today* 32, no. 2 (summer 1989): p. 122.

6. See Derrida's discussion of Levinas's relationship to Parmenides and the Eleatic notion of Being in "Violence and Metaphysics," *Writing and Difference*, translated by Allan Bass (London and New York: Routledge, 1978), especially pp. 84–92. The question concerns the possibility of a break with Greek metaphysics, of "killing a speech" (p. 89) that conceptually shapes alterity as relative to Being. Derrida astutely captures and summarizes Levinas's position in his explanation of how Levinas's notion of alterity is "the other of the logic of non-contradiction," contesting the root of Western philosophy itself.

7. See *CP*, 156 and *AE*, 220–24/*OB*, 140–44.

8. See, for example, *AE*, 113–16/*OB*, 70–72.

9. Fredrich Nietzsche, *The Will to Power*, translated by Walter Kaufmann and R. J. Hollingdale (New York: Vintage, 1968), pp. 302–3.

10. *AE*, 121/*OB*, 75. Also see, *CP*, 115–19 for one place where Levinas expounds his notions of "proximity" and "sensibility." Additionally, see *AE*, 77–124/*OB*, 61–97 and *TeI*, 142–49/*TI*, 135–40.

11. The French cannot be translated unambiguously into English. I have translated *autre/Autre* by "other" and *autrui/Auturi* by "Other."

12. Merleau-Ponty, too, describes night as a deidentifying abyss: "Night is not an object before me; it enwraps and infiltrates through all my senses, stifling my recollections and almost destroying my personal identity"(*Phenomenology of Perception*, translated by C. Smith [London: Routledge, 1989], p. 283); it is an anonymous background, a "spatiality without things," the "uncaused and tireless impulse which draws us to seek an anchorage and to surmount ourselves in things" (ibid.).

13. See the first introductory chapter of *Existence and Existents* for Levinas's discussion of Heidegger in this context. For Levinas, Heidegger deprives death of its full alterity through the thesis of being-towards-death where death is resolutely appropriated and taken over in the angst-ridden apprehension of the possibility of impossi-

bility: of ceasing to be. That is, for Levinas, Heidegger strips death of its sting through a reduction to instrumental worth: the approach of the ultimate negative is turned into the positivity of authentic being.

14. *DE*, 34/*EE*, 26. Also see *TeI*, 151–56/*TI*, 142–46, where Levinas suggests that the insecurity of the *there is* menaces elemental enjoyment of *jouissance*.

15. "Bad Consciousness and the Inexorable," in *Face to Face with Levinas*, edited by Richard A. Cohen (Albany, N.Y.: State University of New York Press, 1986), p. 35. For Levinas's discussion of the significance of the hand, see *TeI*, 169–70/158–62. Additionally, see *TeI*, 181/*TI*, 167: "The hand is by essence groping and emprise."

16. Levinas, *Entre Nous,* pp. 109–10; "Useless Suffering," in *The Provocation of Levinas*, eds. Robert Bernasconi and David Wood (New York: Routledge, 1988), p. 158.

17. Ibid., pp. 116/163. Levinas defines suffering in "Transcendence and Evil" as a "quasi-sensible manifestation of the non-integratable [my emphasis]"(*CP*, 180).

18. Cohen, *Face to Face with Levinas*, p. 35.

19. Ibid., p. 38.

20. Ibid.

21. Levinas explicitly states this in the interview entitled "The Paradox of Morality," *The Provocation of Levinas*, p. 169. It is necessary that the face not have the power of a "force," as that would oblige an irresistible (and a counterfactual) response. Rather, the face is an "authority" that cannot compel. However, this distinction pertains only at the level of the same. It is difficult to make sense of the distinction when applied to the summons of the face, as the response is generated at a "pre-" or "a-conscious" level of absolute passivity that cannot be declined or refused. The important issue here, I would suggest, concerns the transition or translation of the ethical command into the sphere of praxis and thought. I address this topic in "Levinas: the Question of Justice" (forthcoming).

22. Plato, *The Symposium* (Harmondsworth: Penguin, 1983), pp. 81; 203b.

Chapter 4

The Subject and the Other
in Levinas and Lacan

Paul-Laurent Assoun

Ethics and the Unconscious

Rarely has a conjunction been as tempting and as risky, situated in the midst of a contemporary philosophical condition itself so very mined with risky "conjunctions": Lacan *and* Levinas. How is such a connection to be articulated?[1] Where is it to be placed? How is this conjunction to be "pronounced," as it responds to a certain necessity without substantiating its illusion?

It is a fact that Lacan and Levinas come back to the question of alterity: "the Other." The reader is immediately aware that they have, one and the other, only this word on "the tip of their tongues," or rather "at the tip of their pens." All theorization leads back to the Other, however heterogeneous their "points of departure": "knowledge of the unconscious" that reintroduces the question of the law (Lacan) and "phenomenological knowledge" that disengages the question of ethics (Levinas). The overall effect seems the same: to make *the question of the Other* the question of the day for thought, as the reverse side of *the question of the subject.*

Yet if even the slightest legitimacy is to be conferred on such a confrontation, this is at once too much and too little. Until this point it has been a matter of mere *homonymy.* Which Other are they addressing in their writings? What "subject" does it "call into question?" We sense that they are not referring to *the same Other* or the same subjectal [*subjectale*] agency. Still, the insistent recurrence of the same "theoretical signifiers" points to a mysterious affinity, with an insistence that is as equivocal as it is eloquent. The "signature" of a contemporary concern that from time to time takes on the pathos of a "commitment," even a "mission": to oppose "the universal allergy . . . of philosophers" (CP, 91) by returning alterity's meaning to them (Levinas); to oppose the identitarian [*identitaire*] egologism that threatens the future of "Freudianism," even if this means reintroducing a discursive agency of "the Other" that Freud himself did not need (Lacan). With Levinas, the Other makes its entry into ethics. With Lacan, the Other is promulgated in psychoanalysis. The only thing left to understand is what this signifies, and comparing these "operations" may, in fact, help us achieve this.

Nevertheless, it is necessary to explain why, at the very moment of giving in to this "temptation" to meet a theoretical *need,* whose significance we barely glimpse, this "temptation" can appear so "out of place." Complete silence has reigned between Levinas and Lacan. Rarely have interested parties denied so strongly that they are contemporaries, "colleagues" impassioned by alterity, a denial made all the more "violent" by its remarkable serenity. Nothing in Lacan, who was an especially careful reader of Merleau-Ponty, for example, betrays an interest in Levinas—a silence so very symptomatic that it is "resituated" in his philosophical *Belesenheit.* As for Levinas, his reservations about psychoanalysis are well known. It is as if some (mortal?) threat to the very essence of the ethical were associated with it.

Is this "misunderstanding" or "understanding too well" a fundamental divergence? Perhaps, despite this silence and because of this "interdiction," a confrontation[2] comes down to establishing an impossible dialogue. Still, we must dare to pass through this silence (*ad hominem* and reciprocal, as it were), if we are to explain its contrast with that which carries such an eloquent promise of confluence. We must understand why this instance of objective "affinity" can coexist with such sovereign, subjective "indifference"! And, more precisely, what if, reckoning on the resources of our theme, Lacan and Levinas dialogued about "the Other" in and through their decision *not to want the Other of the other?* Each can most certainly live very well and manage his "house" without referring to the economy of his neighbor. But this "allergy" may also bring us to the heart of a field that lives off its contradiction, that is to say, off the conjunction that gives form to an impossible that has interested us for a long time and that finds here precisely a dramatic actualization: "psychoanalysis *and* philosophy."[3] As such, a privileged figure of the eloquent "misunderstanding" of "fields" that returns in philosophical modernity through this disconcerting game of complicity and avoidance that asks to be reconstructed.

From the Double Text to the Name of the Other

To examine the contemporaneousness of Jacques Lacan and Emmanuel Levinas (born in 1901 and 1906, respectively), while satisfying "an archeology of conjunction," whose mode of employment we have defined else-where,[4] it is advisable first to gauge a thought dynamic that, in the works of one and the other can be reduced, without excessive reduction, to a scanning of three periods—where, precisely, the notional pair "Subject/Other" is implied as a "stake" as much as a "theme."

In the 1930s, Levinas started working on his confrontation with Husser-lian phenomenology and Heideggerian ontology; his dissertation on the *Théorie de l'intuition dans la phénoménologie de Husserl*, which anticipated *En découvrant l'existence avec Husserl et Heidegger* (1949), best illustrates this. At the same time, Lacan was elaborating his theory of the mirror stage, with a resounding "false start," at the Congrès de Marienbad (1936) and made an assignation with a theory of the specular imagination, whose title and echoes are all that remain (*Les Complexes familiaux*, 1938). One and the other "launched" a project whose stakes were already perceptible, but that awaited, as it were, their aftereffect.

During a second period, a kind of "central break" appeared in the works of one and the other; we are given the impression of a "tearing open" of a chrysalis, itself revealed in the aftereffect of the war. Apart from Levinas's precursory article "*L'évasion*" (1935), this was the journey from *De l'exis-tence à l'existant* (1947) to the great explosion of *Totalité et infini* (1961), where a major thought revealed itself (let it be noted, after some thirty years of maturation). At the end of the war, Lacan, whose work demands that future historians of his thought examine this as a necessary time of silence and not a "dead time" for his thinking, was reelaborating his aborted announcement of the mirror stage. From the moment that its role at the heart of the formation of the "'I' function" was recognized, the idea of the "imaginary order" was recognized. "*Fonction*" *et* "*champ*" *de la parole et du langage en psych-analyse* (1953) next introduced the idea of a "symbolic order." From then on, the subject and the "ego" [*moi*] were structurally distinguishable with, "fac-ing them," the double function of the "other" [*petit autre*] and the "Other" [*grand Autre*]. During the period of *Totalité et infini*, Lacan's *Seminars*, from *Éthique de la psychanalyse* (1961–1964) to the *Quatre concepts fondamen-taux de la psychanalyse*, reached their acme, as it were, and the sum of the *Écrits* appeared. This chronology seems to encourage us to read a synchro-nous rhythm into these two unfurling movements of a thought that seems, in one and the other, to be "teaching" itself in a thought of alterity [*une pensée de l'altérité*]. This finds its effigy in two powerful appearances associated with the proper names attributed by their authors: on the one hand, the Face (Levinas), and, on the other, the Name-of-the-Father (Lacan).

Since the 1970s, in the backwash of this "central break," we have wit-nessed a change in "style" (to be understood in the strongest sense of the word). Everything was happening as if, in *Autrement qu'être ou au-delà de l'essence* (1974), Levinas was trying to extricate, downstream from the conflagration produced in ethics, the theologico-metaphysical meaning from the event of the preceding decades; this is confirmed with *De Dieu qui vient à l'idée* (1982). Simultaneously, his "Talmudic readings" revived questions about Judaism, associated from the outset with works of philosophical logos. For Lacan as well, the decade opened with the question of "*objet a*" (a concept that appears near the conclusion of the *Écrits*), a question that became increasingly linked to his act of (re)founding psychoanalysis. The quest, via a topology, for a logic of "knotting" the imaginary, the symbolic and the real, compels us to place the center of reflection on the "borders" of the symbolic, Lacan himself suggesting, while considerably refining his path, a displacement of the imaginary to the symbolic in order that it be crystallized *in fine* in a thought about the *real*.

We needed this *course traced* in order to inscribe the embarked-upon confrontation in a dynamic that seems, when all is said and done, to be synchronous, even though its "objects" appear rigorously heterogenous. What is it then that we read there?

Lacan started from a theory of the imaginary that, taking flight from a still "psychogenetic" theory of the mirror experience, disclosed the specular being of subjectivity. He then articulated the structural necessity of the symbolic order as the very destiny of subjectivity, by introducing the category of the Name-of-the-Father to support this "function," before exploring, in an essential inflection, what was missing from the Other as from the other—a "hole" in the symbolic that shows the "*objet a*" in its function of refuse [*déchet*] and a hole in the imaginary itself that makes reflection on the function of the "gaze" possible. In the end, the function of the Other is confirmed as sustaining the unconscious in its subject function, but only as "inconsistent Other." If the Other is not itself crossed out (in the trivial sense of a disappearance—of flight), it is *as* "crossed through" that it fulfills its function, "signifying the lack in the Other, inherent in its very function of being the treasury of the signifier."

Levinas started from a metaphysics of the "*there is*," disclosed as the limit of "phenomenological" and Heideggerian descriptions. From there he had access—via a reflection on temporality—to a position of alterity where ethics comes to be identified with "first philosophy" (classical metaphysics). This position is conceivable through his thesis of the irreducibility of the "infinite" to a logic of "totality." This, in turn, reintroduces a conception of transcendence as if the revolution in ethics were inscribed on its reverse side as a call for reformulation in metaphysical understanding.

One understands how he who organizes all of his thought around psychoanalysis and he who in fact places psychoanalysis beside his thought meet up, in an intense paradox, in this idea that the subject—the *unconscious, eth-*

ical subject—comes back to the question of the Other in its "symbolic" function as in that which it leaves outside itself (the real).

In the same way, we tame the confrontation's original paradox when we understand how the sovereign reciprocal indifference of their projects can accommodate an impression of affinity of "interests." In the final analysis, the "Other" and its subject may perhaps be simple "homonyms," yet this homonymy points decidedly to a secretly homologous event that it is a question here of beginning to bring up to date.

Still, there remains a positive sign in that Levinas and Lacan admitted, as it were, and quite independently of one another it is true, to being contemporaries in the debate over (post)–structuralism and its corollary, "the quarrel over humanism." If Lacan explicitly articulated his position in reference to antihumanism, precisely as it relates to the status of the subject of psychoanalysis, Levinas himself defined, in *L'humanisme de l'autre homme* (1972), an original position where the ethical reference to the Other finds a way not only of radically destabilizing traditional humanism's identitarian belief but also of redirecting toward structuralist thought the challenge of the thought of the Other, the forgetting of which would be confirmed by structuralist thought. There, beyond the conjunction, lies the moment of truth—still indirect—of this "shock" between two thoughts of alterity, put up against the wall of the problematic of alterity at the very moment when is being defined, a counterposition that allows its reciprocal state to be grasped at the same time.

It becomes clear in light of what precedes: the confrontation has meaning and value only when resting upon the dynamic of their projects taken as a whole, their original humus, and their "indigenous" presuppositions (Lacan and Levinas think in terms of "every man for himself," once and for all). But, by force of its own commitments, this monologue becomes "dialogued." In this way, the debate over humanism becomes invaluable, provided that it is examined as the outcome of an entire movement of thought that finds there something to be known.

Double Reformulation in Understanding through Alterity

The reconstitution of the "kinetics" of two journeys, based on a reading of their dynamic, carries in itself a first "lesson." On the one hand, "the Other" is not merely a *theme* among others but the operator of a "reformulation in understanding"; on the other hand, the thought that realizes this "reformulation" must take flight from a certain anterior "blind spot" against which it stands out. This at once precursory and "protohistorical" "blind spot" is, respectively, the Levinasian "*there is*" and the Lacanian "mirror stage."

By explaining this double consideration, we are able simultaneously to take on the confrontation and to have pointed out to us an entry into their "crossed logics."

How is it possible to assess Levinas's pretense of reintroducing the consideration of alterity into philosophy when philosophy seems to have made it one of the central and consistent themes of its reflection? It must be clearly understood that philosophical logos regularly comes up against this theme of the Other, only with the ("unconscious"?) intention of reducing the Other by "saving" the identity of the thinking subject, a somewhat "Odyssean" "complex" that makes Levinas a watchman over an "alteritarian [*altéritaire*] understanding" situated at the heart of the identitarian rationality of philosophical logos. It is in this sense that the following "charge" must be understood: "Philosophy is produced as a form in which the refusal of engagement in the other [*sic*], the waiting preferred to action, indifference with regard to others, the universal allergy of the early infancy of philosophers is manifest. Philosophy's itinerary remains that of Ulysses, whose adventure in the world was only a return to his native island—a complacency in the Same, an unrecognition [*méconnaissance*] of the other (*CP*, 91)."[5] Interest in the Other, "thematized" to this end, would be thus only feigned and "conditional" for "philosophy." On the contrary, Levinas's intervention is made in the context of a "passion for alterity," which is truly an effect of the return of Eros to solipsistic thought. Against "complacency" in the Same, it is a question of awakening the "pleasure" of the Other and of providing the means for "recognizing" the Other in order to frustrate the temptation of misrecognition [*méconnaissance*]. In brief, it is a question of creating a saluatory "allergy" that gives courage to logos, with its "identitarian" inclination, to support alterity's explosive charge. It appears as if all the steps in Levinas's thought proceeded from this central intention. In the name of the Other and its right to be recognized in and by thought, he uses, evaluates, challenges, and repudiates all attempts at thought that he encounters.

This also is the basis of his recourse to Judaism, the biblical text containing this thought of alterity in respect to which the philosophical text so regularly "sins." If, in his thought, there is a resolved duality between the "'field' of his research" and a refusal of apologetic eclecticism, then one must note that the recourse to alterity said in the text assures the philosopher Levinas, reader of the Talmud, that he has "something to lean on" for reintroducing, to the heart of the economy of the philosophical text itself, this "reminder of alterity." Not Being, as Heidegger maintains, but "the Other," is the Object of what has been forgotten. This also is what engages Levinas in a search for "mechanisms" in the literary text for *saying* alterity in some "alternative" way.

We understand at once how this operation, so valued by philosophers, does not promote itself without tending somewhat to "manhandle" the philosophical text itself in its "auto-referential" practice. Against the overly "civilized" passion of the Same of Logos is a certain indecent "barbarism" of the Other that it is a question of unleashing. This philosophy of "peace" is promulgated within the philosophical empire of the Same as a declaration of war in the name of the rights of alterity, and it is only in this context that it is intelligible.

When we turn to Lacan, we discover that his "return to Freud" was only to reintroduce reference to the subject—by making the "unconscious subject" the subject *of* the unconscious—and to the Other. If, in fact, "man's discourse" is the "discourse of the Other," then it is the reference to the agency of alterity (uppercase) that allows the "knowledge of the unconscious" to be inscribed in anthropology in a radical decentering, which radicalizes Freud's "post–Copernican revolution." Such a *formula* acts as a "wake-up" call to a psychoanalysis that would take itself for a psychology. Lacan's taste for "shock formulas," which mark his style, translates perhaps in an essential way his intention to make "the Other" not yet another theme but instead an *operator* intended to jolt ego-psychology, whose touchstone is the belief in the *self*, from its identitarian sleep.

This very discussion presents the problem of passage from Freud to Lacan. Since, as we know, when it comes to the use of the term *Subjeckt*, Freud is quite sparing;[6] when it comes to "the Other," this term would explode within a discourse that makes of science its only semantic legitimacy. From here on in, this is what gives the Lacanian version of psychoanalysis a particular "ethico-metaphysical," even "theological," resonance—even though there is no worse misinterpretation than to confuse the theological thesis of the "consistent" Other with that of the "inconsistent" Other to which the unconscious subject, nevertheless, shows its "attachment." "In-consistent," certainly, but not "in-existent," and Lacan's entire thought process, through his, when all is said and done, violent rereading of Freud, draws the inference of this "fact" of the psychoanalytic experience: that the subject *bears witness*, in the logic of his desire, to his relation with a certain Other (every clinical experience is aimed at the determination of the "nature" and "function" of this relation).

Through "the gnomic formula" that "man's discourse" equals "the discourse of the Other," the link between the "subversion of the subject" and the "dialectic of desire" already makes itself known. "The unconscious is *discours de l'Autre* (discourse of the Other), where the *'de'* is to be understood in the Latin sense of *de* (objective determination). But add that man's desire is the *désir de l'Autre* (desire of the Other) where the *de* provides what grammarians call 'subjective' determination, namely that it is as Other that he desires (the true significance of human passion)" must also be added.[7] Through this "grammar lesson," Lacan introduces the fundamental "injunction" of analytic experience.

But precisely the "ungluing" of this thought of the Other proceeds from the "time for comprehending" the necessity of a break with imaginary adhesion. This is the decisive moment between pinpointing the mirror experience and identifying it as an "imaginary order," "calling" for the "symbolic order." In this way, the dimension of language is introduced, the unconscious showing itself to be "structured like a language" in solidarity with its function as "discourse of the Other." Hence the meaningful tautology, "There is no Other of the Other."

Language is essential for one and the other. However, for Lacan, it is as theory of the subject and the "signifier"; whereas, for Levinas, it continues to acquire importance—until the last philosophy that turns the opposition between the "Saying" and the "Said" into an instance of alterity's authentification—a kind of reviving of the opposition, a decisive moment in Lacan's work, between "full speech" and "empty speech."

Time, the Subject, and the Other

We can now dare to say that, for both Levinas and Lacan, it is reflection on *time* that made possible the advent of a thought of alterity [*une pensée de l'altérité*]. *Le Temps et l'Autre* marks the occasion of Levinas's engagement (1946–47) with this link, at the precise moment—what a providential confrontation!—when Lacan, in referring to the "paradox of the prisoner," is defining temporality as a relation with the desire of the other in its "three ekstases": "the instant of the gaze," "the time for comprehending," and "the moment of concluding."[8]

But it is also at this point that a difference [*divergence*] in alterity—a radical sense—is clearly made known, as revealed by the function that temporality plays in alterity.

In contrast with the time structure of subjectivity, Levinas understands time as "a subject's relationship with others."[9] Reacting against the representation of a "solitary *Dasein*," attributed to Heidegger, a strategy of truly "overcoming" solitude, of "evasion," takes shape—a metaphor instituted henceforth as the axis of Levinasian conceptuality, the place of the revelation of suffering and death. From then on, it seems that "the approach of death," a shadow cast upon existence, symbolizes the rupture of identity. "Something whose existence is made of alterity" depends on it. We must keep in mind the idea that it is through death that the announcement of the "wholly other" to the *existent* occurs, since we will find it again in the very experience of ethical alterity. Would the confirmation of this death threat not be reflected in the face of the other? In this way, "alterity" and "exteriority" are linked, since the threat that is directed toward me suddenly appears *from the outside*. It is on this horizon, in any case, that "the relation with the other" will take hold of the subject. Eros itself reveals its function, assumed to be as "strong as death!"

Here we touch upon what constitutes the originality and style of the Levinasian philosophy of alterity, emerging as this "non-dialectable," [*indialectisable*] the very opposite of an "alter-ego." Even before *Totalité et infini* worked out all of its conclusions, there was no question of making the relation with the Other depend upon a dialectic of recognition, where the conflict [*affrontement*] of desires would condition the advent of self-consciousness and its overcoming in its relation with the desire of the Other. For Levinas, ethics is to be situated on the side of this "undoing" of desire's relation with time. Such a relation with the Other would only be "conditional," whereas the Other signifies itself, in all of its "manifestations," as an appeal as mysterious as it is unconditioned, that inscribes a breakdown at the heart of the subject's "powers."

In contrast, it is not by chance that, at a decisive moment in his journey, Lacan sought reference for his theory of unconscious desire in the Hegelian master-slave dialectic. This "bifurcation" in the history of French thought, implying the Kojévean reception of Hegel in particular, demonstrates a significant divergence in strategies. One would be mistaken to reduce this divergence to a difference in philosophical allegiance ("for" or "against" Hegel). Instead, it is a question of understanding what position the subject's desire maintains in relation to the desire of the Other. What does "it learn"? What does it miss? Is this "logical temporality" to be understood on the side of desire, or is it a break in a logic of recognition?

A significant yet compressed summary suggests that here lies the relation between the "ethics of psychoanalysis" and "plain" ethics (an equivocal expression) that plays itself out between Lacan and Levinas, a terrain mined with "paralogisms," but also the "royal path" of the "ethical and unconscious" problematic.

From the Real to the Other: The "There Is" and the Mirror

Rarely has a philosophical category emerged with such radicality in a text: the somewhat "epiphanic" emergence of the Other in the encounter with the face [*visage*] that forms the heart of *Totalité et infini*.[10] Perhaps there also is a trap here, a temptation to take the face, in that it leads to existential experience, for some incarnation of the Other; whereas, it is precisely the dimension of absence that the face presents, by offering up precisely the truth about ethics. But viewed from within the genesis of the Levinasian journey, this propulsion of the Other *is not* originary. It is taken up in the antecedence of a "first philosophy" centered around the "*there is*" [*il y a*] and around the experience of the "neuter" that the latter organizes. It is more than simply a question of intellectual biography. Levinas's philosophy is, by vocation, situated in the process of auto-revelation of alterity's experience, which requires, therefore, thinking not only about how one moves from a phenomenology of the *there is* to an ethics of the face, but also about what is retained of the *there is* within the very heart of the ethical revelation of alterity. This is such a complex question that we do not have at our disposal, in this so fundamentally contra-Hegelian[11] philosophy, the resources for a "dialectical" model of negation/overcoming.

It is precisely against a backdrop of "detachment" of the *there is* that alterity is promoted both as the event of the Levinasian text and the reality of an "ethical experience," such as this text seeks to understand it.

To ward off any "personalist" reading of Levinasian ethics, it seems essential for us to grasp this relation of the philosophy of the *there is* to the epiphany of the face. The *there is*, the central operator of *De l'existence à l'existant*, slips into the background in *Totalité et infini*, as if it were eclipsed by "the face." Yet, it is essential to grasp why the *there is* is the initial pole for the crystallization of Levinas's reflection—out of which emerges a highly original phenomenology, from "exoticism" to "insomnia"—in this "neutral" home, a rather horrifying point from which a relation of the ego [*moi*] and the world and of the subject and the Other will emerge.

What is thought here? "It is because the *there is* has such a complete hold on us that we cannot take nothingness and death lightly, and we tremble before them (*DE*, 21/*EE*, 20)."[12] Here is a conception of anxiety, whose oppressive "realism" is confirmed by the psychoanalytic clinic (in other respects, so foreign to Levinasian conceptuality): the relation to a "lack" (in the subject) that is manifested on the outside through a "too much of the real." Here insomnia finds its function as the absurd *cogito* of the "it watches," face to face with anonymity and its impersonal—an extreme passivity and underemployment of an ego that drowns in the "rustling of being" and no longer finds distinctive "inside" and "outside" reference points.

It is not by chance that Levinas finds the most fitting description of this vertigo of subjectivity in Blanchot's work. The reader of *Thomas l'Obscure* dedicated a text to this position of the "neuter" that the most originary "prereflexive" would not know how to approach: "The presence of absence, the night [*sic*], the dissolution of the subject in the night, the horror of being, the return of being to the heart of every negative [*sic*] movement, the reality of irreality are there admirably expressed (*DE*, 103/*EE*, 63)." What emerges from this entanglement of the "inside" and the "outside" is a veritable *ventriloquist subject*. "A kind of integral ventriloquist; I cried out everywhere I was not, or I was in all parts equal to silence." Is not the ventriloquist–subject the one who without moving his lips, makes the Other speak? Then, does the ventriloquist–subject allow the Other to speak "through him," or is he expelled into an "outside" without interiority? Through contact with Blanchot,[13] Levinas enters into this mode of "thought of the outside,"[14] which constitutes one of the most profound "adherences" of his thought. The experience of the face could well be the ultimate avatar, the most original and the most radical avatar; it would be, in fact, a matter of letting oneself be affected by the event of the Other as an "outside," a "receptivity" that expels the "ego" [*moi*] from its intimacy. This is an extravagant formula, one that becomes explosive if taken to the letter: "If *there is* . . . of *the Other*, what becomes of . . . the *I* [*je*]?" This is a "psychosis-inducing" vacillation of a real that begins "to chatter to itself."

The mirror experience, however constitutive it may be of subjectivity, takes note of this function of the outside. Everything begins, in fact, in Lacanian description, with the irruption of a certain "outside"—what Wallon named, significantly, the "exteroceptive"[15] aspect—from which the interested one cannot be distracted, from stupor to jubilation, from malaise to *jouissance*. This so mysteriously familiar outside contacts the "premature"[16] one and invites him to identify with an "image" so he may then recognize *himself there*, the "pronominalization," which, through separation and distance, makes the "I" [*je*] emerge. This is the effect of the "imaginary captation," which takes flight from an event. In summary, nothing is more "realistic" than this trigger mechanism that gives birth to subjectivity, the inauguration of the "self" through this inauguratory *there is*.

The imaginary threat would be precisely the nightmare of a "too real" [*tout réel*] from which the subject cannot detach himself and which would confuse his voice with the rumblings of the world. It is no accident that this is the first "syndrome" described by Levinas, the very one that one must evade and from which one can *never totally escape* the encounter with the "faceless gods."

"But then what does the advent of the subject consist in? (*DE*, 113/*EE*, 67)" This question, whose explicitness touches upon what concerns us here, emerges *out of insomnia*. It is, therefore—to quickly portray the "situation" in a real-life situation—the aftereffect of the *there is* (whose presence culminates in the nocturnal hypervigilance that hears its rumblings). Paradoxically, it is not as a wake-up call (like the "classic" link between consciousness and the sentiment of self gives substance to), but precisely as the possibility of first falling asleep. The subject inaugurates itself through this heroic possibility of distracting itself from the *there is*, of "forgetting it," and of "suspending it (*DE*, /*EE*, 115)."[17] To use still more Heideggerian terms: "on the ground of the *there is*, a being emerges (*DE*, 142/*EE*, 83)"; this event is called "hypostasis,"[18] an event that is, in a manner of speaking, "grammatical"; it marks the appearance of the "substantive" that takes over from the verb. This is the possibility for "the existent" to "enter existence."

In this way the "ascent" toward the world is made. The universe of *jouissance* and work[19] comes back to the humanization of the primitive horrors of the *there is* and to "escaping" from "depression." But precisely in the return of alterity—and here we believe that we touch upon the heart of the real that Levinas tirelessly theorizes—within this supposedly "humanized" world, from Death to the Other, from the encounter with suffering to the encounter with the face—what is it, if we pursue this line of reasoning, that comes back, as it were, "in the face [*à la face*]" of the subject, if not the Neuter's primitive shadow reflected in the face [*face*] of the Other?

In this very way, we return to the face [*visage*] of the Other, whose humanity is elsewhere so very poignant, its terrorizing aura, which could be described as the return of the *there is* in its dimension of the anxiety-of-the-real. In the absence of any "diagnostic," how would we not grasp Levinas's invaluable admission that this aura finds its origins in certain childhood impressions: a child feverishly listening in on the "noises" behind the partition, caused by the adults' nocturnal turbulence; the relay of the child's anxiety mobilized by the desire of others . . . ?[20]

The Primal Scene of Ethics

We are coming upon the "scene" that constitutes the dramaturgical framework of Levinas's philosophy, the scene whose *writing*[21] is worked out tirelessly by the text: a description of a "shock" that removes the subject from its (self)-mastery, a failure at every attempt to measure up to one*self*, a fall into the irreversible "outside" of alterity. "The rustling with the *there is* is horror (*DE*, 98/*EE*, 60)."[22] Yet something of this horrifying moment remains sublimated—"thought of height"—in the encounter with the "face."

Without forcing the resources of such an obviously heterogenous style, it is not at all surprising that this reminds us of the experience that Freud called the *Unheimliche*: an 'indecantable' mixture of familiarity and strangeness, of terror and pleasure. Who is this Other who touches me from so near? Who is this "familiar" one who troubles me from so far? The light contact with alterity makes it possible to experience the paradox of an irreversible separation that is combined with an impossibility of detaching oneself.

In "falling" under my gaze, the face of the Other scratches my eyes out, making me fall under the power of an alterity that imposes passivity on me. This too is a mystery of ethics, since, in the end, I can always manage to distract myself from this "spectacle," to elude it in some way or other. The face is not unforgettable for everyone. What matters lies elsewhere. That such an effect exists and finds at least one addressee, this one is *the ethical subject*, identified with the Other as with its "symptom" and as such inseparable from itself.

The question is otherwise (and otherwise complex): What is the "lesson" of the knowledge of the unconscious as it concerns the function of the Other (apparently Levinas's only lesson and one that raises powerful questions about the "symbolic" in Lacan's work)? What is this desire of the Other that supports ethics and reestablishes it as "first philosophy" (that lends distinction to Levinas's project, whereas, for Freud, ethics is but what "goes without saying"[23] and, for Lacan, it refers to the "constraint" of the unconscious)?

Ever since the experience of the "primal scene" [*Urszene*], psychoanalysis has unceasingly experienced this major fact that the Other has hold over the subject through "its" desire (an unspeakable pronoun that has the effect of the subject "taking in" at the same time as its own the Other's desire.) By emphasizing that it is entirely in its "primal scene," we in no way reduce the ethics of alterity. This is the scene in which the subject becomes the symptom of the Other to the point where the ethical disposition yields itself up with all of the features of a "sickness." It plays itself out on the side of a certain "obsession," whose Other is the object, which has the effect of cleaving the "ego" [*moi*] from the subject. This reveals a striking phenomenology of the "superego," which inscribes alterity at the very heart of moique ipseity.

Yet, precisely, by denying any "psychological" consideration, the "ethical fact" appears in Levinas's work as an "absolute" that freezes any "genesis." In this sense, ethics is then the unconscious itself; this is the reason why, for Levinas, the ethical subject makes the *unconscious subject* superfluous and makes the infinity of the "desirable," the desiring-subject, "optional."

Freud articulates the notion of a subject "split" [*gespaltene Subjekt*] at the "moment" of "castration."[24] This "fold" in the structure aligns the subject with an alienation of the object of its own desire. This subject is also taken up in a chronic relation with "prohibition."

Desire, Eros, and the Father

To justify alterity, Levinas's theory leans on a theory of *desire*. This should alert us to the purpose of our own confrontation: What can *this* desire have to do with the agency of "desire" that Lacan institutes from within the Freudian experience?

This is, in fact, a conception of the "desirable," an excess of being—preceding, as it were, all subjective desire—a conception that Levinas places at the foundation of his anthropology in terms that are as Platonic as they are Cartesian and that finds its metaphysical "translation" in the idea of "infinity." It is in reference to this "desirable," which makes its appeal in man even before he *himself* suddenly realizes it, that Levinas conceives of this "infinition of the mode of being (*TeI*, 3–22/*TI*, 33–52)."[25] Nothing is more "objective" than this "infinity," "more objective," precisely, than any "objectivity." And it is exactly this that prepares "the Other's welcome." And, it is in the form of this "desirable" that primal hyperobjectivity reaches the subject and makes itself known. This is not so much an infinite desire as it is desire *as* infinite that "touches" man.

The subject of Lacanian desire is in another sense "inspected" by the Other. It is in no way fortuitous that such a pregnant Heideggerian moment can be found in Levinas and Lacan, a moment that is then criticized and rendered to alterity. At the end of the struggle for recognition, when the subject must admit that "it is as Other that he desires," he places himself instead of the "*Che vuoi?*," "What does the Other want from me?" In a way, the Other is already there, obliging the subject, in order to speak, to enter into the preexisting order of language. But the "symbolic clause," which turns desire into a subject, in psychoanalytic experience—there where the Other was, I must happen upon it as subject—finds itself absolutized in the problematic of ethics. "It is not language that would be the modality of symbolism," Levinas emphasizes, "because all symbolism already refers to language." This is a "masterful" pronouncement that "teaches before all else teaching." The analyst is this other who makes it possible for the subject to confront [*affronter*] the lack in his Other. The Master, according to Levinas, is the other who catalyzes the very Saying of the Other, a knowledge of alterity that is completely different from "reminiscence" where what is already known is *re*cognized. This epiphanic effect can be attested to at the very heart of analysis: "I never would have thought of that!"—the gripping hold of "other knowledge" on the subject.

Now is the time for us to bring forth, from this somewhat architectonic folding of alterity, the event of the "subject." Just as easily, the subject has *being* only as a "respondent" of this alterity; but this is what equips the subject with a form of "autonomy" that is radicalized precisely through its encounter with the Other.

Out of this circle, Levinas proposes the following formula: "It is in order that alterity be produced in being that 'thought' is needed and that an 'I'[26] [*Moi*][27] is needed (*TeI*, 10/*TI*, 39)." One would be mistaken to conclude from this that subjectivity is required only in the "service" of alterity. It is not for nothing that Levinas presents *Totalité et infini* as a defense of subjectivity and that the metaphor of "apology" recurs in Levinas's work in an effort to define the "rights" of the I [*moi*]. Because the being of the "I" [*moi*] is apology—a (*pro domo*) self-defense, as it were—the ethics of alterity is not "an apologetics of alterity," even though a kind of symptomatic *pathos* "signs" this reference to alterity, from the moment that ethics shows *me* to be the symptom of the Other and the Other to be *my* most painful symptom!

From *Le Temps et l'Autre* to *Totalité et infini*, the kind of display of subjectivity that Levinas presents relies on neither a Hegelian nor a Husserlian phenomenology of consciousness. It is a world actor, rooted in the "elemental," in the environment of need and work, a man of *"jouissance"* and "terrestrial food," who, this "history" shows us, is gripped by the experience of suffering and the encounter with death. Through this humiliation inflicted on the "Byronian virility" of the I/ego [*moi*] is achieved a metaphysical detumescence, a moment of affect when the I/ego [*moi*], thinking it is capable of anything, realizes in a "childlike convulsion of sobs" that there is something stronger than it—"death." Out of this, through Eros, it "will counter" this negative alterity, but without dialectizing it: there is no way of making death "profitable" as the energy of negativity. But there is indeed a beyond, the path that leads from Eros to the Father.

A lucidly naive reader could take heed here: Are these not the key words of psychoanalysis, showing us, in its Oedipal drama, only the path from the libido to the Father, "the necessary prejudice" of desire, and thus of its knowledge?[28] And if, as Lacan says, the law is fundamentally the "cause of"—and not the obstacle to—"desire," is there not cause to follow up on this unexpected opening from the Father in the Levinasian sense to the Lacanian Name-of-the-Father, as determining the affiliation of the "ego" [*moi*] (the "ego" of imaginary *jouissance*) to "symbolic" subjection?

It is precisely here, after so nearly coming together, that once again the paths of these two explorers separate—an instance of confrontation's bitter *jouissance*!

Levinas shows the Father's worth in a daring formula. "Freedom comes and time passes not according to the category of cause but according to the category of the father."[29] Is the 'function of the father,' as his letter explains, not really that which psychoanalysis ceaselessly experiences? For the subject, the Father is that strange and structurally ambiguous place of conflict [*affrontement*] of his freedom *and* his relation with prohibition, of his desire and his destiny that knots his relation with the "self" [*soi*] to the relation with the Other [*de alio*].

We can legitimately play with this complicity between ethics and the unconscious, but only to the extent that it comes undone, because the question to be raised is whether the relationship with the father is deduced through a dialectic of "recognition" (in the ringed *supra* sense of the "sopra" reference to the Hegelian moment).

The use of the Father appears with a significant amount of contrast: If, in Freud, "ambivalence is associated with the being of the father," it is, we must not hesitate to remind ourselves, through the son, the "little Oedipus," that the Father intervenes in the logic of desire. It is highly revealing that Levinas himself evokes the very possibility of the father carrying out, as it were, through the son, a perpetuation of the self that simultaneously experiences its own alterity (the son reveals this other of the father that realizes itself there). There where the father (of the unconscious) introduces this "doubt"—upon which the subject's desire feeds—the father of ethics, in his paternity, *gives response* to the question of alterity.

With Lacan, we understand how the father appears as a "metaphor"—being a father . . . only of the Name—which necessarily sustains the constitution of desire. This assumes that three levels are distinguishable. First, the symbolic instance, where the-Name-of-the-Father is found as referent in the speech of the mother and as the condition *sine qua non* of the subject of desire. Second, the imaginary dimension, where the idealized father, constituted at the conclusion of the Oedipus complex, fulfills its function of "diminishing" the mother and bringing about the specular "self." Finally, the basic idea of the real father, who fulfills, through his presence, his function of imposing silence on his *jouissance.*

In contrast, ethics basically comes down to giving substance to a *belief in the Father,* for the purposes of sustaining the symbolic essence; this supposes "boosting up" its ideal somewhat and finally making the real father "profitable" in his maintenance of this function. The Father of the unconscious in this sense mirrors the unconscious, the ethics of the Father. It could be that, in this sense, the Father is the Subject of ethics, even though he is only the function (subject) of psychoanalysis. . . . We know that it is *as dead* that the father, in the aftereffect of the primal murder [*Urmord*], promotes himself as symbolic function: our examination will echo Dostoevsky's theme, so lively in Levinas, of the resistance of the face to the temptation of murder. "The Other is the sole being that I may wish to kill."

From Separation to Teaching: The subject and the Other

It is essential to accept this nature of the Other that "reveals" itself only in the aftereffect of a "separation," the very separation that makes a hole in subjectivity. "This separation must be accomplished in the I," insists Levinas. "The separation of the I with regard to the Other must result from a positive movement (*On Separation,* 53),"[30] in such a way that "the cogito evinces separation (*On Separation,* 54)." Thus, no "fusion mystique"—alterity stands out not in reunion, but by the injunction that, coming from the Other, disturbs my experience of self as separate being. No "dialogism" is possible: in that case, only "other I" *and not Other.*

Levinas gives to the modality of separated being the striking name of "the psychism" and submits it to the "atheist condition": "The soul, the dimension of the psychic, being an accomplishment of separation, is naturally atheist." Nothing is further from this theory of alterity than an interval between "inside" and "outside" than a vague attraction or a fusional complacency for and with the Other: alterity will make itself known the most intensely in favor of a radically separate being, "subjectivity" in this sense. "Without separation, there would not have been truth, there would only have been being"—as "the myth of Gyges," originally interpreted as "the myth of the I [*Moi*]," illustrates. But through this, alterity's eruption—in the face of the other—takes all of its depth from malaise and even *trauma*: What is this outside that, so brutally, results in my separation and my attachment to myself no longer holding, without which I am able to unite immediately with this Other? Herein resides the most poignant aspect of the ethics of alterity, seized by an outside event: "that" which comes to disturb the adhesion of the self to itself and which demands response. In this disturbance, the *ego* [*moi*] of *jouissance*—the *jouissance* that makes "the egoistic being tremble"—becomes the ethical *subject*, summoned as it is, incredibly, to give a response to the event of others in the true vertigo of subjectivity and "hole" in the world, this experimentation with an "outside world" that evokes precisely *jouissance* in the psychoanalytic sense of the word,[31] *jouissance* as distinct from "happiness" and "pleasure."

Levinas's antidialectical relentlessness derives from his will to escape from a logic of mastery that is a logic of war, of "totality," in short. It is a matter of thinking with this "surplus that is always exterior to totality," a teaching by the Other that comes down to discharging from (self)mastery. This "splendour of exteriority or transcendence in the face of others" acts as totality-breaking, although it may mean thinking the scandalous—a thought of history that is "a meaning without context." Escape opens from that moment onto "eschatological" thought.

This "Other's teaching" is "opposite to" that which, at bottom, all experience of transfer demonstrates. And it is this pathos of "transfer" that appears, at bottom, to accompany Levinas. Take, for instance, the intensity of affect that gives his ethics its poignancy—we have the feeling that the thought of the Other is often *on the verge of tears*—though irreducible to some "affectivity." It is simply a matter of noting that the "hold" the Other has on the subject makes its mark on this affect that overflows subjectivity. But in more precise terms, the analytic experience can only refer this Other to the desiring subject: It would not be able to absolutize it—where, when all is said and done, the analytic experience refers to "altruism" that maintains ethics' illusion, fed by the "anaclitic" relationship, which according to Freud is the source of all morality.

This, however, does not exhaust the question: for there is, in the unconscious experience, a certain dimension "inspired by passion,"[32] as it were—tangible in "the love of transfer"—which makes the subject's unconscious, in its *jouissance*, an experience of the Other. The Other would not be capable of being "imagined": nevertheless, at certain moments in Lacan's discourse, a sort of presentification of this Other is perceptible. This is a point of disturbance where the ethical experience "communicates," via desire, with the "unconscious" experience. A privileged moment, where the subject, perhaps, holds the "*objet a*" and the Other in the same "line of sight"—a moment that appears to shed light on the intense instance of the face's encounter (Levinas), where the subject at once experiences and overcomes, in a paroxysm, its own "division."

The Feminine or the Law of the Other

Inevitably, a thought dedicated to alterity encounters the question of the *feminine*. This could very well be the point where ethics and the unconscious reveal their affinity: a question on this side of the law. We only need situate this theme of the feminine to verify its stakes in each of the conceptual economies.

Levinas meets up with the question of the feminine on the wayside of ethics, as if he were providing alterity's "effigy." It is worth noting, moreover, that Lacan, in the last part of his itinerary, gives the question of the feminine a determinative status, when he examines, via "the formulas of sexuation," the notion of a nonphallic *jouissance* called the "*jouissance* of the Other."[33]

Everything happens as if the ethical thought of alterity were destined for sexual metaphor. What is "more other" than "Woman;" this would lead us to infer—with a naivety that says something about the event—that the ethical subject is placed at once on the side of the masculine! This is an idea to correct immediately by saying that ethics is distinguished, as we have seen, from this considerable metamorphosis of the virile "ego" in an experience of a radical *passivity*. This is, in fact, what introduces the feminine in the Levinasian poem of the Other: as "inversion of the face by femininity." "Woman" is identified with "the Other whose presence is discretely an absence and who carries out the hospitable welcome, par excellence, that delineates the field of intimacy." Here the path that distinguishes the ethics of the feminine from its ideological resonances is a narrow one: "The feminine is other in that alterity is in some way her nature." And Levinas sensed this so well that it is around this point that a certain embarrassment, concerning the misunderstanding that this feminine position could give substance to, appears to be the most clearly manifested.

The feminine is in fact this "modality of being that consists in shying away from the light." This evokes, as it were, the flesh and the being of the Law—that the theoretician of the Name-of-the-Father evokes in a mysterious yet impressive way as his intimate and perhaps ultimate perplexity: "How can we know . . . whether the Father himself, the eternal Father of all, is only a name among others for white Diana, she who . . . loses her way in the darkness of time"[34]—radicalizing, in this way, Freud's own stupor when faced with the perpetuity of "Diana of the Ephesians."[35] Indeed, the feminine is the *hic* of the entire theory of alterity: "the Other forever in its *jouissance*. . . ."

Out of this comes the reformulation of the algorithm of "the crossed through Other": "As the place where everything of the signifier which can be articulated comes to be inscribed, the Other is, in its very foundation, the Other. Which is why this signifier, with its bracket open, marks the Other as crossed through—S (A̶) (*FS*, 151–52)."[36] Out of this comes a "theoanalogic" assertion: "And why not interpret one face of the Other, the God face, as supported by feminine *jouissance*? (*FS*, 147)"[37] If the Other requires in Levinas a metaphysics of "otherwise than being," the Other in Lacan leans on an "otherwise *jouir*," whose subject *and* referent is woman.

From the Subject of Ethics to the Subject of Psychoanalysis

We come out of this "confrontation" between Lacan and Levinas—where the term takes up once again its meaning of conflict—with a strangely contrastive impression. Placing these two thoughts "head (forehead) to head (forehead) [*front contre front*]," while everything—context, stakes, content—separates them, reveals an affinity for "reformulation in understanding," whose master word is the Other, precisely destined to thwart the effects of mastery of thoughts about identity. . . . The bringing to the fore of the dynamic and the presuppositions of these two logics of alterity, whose path should serve as an opening for a point-for-point exchange in the future, reveals a stunning game of discrepancies and convergences.

Everything happens as if, by the logic of a thought to which they give their style—there is, in fact, a Lacan style just as there is a Levinas style, styles which are skillfully "disarticulated" to espouse this "alteration" of the thought of the Same—Lacan and Levinas necessarily pass again along the same paths (of which we have prepared the cadastre here), but *never at the same time*, an encounter missed not at all by chance. . . . The "road signs" are often the same: the Other sets in motion the question of desire, of Eros and of the Father, compared with the subject that introduces the question of language. But the punctuation neither is nor can be placed in the same place.

It is not enough to reduce this "difference of opinion" [*différend*] to the simple fact that Lacan begins with "psychoanalysis" and devotes himself entirely to founding its epistemic and ethical status, while Levinas systematically avoids it. For if Levinas fears above all else that the "human sciences" might reduce metaphysical truth to some "fact" (which comes back to postulating an "unconscious fact"), Lacan dedicated himself to helping psychoanalysis "escape" from these " human sciences" and from their logic of "servitude." That one makes ethics his priority necessarily reminds us that the other, at a crucial point along his path, articulates the idea of a necessity of rethinking ethics through psychoanalysis.

Levinas characterizes best his problematic of the subject and the Other (by vigorously differentiating his problematic from Kierkegaard's): "It is not I who refuses myself to the system . . . it is the Other."[38] In contrast with existentialism, which makes "subjectivity" the agency of truth that defies the speculative pretension of the system, Levinas makes the Other the agency of the anti-system.

But here is where the alternative is decided: Levinas's "act" consists in reintroducing the "Other" that is missing and, by making the Other recognized in its dimension of "lack," in somehow giving consistency back to it. Here is where psychoanalysis's suspicion with regard to the *desire of ethics* as sustaining a secret "imaginarization" begins. That this Other could "respond"—to me—such would be the form of this *Wuensch* to which Ethics gives form, relaying, in this sense, the "illusion" that Freud understands to be the driving force behind religion. It is nevertheless a fact that all of the preceding description shows the chronologically and structurally ungraspable nature of the Other: there are no reassurances to be made in this respect, and the subject is sent back to its agony of *not* responding. Yet even this reintroduces an attachment to a certain precious "object"—a sort of *jouissance* of the Other in ethical form—to which the subject does not wish to yield. From here on, it is not a question of examining what underholds this ethical desire itself, since one touches upon here the *nec plus ultra* of the "desirable." This experience, which nicely fits the Lacanian neologism "extimity," in the eyes of psychoanalysis comes back to this at once precarious and nonnegotiable "absolute" that "fills in" the constitutive division of the subject. This is why Eros and the feminine appear in Levinas as "reparation" for the disappointments of the ethical division—the "Desire of the Other" is both *goodness* and aggressivity, whereas, in psychoanalysis, sexuality is the place where what is irreducible in the division of the subject with regard to its desire is experienced once and for all. Freud is definite about this: psychoanalysis must refrain from supplying even the slightest *Weltanschauung* that flatters illusion. Psychoanalysis takes the place of fact through its position in the malaise of the subject, on the side of this reminder of an ethical kind, that *the subject owes something to its Other* (pronounced in the same tone as "a man owes a death to nature").

This traversal of ethics would in the end allow us to hear again the Freudian *imperative*: "It is not a matter of admitting something that would be more delightful, more convenient or more advantageous for life, but instead something that comes closest to this mysterious reality that exists outside us."[39] Such is the "Other": that which summons the subject to confront [affronter], in itself, its most intimate outside. Faced with this "object" of ethics, whose opaque brilliance it sees in the face of the Other—fixing it in this jouissance that supports the very word of the Other, the subject is reduced, to confront [Affronter] promises and defeats, to the resources only of a desire that it offers up once again to itself from the Other. . . .[40]

—Translated by Dianah Jackson and revised by Denise Merkle

Notes

1. This article takes its inspiration from a course given at the Collège international de philosophie between 1985 and 1987, while we were responsible for directing the program "Psychoanalysis and Philosophy." It is a reconstructed outline of summarized assessments and thoughts that anticipated a research project.

2. Translator's note: The word "confrontation" (confrontation, prefix 'con' meaning with) will later be distinguished from "conflict" (affrontement, prefix 'a' meaning against), although the two words are sometimes used synonymously in French, as at the beginning of the last section of this article, "From the Subject of Ethics to the Subject of Psychoanalysis," where Assoun specifies that confrontation has taken on the meaning of affrontement. It is thus essential to recognize the similarities and differences in meaning between the French confrontation and affrontement. Confrontation usually means 'action de confronter (des personnes, des choses) ⇒ comparaison' with the idea of bringing together; affrontement usually means 'action d'affronter (aller hardiment au-devant de—un adversaire, un danger, opposer front à front).' The English 'confront, v.' means 'meet face to face, face boldly, oppose; bring face to face; compare.' The English verb thus encompasses the French confronter and affronter; however, the English noun 'confrontation' does not mean comparison. Despite the semantic differences between the English and French, confrontation is used to translate confrontation. (Sources: Nouveau Petit Robert, 1993, and Canadian Gage Dictionary, 1983.)

3. Here I [Assoun] am referring to the specific "field" of research that delimits the scope of this study—reflections that have led us from the Freudian episteme (see Paul-Laurent Assoun, Freud, la philosophie et les philosophes (P.U.F., 1976), Freud et Nietzsche (P.U.F., 1980; 1982), Introduction à l'épistémologie freudienne (Payot 1981; 1990) to a reflection on analytic ethics in L'entendement freudien, Logos et Ananké (Gallimard 1984), as well as the feminine and the law in Freud et la femme (Calmann-Lévy 1983; 1993), Le pervers et la femme (Anthropos/Economica, 1989), Le couple inconscient (P.U.F., 1992), a question that will be taken up again later.

4. From Freud et Nietzsche (1980) to Freud et Wittgenstein (1988).

5. See "La signification et le sens," CP, 40.

6. See in particular *Nouvelles Conférences sur la psychanalyse*. On the context and problem of the subject in Freud, cf. the conclusion of *Introduction à la métaphysique freudienne* (P.U.F., 1993).

7. "Subversion du sujet et dialectique du désir" (1957), in *É*, 814.

8. "Le temps logique et l'assertion de certitude anticipée," reprinted in *É*, 814. Translator's note: The reference for the English translation of Lacan's paper on logical time is as follows: "Logical Time and the Assertion of Anticipated Certainty: A New Sophism," translated by Bruce Fink, *Newsletter of the Freudian Field 2*, No. 2 (fall 1988): pp. 4–22.

9. Republished by Fata Morgana (1979) and in *"Quadrie"* (P.U.F., 1983), p. 17.

10. Refer to the third part of *Totalité et infini*, entitled "Le visage et l'extériorité," Martinus Nijhof, pp. 161–231.

11. For more about this concept, I refer you to my analysis in the forward to the Franz Rosenzweig edition of *Hegel et l'État* (P.U.F., 1991), where I examine the consequences of the break with Hegel, from Rosenzweig to Levinas, on a philosophical, historical, and political level.

12. For a discussion of the invention of this phenomenology dedicated to the *there is*, see *De l'existence à l'existant* (Fontaine 1946), p. 21.

13. In this sense, we must not underestimate the importance of Levinas's and Blanchot's youthful friendship while Levinas was a student of philosophy in Strasbourg.

14. Cf. Michel Foucault, *La Pensée du dehors* (Fata Morgana 1986).

15. It is well known that as early as 1931 Wallon noted the importance of the mirror experience in *Origine du caractère chez l'enfant*, 1949.

16. In reference to Bolk, Lacan emphasizes, in his 1949 contribution, this determining element in motor delay at the phylogenetic level, the "petit homme" compensated for by this imaginary "anticipation" of his identity, the "precipitation" toward an "imaged real."

17. *DE*, p. 115.

18. Ibid., p. 142.

19. Cf. the second part of *Totalité et infini*, "Intériorité et économie," *"Jouissance et représentation,"* pp. 81–160.

20. *Éthique et infini*.

21. Herein lies the importance of literary writing as access to alterity, from Shakespeare to Proust, including Dostoevsky.

22. *De l'existence à l'existant*, p. 98.

23. On this point, see my analysis of the Freudian position in *L'Entendement freudien, Logos, et Anankè*.

24. *Le Clivage du moi dans le processus de défense* (1937).

25. Cf. the first part of *Totalité et infini*, "Le Même et l'Autre," "Métaphysique et transcendance," pp. 3–22.

26. Translator's note: In "Métaphysique et transcendance," *Tel* Levinas uses *Moi* to refer to I (*je*). Assoun retains the uppercase 'M' in the cited passage, but writes *moi* lowercase in the rest of the text. The word's polysemy leads to ambiguity in the text because in both Lacanian and Freudian terminology '*moi*' refers to the English 'ego.'

27. *Totalité et infini*, p. 10.

28. On this point, see my synthesis, "Fonctions freudiennes du père," in *Le Père* (Denoël, 1990), pp. 25–51.

29. Ibid., p. 86.

30. Ibid., . . . /53.

31. On the link between *jouissance* and the outside world, see my analysis *Le couple inconscient, Amour freudien et passion postcourtoise* (Anthropos/Economica, 1992).

32. I analyze this in the work cited in the preceding note.

33. Seminar *Encore*, 1972–1973 (Seuil 1974).

34. Preface to Wedekind's *L'Éveil du printemps* (Gallimard 1974), reprinted in *Ornicar?*, n⁰ 39. winter 1986–1987, pp. 5–7.

35. Cf. "Grande est la Diane des Éphésiens," (1911) and my commentary in *Freud et la femme*.

36. *Encore*, p. 75.

37. Ibid., p. 75.

38. *Totalité et infini*.

39. Letter to Oho Pfister (February 7, 1930) in Sigmund Freud, *Correspondance avec O. Pfister* (Gallimard), p. 191.

Chapter 5

Death and Sublimation in Lacan's Reading of *Antigone*

Philippe Van Haute

Introduction

The problem of sublimation follows psychoanalysis like a shadow.[1] Many feel called to intervene in the debate over its meaning and status, but only a few succeed in finding a more or less satisfactory solution to this problem. Still, the stake of this debate is difficult to overlook, if only because the attempt is often made to define the aim of the psychoanalytic "cure" in terms of a greater capacity to sublimate. Does psychoanalysis set for itself an aim that it cannot articulate in a satisfactory way? And, for example, when psychoanalysis calls art and religion forms of "sublimation," then must it not also adequately clarify what it means by this? These examples show that a worked-out theory of sublimation is not at all a superfluous luxury with regard either to psychoanalysis *intra muros*, that is to say, to the cure, or psychoanalysis *extra muros*—for instance, its application to theories of art and culture.

It is not surprising that in this connection Lacan too has taken up the task of trying to shed some light—according to his own theory—on what he also considers to have remained enigmatic in Freudian psychoanalysis until now. Here, two considerations immediately come to mind. In the first place, Lacan's theory of sublimation is indissolubly a theory of the status and meaning of the beautiful.

Second, his explanation of sublimation is to be found in a seminar on the "ethics" of psychoanalysis (*Sé VII*). This ethic is, he says, a tragic ethic that cannot be thought apart from the dissolution of an ethics of the sovereign good.[2] I begin with the latter. The development of science and the evolution of culture have made it impossible for us to direct our actions according to a teleological *logos* governing the whole of reality. Aristotle can still begin from the idea that man as "truly" man—that is to say, as a "good" man—conforms to a nature thought to be at one and the same time in both the microcosm of our psyche and the macrocosm of which this psyche is a part. Active in all beings, this nature directs us from out of itself to the sovereign good. According to Lacan, belief in this has become impossible. What remains for us is, on one side, an infinite universe that no longer has anything human about it, which answers to purely quantitative measures only, and, on the other, a psyche whose essentially conflictual and broken character has been shown by Freud and psychoanalysis. It is to this situation that Lacan's tragic ethics of psychoanalysis wishes to offer an answer. What can ethics still be or mean if we are in a universe that no longer has anything to say to us, and if the world of our drives and desires does not prescribe from out of itself an aim that could give our lives meaning and direction? What is a good way to carry on with this "human condition"?

It is in the context of posing these questions that Lacan formulates his insights on sublimation. Furthermore, his theory of sublimation is a response to the impossibility of trusting nature, both inside and outside of us, in defining the good. This implies at the same time that Lacan is trying to replace the "ethics of the sovereign good" by an "ethics of sublimation."[3]

We called Lacan's ethics of psychoanalysis a "tragic" ethics. And Freud introduces the concept "sublimation" in the context of a psychoanalytic theory of art. It will therefore also be unsurprising that Lacan's study of the ethics of psychoanalysis—and thus of sublimation—culminates in an analysis of two of the most remarkable tragedies of Sophocles—*Antigone* and, to a lesser extent, *Oedipus at Colonus*.[4] We also have already said that Lacan's theory of sublimation is in indissoluble unity with a theory of the status and meaning of the beautiful. It is indeed striking that Lacan's analysis of *Antigone* as well as of *Oedipus at Colonus* is centered primarily on the beauty of the (supposed?) protagonists of these two tragedies. In this way, Lacan's insights concerning ethics, sublimation, and the beautiful all reflect on one another. In what follows, I will try to shed some light on this connection from the perspective of Lacan's interpretation of Sophocles' *Antigone* and *Oedipus at Colonus*.

First I will formulate some introductory remarks concerning Lacan's theory of the beautiful. However, good insight into this theory presupposes an explanation of the relation between language, desire, and what Lacan, following Freud, calls *Das Ding*—the Thing. It then becomes possible to bring into discussion Lacan's analysis of *Antigone* and *Oedipus at Colonus*, according to the perspective that I have just sketched.

Boots Are Made For Walking

In his seventh seminar on the "Ethics of Psychoanalysis,"[5] Lacan recounts the story of how, during a stay in a London hotel, his wife drew his attention to the fact that Professor D was also lodging there.[6] Lacan himself had no reason to suspect that this famous professor whom he had known and respected since his own youth was also staying in London. To his question how his wife nonetheless knew that this man had a room in the same hotel as the Lacans, his wife answered curtly, "I've seen his shoes." A shiver ran through Lacan as he heard this explanation. Still, he remained skeptical, for there was no good reason to think that Professor D. was in London. Lacan found the whole incident amusing and attached no further importance to it. It is therefore understandable that he was astonished when, some hours later, he saw the renowned professor from his youth walking through the hallway in his robe.

How are we to understand Lacan's shiver at hearing his wife respond curtly that, "I've seen his shoes"? Furthermore, how is it that this announcement holds for Lacan an almost blasphemous meaning? Just imagine: the noteworthy Professor D., an idealized intellectual hero from Lacan's youth, is recognized here by his shoes. The presence of Professor D.'s charming and impressive personality is confirmed by a detail that seems completely extrinsic to the internalized ideal cherished by Lacan. Everyone wears shoes. There is nothing special about them. No greater blasphemy is possible: Professor D. is recognized in a pair of shoes that in principle could be worn by anyone.

But is all of this anything more than a somewhat pathetic dramatization of what is, in the end, a futile event occurring in everyday life? Why does Lacan attach so much importance to it? The shoes seem extrinsic to the idealized image that Lacan had formed of Professor D. and in which he could recognize himself. Indeed, on further inspection, the shoes are as it were a sort of transition point in the boundary between the personal and the impersonal. True, the shoes recall Professor D.—they are identified as "his" shoes—but they do so in such a manner that the idealized image that Lacan had formed of this man is shattered. For Lacan, these shoes are a sort of sign of transition: they form a sign binding an exteriority that no longer means anything to an idealized image of Professor D. While they do indeed refer to Professor D., they also bring about a reference to something in which we can no longer recognize ourselves. In other words, the shoes situate themselves at a limit. They not only call up the presence of Professor D., but also and at the same time refer to the outside of the idealized image that is without any familiarity to us.

To explain further, our everyday world takes form from our expectations, intentions, representations, and so on that are themselves structured from and through the symbolic systems that define our lives. It is for precisely this reason that the world seems familiar. It is "our" own "personal" world with which we can identify and in which we can recognize ourselves. Professor D. had a clear place in Lacan's "own" world: he was a renowned intellectual, an author of important works, and a high-ranking academic whom Lacan admired. In contrast, the shoes are not at all the shoes of a renowned and admired intellectual. In principle, they could be worn by anyone, and in that respect stand at the edge of the impersonal in which we no longer recognize Professor D. with all of his qualities.[7]

It is hardly cause for surprise that in this context Lacan refers to the celebrated shoes of Van Gogh (*Sé VII*, 343/*S VII*, 297). Here, too, it is a matter of a solitary pair of shoes. For these shoes, like the shoes of Professor D., to appear beautiful, claims Lacan, they must be freed from their usual pragmatic meaning, namely that they "are made for walking." They belong to what Heidegger calls a *"Zeugzusammenhang,"* a pragmatic network of references out of which shoes can appear to us as meaningful. For them to appear beautiful we must, according to Lacan, view them *"Ohne Begriff"* (without concept—the reference to Kant is clear), that is to say, they must loosen themselves slightly from our familiar world in which everything has a place and a meaning.[8] The shoes that stand in relation to a human world by fulfilling a function in it are, according to Lacan, brought by Van Gogh's painting in connection with what no longer has any relation with the meaningful world. The shoes belong to our world and we recognize them ("boots are made for walking"), but they come to us as something having almost nothing more to do with this world. The shoes are barely shoes anymore. They are shoes that no longer belong to anything or anyone. The abandoned shoes of Van Gogh resound as though they were the echo of the outside, the beyond of this world, the echo of that which in no way whatsoever takes account of our feelings, projects, and so on, by which the world precisely as meaningful can appear. They bring us to the limit of the meaningless real [*réel*].[9]

What do these two examples clarify about the experience of the beautiful? They show us, says Lacan, that the experience of the beautiful implies a sort of change of perspective. An object can appear "beautiful" only when it incarnates the transition point at which the world of meaning loses its self-evidence and appears vulnerable. The beautiful is the infinite approach of that in which we cannot recognize ourselves in any way whatsoever. In this sense the shoes are, as a sort of insignificant remainder, the image of human loneliness, of decline and decay. In the experience of the beautiful, we have contact with what evades the meaningful world without it being totally destroyed. In this sense, it is the last defense against the real.[10]

It is striking that Lacan describes the experience of Oedipus at Colonus as well as the figure of Antigone in the same terms he describes the shoes of Van Gogh. He thus says of Oedipus at Colonus that he is the image of a "total absence of charity, of fraternity, of anything whatsoever relating to what one calls human feeling. . . . [He] is nothing more than the scum of the earth, the refuse, the residue, a Thing empty of any plausible appearance (translation modified)" (*Sé II*, 268–70/*S II*, 230–32). And further, Lacan makes the beauty of Antigone the core of his reading of Sophocles' tragedy by that name. If Oedipus as well as Antigone have their own beauty, then this is precisely because they, like the shoes of Van Gogh, allow something to be seen of the limit where form dissolves into emptiness. Both Antigone and Oedipus bring us to the boundary where sense and nonsense, the personal and impersonal, separate. They find themselves—and bring us—to the limit where the world of our natural attitude stands on the verge of collapsing.[11]

But there is more. At the same time, Lacan says about Antigone that precisely in her beauty she shows us that at which desire aims (*Sé VII*, 289/*S VII*, 247). She not only brings us to the limit between the personal and impersonal but also in this way shows us something about the truth of our desire. This seems to mean that of itself desire brings us to the limit where we risk destruction. In light of the preceding, this can only mean that desire is directed to a point lying beyond all possible experience, *jenseits* the phenomenal world such as we described it. Lacan also explains this thought by saying that desire must be characterized as essentially desire for the Thing.

One Thing Is Not The Other

To clarify Lacan's insights concerning desire as desire for the Thing— and to illuminate the significance of the figure of Antigone for his thinking— it is first necessary to formulate some remarks on Freud's use of the same concept. Lacan does indeed introduce the notion of the Thing in direct reference to the *"Komplex des Nebenmenschen,"* such as Freud sets it forth in his *Entwurf einer Psychologie* (1895). But in this Freud is certainly not Lacan's only source of inspiration—one thinks here of Kant's "Thing-in-itself" as well as Heidegger's lecture on "the Thing"—but in this context he is for us the most useful one. To not overburden my story with all sorts of complex references to the history of philosophy, I restrict myself in what follows largely to the reference to Freud.[12]

In the *Entwurf* Freud brings in the *Nebenmensch* Complex to clarify the emergence of human knowledge and the capacity for judgment. Freud asks himself how it is that we come to know and judge an object. According to him, knowledge and the capacity for judgment come into being in relation to the first object of satisfaction. The perceptual system—that which one perceives of the other—that issue from this first Other can be joined partly to similar perceptions that the infant has had in connection with his or her own body. When, for example, another person cries, this will call up in the child memories of his own crying and in turn also of the painful events accompanying it. The child "understands" the other because what she or he perceives in her or him can be brought into connection with what she or he has experienced. Here, then, it is a matter of perceptions of the other person that we can give a place in our own world of representations, and precisely this reduction of the other to perceptions that we can recognize in ourselves is according to Freud the first form of knowledge. Still, the other can never be reduced entirely to our own representations. The *Nebenmensch* Complex thus falls into two parts. Besides perceptions, such as crying, which the child can connect with his or her own world of (bodily) experiences, there exists another sort of perception, such as the facial expressions of the other, for which this recognition is not possible. The child, says Freud, cannot compare the continually changing facial expressions of another person with any similar perceptions of his or her own body. And for precisely this reason they cannot be understood, since to understand means to couple perceptions of the other with one's own bodily experiences.[13] Well then, the Other insofar as it essentially evades my own world of representations, is called by Freud the Thing.[14]

In light of the foregoing, it is clear what Lacan attends to in Freud's consideration of the *Nebenmensch* Complex: the Thing is the Other insofar as he evades my world of representations, and it appears at the point where the personal—that in the other person which I can give a place among my own intentions, expectations, and so on—passes over into the impersonal. Moreover, according to Lacan, Freud suggests that this Other—this Thing—is the *terminus ad quem*, not only of human knowledge but also and at the same time of desire. In a letter to Fliess,[15] Freud does indeed claim that what is aimed at in and through a hysterical attack is nothing other than the prehistoric unforgettable other against which all subsequent others appears lacking. In and through the hysterical attack, the hysteric tries to recuperate this other so as to undo an original, "unpleasurable" experience. According to Lacan, this prehistoric other of hysteria can be nothing else than the Other as Thing (*Sé VII*, 81–82/*S VII*, 66–67).

To understand Lacan well it is not without importance here to make note of a fundamental shift in meaning he introduces into Freud's text.[16] Freud connects the Thing with the other person's perceptual system that I cannot bring into connection with my own bodily experience. Naturally, this does not rule out that these complexes leave behind memory traces. In contrast, the Lacanian Thing appears at a point where the phenomenal world collapses. It lies radically beyond the representable and all possible meaning-giving.[17] Of this

Thing we have no memory-traces. On the contrary, according to Lacan, we can only try to reach this Thing via memory-traces which, however, can never give us the Thing itself.[18] For Freud, the Thing is thus the whole of the perceptual system, or memory-traces, of the Other which we cannot bring into connection with our own bodily experience,[19] whereas for Lacan the Thing lies beyond all memory-traces that at the same time present us with the only available path to it. Here, in short, Lacan seems willing to think an alterity more radical than Freud has in mind. In Freud it is a matter of a split between two different sorts of memory-traces, in Lacan of an original split between the memory-traces and that which in essence eludes them. What does this mean?

Lacan aligns the Freudian Thing with the prehistoric Other that is lost to me forever. Furthermore, according to Lacan, this first Other is not only lost forever but in fact has never been present as such. Contact with the first unforgettable Other is from the very beginning concretized in a multiplicity of particular experiences of pleasure and unpleasure of which we possess the memory-traces, but which never give us the Other as such. This means we can seek the Other only via this multiplicity of particular memory-traces, which at the same time, precisely as *particular* memory-traces, ultimately deny us access to that Other. However far I may go in my pursuit of the Thing, or the Other, I will never find anything but one or another particular memory-trace that at the same time also prevents me from reaching the Other. According to Lacan, the multiplicity of memory-traces that Freud had in mind must then also be understood in terms of and as a sort of gravitating movement around a point—the Thing—which they can never make present as such, but which at the same time both commands and supports them as an always absent *terminus a quo* and *ad quem*. Or better, it is only on the basis of this gravitating movement that can be thought a *Jenseits* the appearance of which would mark an end to that movement once and for all (*Sé VII*, 101/*S VII*, 83). However, the appearance of this *Jenseits* would at the same time mean the end of every meaningful world. Lacan therefore also calls desire an "antipsychical power": it is a death drive (*Sé VII*, 142–43/*S VII*, 118).

Language And Desire

Those familiar with Lacan's work will probably already be clear about the manner in which he is able to reformulate the *Nebenmensch* Complex in terms of his own thinking. What else can the gravitating movement of memory-traces be, Lacan asks, than the movement of differential signifiers which in principle can never end. The word, he says in line with Hegel and Kojève, is death of the thing (*É*, 319). Just as memory-traces refer to the Thing without ever making it present, so the word renders that to which it refers present only in its absence. In the word "being," for example, being itself is not present. The word "being" makes being present only in its absence. Moreover, since the signifiers signify only on the basis of their difference, their movement around that to which they refer without ever making present can never be brought to an end. Just as we in our pursuit of the Thing pass from one memory-trace to another without ever reaching it, so one signifier takes the place of another in endless movement around something that was originally excluded—the Thing. And just like Freud's memory-traces, Lacan's signifiers refer to something lying beyond, which itself can no longer be expressed in their order. Finally, since according to Lacan there can be no meaning outside of the order of language, this Thing lies beyond meaning and every possible experience.

When we called desire a death drive, it should have been clear that the death Lacan has in mind here is not biological. Of death as a sheer biological given, one cannot say that it falls wholly outside of the world of human meaning. This death can be described in scientific terms, and of the dead body, for example, it can be said that it returns to—and thus has a place in—the ongoing process of passing away and becoming what we call "nature." In this way, we can still assign a function to biological death. In contrast, the death entailed in desire as a death drive is, according to Lacan, a "second death" [*une seconde mort*]. Desire directs us to a point lying beyond every possible meaning and experience. Only this second death can rightly be called, in the most literal sense, "ob-scene."[20]

Oedipus: Better Never To Have Been Born

Desire is desire for the Thing because and insofar as one is marked by the order of the signifier. Lacan never tires of repeating that the subject is in the grip of this order. The signifier rules over the subject. What this might mean and in which manner it fits together with what has been said here about desire as a death drive is, according to Lacan, never clearer than in Sophocles' *Oedipus at Colonus*. The being of Oedipus, says Lacan, is completely enclosed by the prediction of the oracle at Delphi. Oedipus is nothing other than "le noeud central de la parole," that is to say, "the central knot of speech," the place where the word, or the prediction, of the oracle realizes itself. He exists under the sign of a word—or, as one might better say—in a "chain of signifiers" from which Oedipus functions as a pure point of passage (*Sé II*, 269/*S II*, 230). This word is not a word of Oedipus: true, this word bears his existence and determines its course, but at the same time it comes from the Other and eludes his—Oedipus'—grasp. It realizes itself in spite of Oedipus and, as it were, behind his back. Whatever Oedipus might think about his own actions, whatever picture he might develop of his own existence, whatever ideals he may serve, he remains subject to the curse of the oracle at Delphi. The life story of Oedipus unfolds in function of the oracle and the fact that he is other than what his history first leads him to believe. He is the son of Laius and Jocasta, and he executes his existence without knowing this (*Sé II*, 245/*S II*, 209).

What remains of Oedipus, Lacan asks, when the oracle is fully realized? It is precisely at this point of his analysis that Lacan describes Oedipus as the image of a "total absence of charity, of fraternity, of anything whatsoever relating to what one calls human feeling . . . nothing more than the scum of the earth, the refuse, the residue, a Thing empty of any plausible appearance" (*Sé II*, 269–270/*S II*, 230–232). The oracle that determined and gave shape to Oedipus' existence from before his birth has realized itself completely. At that same moment it becomes clear in a shocking manner what Oedipus is when detached from the signifiers that had determined his existence until then. Oedipus stands, according to Lacan, on the verge of the formless, of that which can in no way be recuperated into the order of meaning. He finds himself at the limit where the Thing emerges all too plainly. He is no more than refuse, residue: "Am I made man in the hour when I cease to be?" (*Sé II*, 268/*S II*, 229). The chorus summarizes in pregnant manner what for Lacan is the proper theme of Oedipus at Colonus: "*Mè funaï*"—(better never to have been born).[21]

"*Mè funaï*"—this, says Lacan, is the refusal in which culminates a truly human existence. When everything is said and done for Oedipus, he withdraws to die. He withdraws from an existence that has lost all meaning. The death of Oedipus is "like . . . a terrible spectacle . . . unbearable to human eyes."[22] Lacan comments, "The malediction is freely accepted on the basis of the true subsistence of a human being, the subsistence of the subtraction of himself from the order of the world. It'is a beautiful attitude. . . ." (*Sé VII*, 353/*S VII*, 306). Oedipus' bearing can appear to us as "beautiful" because it makes possible a change of perspective that we took note of before as a prerequisite for the experience of the beautiful. Oedipus takes us to the limit—unbearable to human eyes—where the personal sinks into (passes over into) the impersonal form into emptiness.

How are we to understand this in terms of what has already been examined concerning the relationship between desire and language? Desire, as desire for the Thing, is an effect of signifiers that refer to something beyond and which itself can no longer be expressed within the order of signifiers. These signifiers at the same time determine our fate as mortals. In the most literal sense, they determine our existence, just as the oracle at Delphi determines the existence of Oedipus. Following Lacan, the figure of Oedipus illustrates two mutually related existential truths. On one hand, Sophocles' *Oedi-*

pus at Colonus shows what happens when we focus on the Thing too directly: we then come inevitably to a point where the signifier falls short and where the Thing thus manifests itself too immediately. On the other hand, it becomes clear here that the signifier directs us to the Thing not only *in abstracto*, but also and at the same time determines the way in which and along which we move toward It. It is true that the Thing is the *terminus a quo* and *terminus ad quem* of everyone's desire, but the way along which we can reach it is determined by the fundamental signifiers which specify and give form to our existence.

The Unicity of Polynices: The Story of a Passion

We are now fully armed to undertake our reading of *Antigone*. Traditionally—one thinks, for example, of Hegel (*Sé VII*, 292/*S VII*, 249)—this tragedy is understood according to a contrast between two opposed principles of justice or between two types of discourse that must finally be reconciled with one another. Antigone, so one then thinks, defends the laws of the gods. She affirms these laws unequivocally over against the laws of the state that Creon defends just as unequivocally. Lacan rejects such a reading from the very beginning. According to him, what is at stake here is not a conflict between two contrary principles, each of which can make claim to equal justice or injustice, it is in fact, says Lacan, a matter of a conflict between, on one hand, Creon, who makes a mistake, and, on the other, Antigone, who is found, as it were, *jenseits von Gut und Böse*. Thus, according to Lacan, the behavior of Creon is marked by *hamartia*: he makes a mistake in judgment. Still more, he commits stupidity (*Sé VII*, 300/*S VII*, 258). For, indeed, Creon locates himself at the standpoint of the state. He is the politician who wishes to realize "the greatest happiness for the greatest number" (*Sé* VII 301/*S VII*, 259). Yet, at the same time, says Lacan, he goes too far in this: political power applies to the living, not the dead. By refusing burial to Polynices, he wishes to still punish him after his death for the harm he has done to the state. Creon transgresses the limits of the political that he was supposed to represent. And apart from this, he also makes a major political miscalculation. It is all too clear, Lacan says, that no one asks Creon to pursue Polynices, even into death.[23] Indeed, both Haemon and the chorus point out to him that the people in whose name he acts take the side of Antigone and reproach him for his tyranny. Also from a purely political standpoint—that is, from the standpoint of political "wisdom"—Creon should have permitted Polynices burial according to the usual rituals. In contrast with the classical Aristotelian interpretation according to which there can be no tragic hero without "hamartia," Lacan reduces Creon—precisely insofar as he falls into error—to an "anti-hero" or "secondary hero" (*Sé VII*, 323/*S VII*, 277). The disproportion here is total: Lacan situates Creon and Antigone on wholly different levels.

But how then does Lacan understand the figure of Antigone? Why, according to him, is she, in contrast with Creon, a tragic heroine? What, for Lacan, is the tragic? Lacan concentrates mainly on the manner in which Antigone accounts for her stubborn resistance to Creon. Antigone wishes to bury Polynices at any cost. With a wondrous insistence, she defends the right of Polynices to be returned to the earth according to common practices, just as had been granted his brother Eteocles. Creon's argument makes absolutely no impression on her. He rejects the thought that a traitor to the state should be treated in the same manner as someone who has remained faithful to it and has defended it to the death. But this is not Antigone's concern. Polynices is "*autadelphos*": "For was I the mother of a child, or were the dead man lying there my husband, then I would never, as enemy of the people, have done this. According to what principle to I say this? Well, if my husband died, I could find another; a child? if necessary from a new marriage. But since my parents are in Hades, there is no question of having new brothers."[24] In other words, Antigone bases her resistance on the unicity and irreplaceability of Polynices.

The passage just cited has long been a thorn in the eye of many interpreters. Hence did Goethe say to Eckermann that he hoped one day someone would show that it was apocryphal? In contrast, for Lacan, this passage is not so much interpolated after the death of Sophocles as it lays bare the truth of the tragedy. Nowhere more than here is the aim of Antigone's desire so clear (*Sé VII*, 297/*S VII*, 254). What does this mean?

Were Polynices my husband, I could now seek a new one. Had he been my child, I could try for another. But now that my parents are in Hades, my brother is irreplaceable to me. The unicity of Polynices cannot be located in any one of the properties ascribed to him during his life. We can say of Polynices that he was cowardly or brave and that he fought for a just cause or was a traitor to Thebes. These are properties Polynices shares with others in greater or lesser degrees, and on that basis he is comparable to them. For example, we can say Eteocles was just as courageous, or even more so, and that the cause he defended was at least as just as that of Polynices, if not more so. What interests Lacan here is that what makes Polynices unique and incomparable eludes expression in the signifiers of language. His unicity does not lie in anything that can be said of him. It does not lie in properties that can be articulated in linguistic signifiers. Consequently, what Antigone defends is Polynices in what he is beyond all the good and bad things that can be said of him: you may say what you will of Polynices, and it might even all be true, but he is still more than that—he is and remains my brother. According to Lacan, the "more" to which Antigone refers here is nonetheless inarticulable in language. It is essentially unspeakable (*Sé VII*, 325/*S VII*, 279).

It is not difficult to see in Lacan's analysis of the notion of "*autadelphos*" the same structure as that which we saw earlier in connection with the relation between the Thing and language. For what else are the so-called "properties" of Polynices than signifiers invoking a "*jenseits*" that can no longer be articulated as a supplementary property? What Antigone aims at in Polynices is thus nothing other than the Thing. Her desire then turns exclusively around the body of Polynices as a sort of quasiobject that must be covered because it reminds one too explicitly of the outside of the world of human meaning.[25]

This latter point brings us inevitably to the problem of burial and the tomb. The burial place, writes Lacan already in his "Function and Field of Speech and Language" (1953), is the first symbol in which humanity can recognize itself. Only humans bury their dead and erect monuments to them because only humans are in the full sense of the word "mortal."[26] The death of the individual animal changes nothing. It makes no difference whatsoever. Is today's mosquito the same as those from last year? It might well be, but in any case it makes no difference. Animals remain the same unto themselves as do waves on the sea. They are completely taken up in the process of coming to be and passing away. In contrast, the problem of a unicity and an irreplaceability that must be protected and remembered presents itself only to speaking beings. It is only from within language that reference can be made to a *jenseits* that cannot be taken up into any comparison (*Sé VII*, 325/*S VII*, 279). Or, to express this same thought somewhat differently, the animal knows only biological death, but humans also are eventually confronted with what, as we have seen, Lacan calls "a second death." And it is precisely at that point that the problem of our unicity and incomparability presents itself.

Naturally, this means that the problem of the burial of the dead, which in many respects governs Sophocles' *Antigone*, is wholly at one with the Lacanian problem of desire as a "death drive," such as we have described it and such as it takes form in exemplary manner in the figure of Antigone. Here it is necessary to take one more step. When Antigone says, "My brother is what he is," an analyst will hear the inverse form of her own message: "I am only his sister, I am only a sister."[27] Lacan points this out by calling Antigone an "absolute individuality" (*Sé VII*, 325/*S VII*, 278). She has absolved herself—made herself absolute—from everything that binds her to this world—from her relationship with Haemon, as well as from her relationship with Ismene, whose help she haughtily casts aside—all so as to be only a sister for her brother. Antigone's desire is, as Lacan says, an absolutely "pure" desire (*Sé VII*, 328/*S VII*, 282). It is purified from every calculus and every attachment that would make her anything other than "a sister." Lacan can then also say that Antigone represents the "signifying bar": she is directed exclusively to the point where the signifier falls short of articulating that in which Polynices would be absolutely singular (*Sé VII*, 325/*S VII*, 278).

We now also understand why Lacan can write of Antigone's behavior that "it is a matter here of the evocation of what is in effect of the order of the law, but which is developed in no signifying chain, in nothing" (*Sé VII*, 324/*S VII*, 278). Antigone does indeed obey the law of "pure" desire. She aims at the Thing, which cannot be expressed by any signifier. Lacan says in this same line, "Antigone, faced with Creon, is situated as synchrony, as opposed to diachrony" (*Sé VII*, 331/*S VII*, 285). Antigone defends something in Polynices that cannot in any way be affected by the praise—or blameworthy deeds he has or would have committed in the course of his life. Moreover, it is for this same reason that Antigone is "without fear and pity." We are always afraid of what threatens our lives or that of our fellow humans, insofar as we can relate to them. Likewise, our compassion concerns only those who appear in one or another manner as an alter-ego. Compassion and fear are therefore affects that play a role in the world insofar as we can experience it as "familiar" and "proper." In contrast, Antigone's desire seeks something that lies precisely "beyond" this world (*Sé VII*, 372/*S VII*, 323).

The Tragic

What is it that drives Antigone over the limit? Why does Antigone give such importance to the burial of her brother? Why especially does she, after a first attempt at burying him, return to his body to try again? Did she not fulfill her duty that first time? Antigone bases herself on the chtonic laws of the blood. One can understand her resistance and stubborn perseverance as a sort of overvaluation of blood ties. According to Lacan, this overvaluation must also be understood in the context of the history of misfortune (as well as madness)—the *atè*—of the Labdacidean family with which she identifies (*Sé VII*, 333/*S VII*, 283). In this respect, Antigone is no more than an exponent of this history and of what determines it—the oracle at Delphi and the curse by Oedipus on his two sons (*Sé VII*, 329/*S VII*, 283). Just like Oedipus at Colonus, Antigone is for Lacan nothing other than "the central knot of speech." More precisely, she is the place where the fundamental words bearing the Labdacidean family realize themselves. And when the chorus says Antigone will go *Ektos Atas*—beyond the *atè*—for Lacan this means nothing other than that Antigone seeks the point reached by Oedipus at the end of his existence. Antigone aims toward something lying beyond the signifiers in which takes form the Labdacidean family *atè* (*Sé VII*, 315/*S VII*, 270). She stands, just like Oedipus, on the verge of the formless, at the limit where the Thing emerges all too plainly. According to Lacan, nowhere is this expressed more clearly than in the long lamentation of Antigone occurring at the end of the tragedy, as she makes her way to her self-chosen tomb. " Ah, wretched as I am . . . to dwell not among the living, not among the dead."[28] Sophocles, says Lacan, situates the heroes of his tragedies in a zone where death seems to overtake life. Antigone is found in a zone where death breaks in on life. Still living, she belongs to the realm of the dead.[29] For Lacan, the *tragic* is precisely this paradoxical confrontation with the second death, with the nothing to which desire conducts us.[30]

Beauty and Sublimation: Catharsis

Antigone is found in a zone where death breaks in on life. She puts herself on the verge of the second death. This zone, says Lacan, has a special function in the effect that tragedy is supposed to achieve (*Sé VII*, 290/*S VII*, 248). This effect is traditionally thematized as "catharsis." The classical Aristotelian definition of tragedy is well known: by stimulating anxiety and compassion, tragedy makes possible a catharsis of these feelings in the spectator. To some extent, Lacan follows this definition, but he also reinterprets it in light of his reading of *Antigone* and *Oedipus at Colonus*. To understand this, we must first go more deeply into the status of the beautiful in art.

What is the particular function of entering the zone where death overtakes life? According to Lacan, what appears at the moment of Antigone's lamentation is *"imeros enargeia,"* that is to say the becoming visible of desire (*Sé VII*, 311/*S VII*, 268). And, he adds, "The violent illumination, the glow of beauty, coincides with the moment of transgression or of realization of Antigone's Atè" (*Sé VII*, 327/*S VII*, 281). Where desire appears as pure desire, beauty also lights up. Beauty, Lacan goes on, has an essentially blinding effect [*"un effet d'aveuglement"*]. Besides what shows itself in beauty, there also happens something that cannot be seen. Oedipus dies in loneliness and so, too, the death of Antigone withdraws from the eye of the spectator (*Sé VII*, 327/*S VII*, 281). What plays itself out in Antigone's self-chosen tomb is, like the end of Oedipus at Colonus, "unbearable by human eyes." Here one sees how the meaning Lacan wishes to give the beauty of Antigone runs perfectly parallel with what we said earlier about the shoes of Van Gogh and about Oedipus. Like the shoes in Van Gogh's painting and like Oedipus at Colonus, Antigone is an image of human solitude, of decline and decay. Like Oedipus and the shoes, she is found at the limit of the *jenseits* in which form and meaning dissolve into emptiness. In the experience of beauty that comes to light here, we have contact with what eludes the meaningful world without destroying it. In this sense, beauty is also the last defense against the real.

This also makes it clear why Lacan wishes to ascribe to beauty a "sublimatory" effect. Indeed, for him, "sublimation" means nothing else than the possibility of coming into contact with the Thing without losing oneself as a subject. Here, sublimation is no longer, as it is in Freud, primarily related with an internal transformation of the sexual drive, but with the possibility of a nondestructive relation to the Thing. This Thing, we said, lies beyond the proper, trustworthy world with which we can identify and in which we feel at home. In the experience of the beautiful, we are for a moment, as it were, cut loose from this world. The self-absorbed ego is here confronted with its own outside which it wished not to know about, but which, as *terminus a quo* and *terminus ad quem* of desire, nonetheless and from the beginning, forms the unspeakable background against which our existence is always exercised.[31]

In sublimation, we are loosened from the proper, familiar world. All categories (including good and evil, sense and nonsense, etc.) by which we judge this world and from which they can appear as meaningful are thus—if even for only a moment—placed between brackets. At the limit where the Thing appears, they lose their meaning. It will then come as little surprise—so says Lacan—that in the presence of Antigone the chorus loses its way.[32] Is Antigone's behavior right and just? Has she earned our praise and admiration or is her stubborn resistance reprehensible? According to Lacan, such considerations lose their relevance with regard to Antigone. She brings herself to a point beyond the "proper" world in which they can be meaningfully used.

Hence is it also clear in which manner tragedy can "purify us of our feelings of compassion and fear"? Earlier we said Antigone is without these feelings because she aims at a point that is literally no longer of this world. In contrast, fear and compassion are affects that play a role in the world insofar as we can experience it as "proper" and "familiar." Thus, precisely to the degree that in and through sublimation we are loosened from this "familiar" world, it also makes possible a catharsis of these affects.

The Object Rises to the Dignity of the Thing

We now understand why Lacan says that tragedy—and the work of art in general—can initiate a sublimatory effect on the spectator. But is sublimation not first the work of the artist and only secondly—that is, in a second moment—of the spectator? Did Freud not introduce the concept of sublimation in the first instance to clarify the activity of the artist? In Freud, sublimation is related first to the transformation of sexual drive in and through the creation of a work of art: sexual drive is diverted from its original object and aim and employed in a "socially acceptable manner." Consequently, when sublimation is said also of the beholding of a work of art, then it seems that for Freud this can only occur in a derived, secondary manner. Lacan sees it no differently: for tragedy—or, for that matter, any other work of art—to have a sublimatory effect, it must raise the object—in this case, Antigone or Oedipus—to the dignity of the Thing (*Sé VII*, 133/*S VII*, 120). This, then, is sublimation in its proper sense. What does this mean?

In the image of Antigone, we know, one comes into contact with the Thing (with the "second death") without being destroyed in the process. The image of Antigone is the image of a passion. From the foregoing we know that the beauty of Antigone is directly connected to the fact that she is found at the limit of the "second death." In this light, we could also say that "tragedy is that which spreads itself out in front so that that image may be produced" (*Sé VII*, 318/*S VII*, 273). This can only mean that tragedy, on the ground of a systematic and deliberate use of the signifier, as such, places the object in a particular relation with the Thing through which the latter in its absence is made present. Lacan says in this connection, "The object is established in a certain relation to the Thing and is intended to encircle and to render both present and absent" (*Sé VII*, 169/*S VII*, 141). In precisely this way, the object acquires the dignity of the Thing and makes catharsis possible in the spectator. This is sublimation.

Conclusion: Toward an "Ethics of the Bien-dire"

Tragedy elevates the object to the dignity of the Thing. It shares this property with the other art forms. But although all arts are forms of sublimation, Lacan still affirms unambiguously an essential primacy for those working with *words*. Art is essentially *Dichtung*—poetry (Heidegger). Hence does Lacan say of Cezanne's still life of apples that the more the object is represented *as* imitated, the more it opens us to the dimension in which the illusion itself is, as it were, destroyed, and it begins to point us toward something else. Lacan says: ". . . the illusion (that it imitates) . . . transcends itself, destroys itself, by demonstrating that it is only there as a signifier" (*Sé VII*, 163/*S VII*, 136). Cezanne's apples are like signifiers calling forth a *jenseits* that itself can no longer be articulated in the order of the signifier. The order of the signifier is nonetheless primarily the order of language. According to Lacan, we therefore cannot help but affirm the primacy of *Dichtung*. Could it be otherwise when, on one hand, every form of art must raise the object to the dignity of the Thing, and, on the other hand, the problematic of the Thing emerges only from out of language—and for a speaking being?

Whenever art thus succeeds in bringing about a relation to the Thing such as I have described it—again, whenever it succeeds in raising the object to the dignity of the Thing—then it is, says Lacan, a *bien-dire*. Art does not teach us what we must do. It has no moralizing significance. It does not tell us what the good life consists in [*"Elle ne dit pas le bien"*]. It can only, on the basis of "a systematic and deliberate use of the signifier as such"—that is to say, as a *bien-dire*—bring about a nondestructive relation to the Thing. In this way, art brings us into contact with the ultimate truth of our existence, without that truth being able to overwhelm us.

But, naturally, sublimation is not the privilege of art. I said in my introduction that the aim of a psychoanalytic cure is often defined in terms of a greater capacity to sublimate. An ethics of the sovereign good has become impossible. This directly implies that psychoanalysis is also unable to teach us what the good (and happiness) consists in. It has no more moralizing significance than does art. Like art, it can only aim at a *bien-dire* that would enable us to carry out our mourning over the loss of the sovereign good.[33] In other words, analysis must make possible such a relation to the Thing—without our misrecognizing it—and without our being overwhelmed or destroyed in the process. And perhaps—but I would like to think more about this—Lacan expects of psychoanalysis nothing other than that it help us to make of our existence a work of art anew.

Notes

1. This paper was read at the Slade Center of Art at University College, London (October 18, 1995).

2. It deserves attention that whereas the ethics of the sovereign good is historically subsequent to tragedy, Lacan's thinking in a certain sense proceeds in the reverse.

3. In Freud, sublimation is a specifically psychical process. In Lacan, it takes on a more general "philosophical" meaning. We will come back to this difference later.

4. For Lacan's reading of *Antigone,* see especially *Sé VII*, 285–333/*S VII*, 243–287; for Lacan's reading of *Oedipus at Colonus,* see *Sé II*, 267–74/*S II*, 304–08.

5. Cf. to what follows, Paul Moyaert, "Sur la sublimation chez Lacan: quelques remarques," in Steve G. Lofts and Paul Moyaert, *La pensée de Jacques Lacan: Questions historique—Problèmes théoriques* (Louvain: Peeters, 1994), pp. 125–46. This extremely interesting article inspired my whole reading of Lacan's reading of Sophocles' *Antigone.*

6. For what follows, see *Sé VII*, 343–44/*S VII*, 296–97.

7. Here one could probably also think of the unbearable sight of the heaps of shoes in the concentration camps. What makes this sight so unbearable is precisely the fact that here—much more than in the case of Professor D.—every reference to something "proper" or "personal" has become impossible. It is useless for us to connect these shoes with the representation of a familiar face. They have become nothing more than shoes.

8. "You must imagine Professor D . . .'s clodhoppers *ohne Begriff,* with no thought of the academic, without any connection to his endearing personality, if you are to begin to see Van Gogh's own clodhoppers come alive with their own incommensurable quality of beauty" (*Sé VII,* 343/*S VII,* 297).

9. "They are simply there. . . . This signifier is not even a signifier of walking, of fatigue, or of anything else, such as passion or human warmth. It is just a signifier of that which is signified by a pair of abandoned clodhoppers, namely, both a presence and an absence—something that is, if one likes, inert, available to everyone. . . . It is an impression that appears as a function of the organic or, in a word, of waste, since it evokes the beginning of spontaneous generation (*Sé VII,* 343/*S VII,* 297).

10. See *Sé VII,* 135–36/*S VII,* 113–14; 271–81/231–40; 289–91/247–49.

11. "*C'est de cela qu'il s'agit dans le cas d'Oedipe. Oedipe, tout le montre depuis le début de la tragédie, n'est plus que le rebut de la terre, le déchet, le résidu, chose vidée de toute apparence spécieuse*" (*Sé II,* 269–70/*S II,* 230–32). Cf. to Antigone, for example, *Sé VII,* 289–92/*S VII,* 247–50.

12. For what follows, see Sigmund Freud, "*Entwurf einer wissenschaftlichen Psychologie*" in *Aus den Anfänge der Psychoanalyse. Briefe an Wilhelm Fliess, Abhandlungen und Notizenaus den Jahren 1887–1902* (Frankfurt am Maim: S. Fischer Verlag, 1962), pp. 336–41.

13. Ibid., p. 337.

14. "*Und so sondert sich der Komplex des Nebenmenschen in 2 Bestanteile, von denen der eine durch konstantes Gefüge imponiert, als* Ding *beisammenbleibt, während der andere durch Erinnerungsarbeit* verstanden, *d.h. auf eine Nachricht vom eigenen Körper zurückgeführt werden kann*" (Ibid., p. 338).

15. Letter 52, ibid., p. 156.

16. For Lacan's comment on the passage on the "*Nebenmensch,*" see *Sé VII,* 55–70/*S VII,* 43–70.

17. "The *Ding* is the element that is initially isolated by the subject in his experience of the *Nebenmensch* as being by its nature, alien, *Fremde. . . . Das ding* is that which I call the beyond-of-the-signified" (*Sé II,* 66–68/*S II,* 52–54).

18. "Right at the beginning of the organization of the world in the psyche, both logically and chronologically, *das Ding* is something that presents and isolates itself as the strange feature around which the whole movement of the *Vorstellungen* turns—a *Vorstellungen* that Freud shows us is governed by a regulatory principle, the so-called pleasure principle. . . ." (*Sé VII,* 71/*S VII,* 57).

19. This does not rule out that these memory-traces could still be integrated in further stages of psychic development.

20. *Sé VII, passim.*

21. Cf. to this Patrick Guyomard, *La jouissance du tragique: Antigone, Lacan et le désir de l'analyste* (Paris: Aubier, 1992), p. 91. In his seminar on ethics, Lacan lies these words in the mouth of Oedipus, where in fact it is the chorus that proclaims that "one should better never to have been born" *(Oedipus at Colonus*, lines 1225–28).

22. *Oedipus at Colonus*, lines 1652–53.

23. *Sé VII*, 301/259. One can doubt the historical correctness of Lacan's reading at this point. Creon is right from the point of view of the city. He is doing what would be done in Athens. At the same time in the tragedy the city puts itself into question through the intermediary of heroic myths, the old legends that belong to the city's past. See Jean-Pierre Vernant, "Greek tragedy: problems of interpretation," in Richard Macksey and Eugenio Donato, *The Structuralist Controversy: The Languages of Criticism and the Sciences of Man* (Baltimore and London: Johns Hopkins University Press, 1982), pp. 281–82.

24. *Antigone*, lines 905–12.

25. *Sé VII*, 307/*S VII*, 264. See also in this context Lacan's interpretation of Edgar Allan Poe's "The Facts in the case of M. Valdemar," in *Sé II*, 270/*S II*, 231–32.

26. *É*, 319; see also in this context George Bataille, "Hegel, la mort et le sacrifice," *Deucalion* 5 (1955): pp. 21–43.

27. Cf. Guyomard, *La Jouissance*, p. 55.

28. *Antigone,* lines 850–52.

29. "Sophocles . . . situates the hero in a sphere where death encroaches on life. . . . (*Sé VII*, 331/*S VII*, 285).

30. Cf. "Dead is all that I am," *Oedipus at Colonus*, line 1613.

31. See *Sé VII*, 105–94/*S VII*, 87–166.

32. *Antigone,* line 801.

33. See *Sé VII*, 337–75/*S VII*, 291–325.

Chapter 6

Ethics with Psychoanalysis

Alain Juranville

Must one with psychoanalysis go beyond guilt? Or, for psychoanalysis, is there in transgression [*faute*]¹ something irreducibly objective—that would presuppose an ascribable absolute Good?

Through guilt is maintained a relation with an ideal of mastery that one must relinquish during the cure by confronting the truth of unconscious desire, unmasterable in knowledge. Beyond guilt, anxiety would mark the trial [*épreuve*] of the effacement of mastery and would be the passion linked to the ethical act. Ethics with psychoanalysis would find again, in this way, the essence of thoughts of existence, in particular Heidegger's.

But the ethical work of the cure supposes the discourse of the psychoanalyst, a discourse that puts forward the hypothesis of the unconscious and, calling for its confrontation, determines an ideal, a Good. The possibility, impassable for man as finite being, of fleeing this confrontation would thus be objective transgression. This is what Lacan evokes when he says that "from an analytical point of view, the only thing of which one can be guilty is to have given ground relative to one's desire,"² and that is always, at bottom, what the subject feels guilty about.

Would affirming such an objectivity of transgression and of the Good not represent, however, a return to the idealism of metaphysical thought, called into question by the thought of existence that holds that the Good can neither be posited as ideal nor expressed in discourse? This thought, taken up repeatedly by thinkers from Kierkegaard to Levinas, is captured in Wittgenstein's formula, "ethics cannot be put into words."³ And the unconscious taken up anew by Lacan appears to be the concern of an identical impugnment of the master-of-his-world subject of modern metaphysics in the name of an essential relation with an absolute Other. To be able to establish an objectivity of transgression, it is important then to investigate what can be made of *ethics with psychoanalysis* in general.

Ethics requires an objective Good that can be stated in discourse and in relation to which something like transgression can be determined. On the one hand, it is necessary that the finitude of freedom and the violence of being, given prominence by the thought of existence, may be assumed by an absolute freedom that experiences guilt. This is what Levinas has insisted upon in his ethics-based critique against Heidegger: for Levinas, the absolute Other who, on this side of every possible choice and commitment, appoints us responsible for the Other [*autrui*], summons us to substitute ourselves for the other as victim and to renounce being. But, on the other hand—and this goes in the opposite direction of Levinas—it is necessary that this absolute freedom that assumes the violence of being and finitude be able also to act according to the Good and choose in full autonomy, without submitting to a law received from the Other. If being is irreducibly nonmeaning and violence, this violence must itself be capable of being desired as a Good. This brings us to the heart of the act of creation—positive essence implied in transgression—that ethics would consist in disengaging.

Does psychoanalysis make it possible to give reality to this idea of ethics? In his first conception, Lacan maintains the general perspective of the thought of existence. The unconscious is the Other of language, knowledge that is outside the subject, law that determines the subject to be and to desire according to an impassable violence. Yet his search for an ever more rigorous thought of the unconscious led him finally to question his initial position, to go beyond the Other of the thought of existence. The unconscious is the Thing, the innermost heart of the subject, that poses the Other of the law to which it submits by existing. The suffering of desire is now no longer violence proper, and the idea of full ethical autonomy in guilt itself can be upheld.

Taking psychoanalysis as my point of departure, I would now like to try to demonstrate the following:

1. The Good is intelligible and statable, and a transgression can thus be objectively determined in relation to it. For if the Good is in the act against discourse, as the thought of existence wants it, what acts [*faire acte*][4] in history is a discourse, philosophical discourse that, in taking up the partial truth of psychoanalysis within the framework of a total truth, states in fact the Good.
2. The Good is attainable, despite irreducible finitude and transgression. If, as the thought of existence has shown, the act must be carried out by passion, guilt as fundamental ethical passion—for example, that of the analyst provoking the trial of anxiety in the patient—can be fully wanted again in an absolutely free act that, for man, is transgression.

It is a question of wanting again the four moments [*temps*] just indicated of ethical work, which traverse the entire neurotic structure that constitutes man. To use the terms of the Borromean knot, they are: (1) the imaginary, or consistency, produced effectively in the act (for ethics, in general, this is religion); (2) the symbolic of knowledge where this consistency is founded (this is philosophy); (3) since both terms are confused in the neurotic imaginary of the ideal, an additional symbolic is needed—the symptom, which is ethical exigency (on a general level, this is psychoanalysis); and (4) finally, the real of the creative act, of transgression (ethics then encounters art). This quaternary movement is found at every level of analysis.

Let us begin by showing that the Good is intelligible and can be stated objectively, that there is an *ethical discourse*. Stating the Good in the universal, ethical discourse establishes it as justice and, against any risk of imposture, establishes it as truth. But if justice and truth are obviously in harmony for metaphysical thought, with the thought of existence it appears that justice as the consistency of the world is contradicted by truth, which is outside the world and outside discourse. The Good is then no longer in discourse or in the act that conforms to it, rather the Good is in the pure act, against discourse. But this antinomy can be resolved with the thought of the unconscious. Psychoanalysis, posing the partial truth, outside of the world, of the unconscious, is discourse that acts in the social world. And philosophy recaptures this truth in the framework of a total truth that acts in history. The Good, then, is intelligible and statable in its objectivity. In the movement to determine ethical discourse, let us now look at how it relates to fundamental practices (politics, religion, therapeutics, history) that aim at the Good in accordance with the constituent discourses of the social world.

The antinomy of ethical discourse relates the Good, on the one hand, to politics and to the discourse that Lacan calls the master's discourse (metaphysical or dogmatic discourse) because a Good that can be articulated in discourse is necessary, and, on the other hand, to religion and to the discourse that Lacan calls the hysteric's discourse (empiricist or sceptical discourse), because conformation to a norm of discourse and reason cannot lead to a Good, an antinomy that to be articulated supposes the *justice* antinomy resolved. Must one conform to a model that already exists, or must one introduce one's own model? On the political level, where the objective universal is presupposed and aimed for, this contradiction is effaced. It is asserted and resolved on the religious plane: to the impassable violence of social existence is opposed the just law that can only come from God. But, when it is abstracted from the rational determination of discourse, is the Good not threatened with imposture?

Ethics relates first of all to *politics*, inasmuch as it posits the Good in discourse, thus establishing an ideal after which one's actions are to be modeled. It is on this plane that metaphysical thought, which determines Being [*être*] from the world and its finalism, is confined. For metaphysical thought, ethics consists in allowing the timeless essence present in everyone to emerge. In the perspective of such an idealization, it is impossible to desire evil. According to the Socratic formula, "Nobody desires what is evil." [5] In fact, transgression is only an error and cannot be properly understood.

For Aristotle, ethics is essentially tied to politics; it is Πολιτική τις [*politiké bis*], as he writes in Book One of the *Nicomachean Ethics*. Ethics aims at the acquisition of virtue, that is to say, the predisposition to act in conformity with the Good determined in discourse. Perversion, evident in behaviors and vice as evil disposition, is not insurmountable. Perversion results either from a monstrous act, which is always possible but exterior to ethics, or from bad education. Through good education, virtue is acquired by means of associating pleasure and pain with good and bad actions, and by means of imitating good men who are the city's legislators.

For Descartes, by contrast, ethics excludes politics. Through wonder, the "first of all passions," [6] one risks settling for necessarily imperfect human models. Only God is the model. What is worthy of admiration in man is that which "renders him in a certain way like God by making him master of himself," "the exercise of his free will and the control he has over his volitions": [7] this is the generosity by which he esteems nothing but the good use of this freedom. Yet the virtuous humility accompanying it knows that, just as the passions are all by nature good and everything depends on what use is made of them; no human behavior is in itself worthy of being imitated.

Kant restores a political perspective to ethics. Morality does not reside in any material pretext of action [*matière de l'action*]. Every model to which it would conform would come under the phenomenal and the pathological. Only a will that envisages the pure form of the law, when it acts, is free. Respect rather than wonder is the primordial ethical sentiment: no longer grandeur in the other, no longer anything that renders him like God, but the same exigency that one finds in oneself and that unfolds from the presence of the moral law. Yet, because action must nevertheless give itself a material pretext [*se donner une matière*], from the pure formalism of duty results the pursuit of "a kingdom of ends," an ideal world the realization of which receives no objective guarantee.

Finally, for Hegel, who concludes the ethical movement of metaphysical thought, politics is the essence of ethics. Man is first of all a member of a community. The spirit of the people is primordial morality. There are then models and virtue such as Aristotle had conceptualized. If subjective moral exigency can appear, it is because of the degree of historical development of this ethical substantiality. Particularity would not, without immorality, be able to rise up against it and its institutions in the name of formalism. It is justified in its affirmation of an ideal beyond the spirit of the people only insofar as it contributes to bringing about a new historical age. The moral being is eminently the great historic figure.

But we must go beyond the relation between ethics and politics to the relation between ethics and *religion*. This is the level disclosed by the thought of existence in emphasizing the violence of discourse, for example, in the theme of ideology. Against the idealization that denied existence and the nonmeaning it implies, as well as against refuge in the idea that meaning has always already existed there, ethics consists in confronting this nonmeaning and firmly establishing it by producing a new meaning, according to an act that one can with psychoanalysis call "sublimation." The affirmation-to-the-end of the ethical Good leads, by dint of the finitude of human sublimation, to the act of faith that places infinite sublimation in God. Transgression now is no longer error, but sin. Will to evil. Movement to content oneself with man's dreamed-of mastery. Implacable perversion.

In his theory of the spheres of existence, Kierkegaard shows that ethics leads to religion. Ethics is distinguished from aesthetics that, through conformation to models or complacency in particularity, dissimulates the contradiction of existence, synthesis of subject and object, of freedom and necessity. Ethics is suffering in contradiction, passionate desire to efface the contradiction effectively and to realize the ideal—that cannot, if there is an impassable truth of existence, but lead to failure, despair, and absolute evil. The Good is produced by a "teleological suspension of the ethical," in the religious,[8] the acceptance of existence in its contradiction, the will even to repetition, because beyond reason, *quia absurdum,* that which can give it meaning is recognized and loved, an act of faith that supposes that God has revealed himself.

For Nietzsche, on the contrary, the essential ethics, which is indeed the acceptance of existence and the will to repetition, excludes every religious concept. For the will to repetition, not some act that is supposed to be in God, gives it meaning. To the morality of the masters that affirms life in all its aspects, according to the *Stimmung* of the eternal recurrence,[9] is opposed the illusory morality of the slaves that negates the morality of the masters and supposes ideal authorities that could be blamed for suffering. Religion is that which gives reality, initially, social, to this negating idealization where the nonmeaning of life is effaced. That which leads to the affirmation of life is art: ideal, divine figures are doubtless produced there, but never presupposed, and always in the end drawn into the very movement of life.

Heidegger once again gives ethics a religious perspective. Existence is not simply duality of subject and object, the duality that maintains the fundamental categories of metaphysics, but ex-position to the truth of Being [*être*] beyond being [*étant*], relation with the absolute Other, which happens in language. Ethics consists of appropriating this original relation of "appropriating disappropriation," produced in the poem as the essence of the work of art. But art comes back to the religious: on the one hand, appropriation comes up against its necessary limit, against the disappropriation that releases the figure of the Other in its irreducibility; on the other hand, in order to appear, the work of art presupposes the opening of Being, the space of the sacred, where it can be received by a people.

For Levinas, with whom the ethical movement of the thought of existence reaches its conclusion, religion is the essence of ethics. For ethics cannot reside in the trial of disappropriation that Being inflicts and of the violence of the sacred, but in the assumption of violence to which the other is submitted, in substitution for the other and in the renunciation of Being. What is original is not the relation with the neutral Other of Being, but the ethical relation with the Other who commands me not to kill and to enter into spiritual communion with him, beyond Being—and the face of the other is in the trace of this Other. Dissimulated in sacrificial religions, liberated in revealed religions where the divine appears in its sanctity, this relation that is the essence of ethics is also the very essence of religion.

Psychoanalysis, and its hypothesis of the unconscious, makes it possible to resolve the antinomy that relates ethical discourse to politics because the Good must be articulated in discourse, and to religion, because the Good resides in the act beyond the human order of discourse. Ethical discourse is thus related, on the one hand, to the therapeutic because it must be a discourse that acts; this is what psychoanalytic discourse brings about in the social world by making the individual experience as Good that which it articulates. Ethical discourse is related, on the other hand, to history because psychoanalysis cannot articulate an absolute Good in its objectivity nor establish it for everyone and forever. Only philosophical discourse linked to what Lacan calls "the discourse of the university" can do that, and that turns it into an act, not in the social world, but rather for instituting a new social world in history. The solution to the antinomy of ethical discourse supposes the antinomy of *truth* resolved. Can that which presents itself as total truth appear as truth to the individual, answer his questions, and allay his doubt? Yet, must the absolute Good not be total truth? Effaced on the therapeutic level where efficacy allays the question, the truth is proclaimed and resolved in history, inasmuch as the confusion between partial truth and total truth that characterizes traditional societies founded on sacrifice is called into question.

Ethics is related to the therapeutic in that the Good must be able to become effective and efface the individual's suffering. This was Aristotle's aim in identifying the Good with happiness, and this is what happens in psychoanalysis, what opens the space of the cure. Ethical space for a work of sublimation. But merely partial sublimation. Acting in the social world, psychoanalysis must content itself with the partial truth of unconscious desire, which at this level appears as sexual desire. No longer error or sin, transgression is now nothing but suffering.

For Freud, ethics is essentially linked to the therapeutic. First, he introduces the hypothesis of the unconscious to treat neuroses, independently of ethics. The cure aims to achieve the highest degree of happiness possible, the most harmonious relationship between the sexual drives, under the control of the pleasure principle, and the ego drive, attached to the reality principle—a mere extension of the pleasure principle. When he then proposes a new duality of drives—the life drive and death drive—it becomes impossible to suppress the suffering of being [*mal d'être*], the relation with the constituent authority agency,[10] the superego, which establishes true ethics. In the instant of ethical choice, the victory of the life drive remains nevertheless that which happiness and harmony aim toward.

With Lacan, on the contrary, ethics at first excludes the therapeutic. For him, the unconscious is the absolute Other of language and knowledge, pure play of the signifier identified with the symbolic, place of a merely partial ontological truth, that like Heidegger's Being, assigns to us our destiny as desiring beings. Passing through the imaginary plenitude of the mother-child relationship, the law of language, which incarnates the father figure, becomes in effect an Oedipal prohibition. Against the imaginary and the therapeutic aim, it is a question in the cure of taking up again the confrontation with this symbolic of desire and the death drive.

Later, Lacan returns to the therapeutic perspective of ethics. To enter into the actual work of ethics is to direct oneself to the forbidden absolute mythical object where one places the Sovereign Good, the absolute significance that Lacan calls *das Ding*.[11] Not the plenitude of the Thing, but its incompleteness is encountered thereafter. Not a separation [*faille*], nevertheless, that it receives from the other, but that it itself opens by posing the Other of the law. This Thing, and not the Other, is the proper and radical truth of the unconscious, beyond existence. If suffering does not come from the Other, the confrontation with desire in ethics no longer occurs against the illusory of the imaginary, but by another imaginary than that of neurosis, by the positive imaginary of sublimation, by an effective plenitude (happiness, therapeutics) that permits only the fixation of the absolute object's lack.

At the level of psychoanalysis, therapeutics is, in the end, the essence of ethics. Psychoanalytic discourse acts in the social world only because it states a mere partial truth and, beyond the evident finitude of human sublimation, appeals only to an equally partial sublimation—for psychoanalytic discourse, there is no Sovereign Good. But it is, in itself and in the analyst who incarnates it, sublimation in action, proof of pure *jouissance*, "constitutive of the speaking being," and the very essence of the unconscious, which it is a question of disengaging from sexual pleasure in the cure. And it is through this *jouissance* and this happiness that in the transference the ethical space of the cure is opened for the patient.

Ethics in its truth is related finally to *history*, because the Good must impose itself on all objectively, beyond therapeutic efficacy that would not know how to respond to the absolute of the question. This is what philosophy accomplishes by acting in history. Philosophy does not open the space of ethical work, but establishes the Good through analyses that will later be taken up in the whole of the social field, beyond the antagonisms of discourse. The total sublimation that it requires does not contradict the finitude of sublimation, but finally allows it to be properly conceived as transgression.

Ethics, at first, appears to be essentially linked to history. The traditional world, which is given as harmonious totality, is, in fact, founded on the relation of fascination, which reproduces the illusory complementation of fantasm, and that the violence of sacrifice determines. Psychoanalysis calls it into question because it is discourse that posits the partial truth of desire, irreducible nonmeaning, or, to use Lacan's term, the *real*. But it can only open onto a new social world and be the essence of every historical rupture through meaning, through its own absolute consistency of discourse, through this total truth that Lacan himself, bringing together absolute, philosophical, or religious, thought, presented in his ultimate theory of the Borromean knot. That is, through absolutely pure ethical law.

But it then seems that ethics must exclude history. Psychoanalysis is indeed ethical discourse in the full meaning of the word, through the total truth that it contains; but to act in the social world, it must silence it, not present it as such, set aside every historical dimension. It is philosophy as absolute thought articulated in the discourse of the university that can, through its relation with psychoanalysis as that which problematizes the social field and incarnates the question, tell the total truth of the pure signifier. It justifies the historical world and conveys the rupture with psychoanalysis. Yet because of its knowledge and affirmation of total truth, philosophy would not be able to act.

Philosophy, however, once again gives ethics an historical perspective. Beyond the power of psychoanalysis, alone effective, but which has relinquished any political perspective, the discourses that enter into battle in history are the master's discourse and the clerical discourse, or the discourse of the university, that wins in the end. As *ideology*, an attempt to exercise in a totalitarian way its power that is only formal, the university discourse leads to the extremes of social violence. As *philosophy*, which is the critique of ideology in its lure of human omnipotence, and declaration of impotence, recognition, at the extreme point of knowledge, of the power of the sacred—and philosophy here finally finds ethics and its partial truth—it calls into question on the social level the relation of fascination and accomplishes the historical act.

We can finally conclude this questioning of the general possibility of ethics by asserting that history is the essence of ethics. For if the essence of religion is the relation between the sacred and the saint, in God himself and repeated from man to God, it is "naturally" dissimulated by its form, a specifically sacrificial confusion between, on the one hand, the sacred, which is total sublimation that undoes itself and results in the mere partial sublimation of social existence (it is the act of creation that posits finitude and the universe of transgression—*univers de la faute*),[12] and, on the other hand, the saint, who is totally pure sublimation to which even human beings are called beyond partial sublimation, whence the necessity—so religious law is not the violent law of sacrifice, but the pure law of ethics—of a *revelation*. First, of the good law, in Judaism—but the traditional religion of a people, the Jewish religion, despite the ethical perfection of its law, does not free the space for the autonomy of the ethical act. Then, of the character for man who is always sacrificial of his religious relation to the law, in Christianity—through politics and history, the Christian religion establishes the secular world where the truly ethical act is possible.

Let us now look at how the Good can be realized, how the *ethical act* is performed. Aiming at the realization of the Good, it is will; breaking with the hold of the relation to fascination and of the fantasm, it is freedom. If for metaphysical thought, the idea of free will presents no difficulty, for the thought of existence, the will that strives for the totally consistent world of the ideal is the refusal of existence and thus nonfreedom, passion. If there is to be an act, it can be carried out only through the trial of passion and of finitude, the passage beyond the illusion of an absolutely free act. But must not an ethical act be precisely an absolutely free act? With the thought of the unconscious and psychoanalysis, this antinomy can be resolved. For if in the cure the act starts out on the side of the patient with anxiety and the trial of finite freedom, it is brought to a close as an ethical act in the position of the analyst who assumes, in absolute freedom, this passion is sustained in the other. Beyond guilt, the ethical act is transgression, fortunate repetition of the very essence of all transgression. In the movement of the effectuation of the ethical act, we must elucidate how the ethical act traverses the fundamental passions (shame, fear, anxiety, guilt), each of which determines the relation with the other according to one of the structures of existence.

The antinomy of the ethical act is encountered when we enter into the actual work of ethics. For, on the one hand, only passion can act, from the moment that finitude is impassable—that which involves traversing the trial of shame and of sublimation in the other. But, on the other hand, it is necessary to act against passion, because posing sublimation in the other comes back to idealizing the other, and would not know how to act—which causes one to traverse the trial of fear and madness in the other. An antinomy that cannot be displayed until such time as the *will* antinomy has been resolved—is it not flight from existence? Is it not, nevertheless, constitutive of ethics? Effaced in the trial of shame, where one renounces the will in the name of an ideal, the antinomy is posed and resolved in the trial of fear, where one comes to will [*vouloir*], not an ideal, but the nonwill [*le non-vouloir*] itself, the confrontation with the present and the threat of death. Thus is the ethical act not doomed to this unacceptable contradiction of being freed only by and for death? The *tragic* moment of ethics, necessary if the exigency of total sublimation beyond partial sublimation is experienced, and for it to be insuppressible. In discourse, it is marked by *irony*.

Ethics, initially, involves traversing the trial of *shame*, for it poses the exigency of total sublimation and absolute freedom; he who is fascinated sees it realized in the other who fascinates him, whence the trial of shame. That unsurpassable finitude, impossible infinite sublimation for man, might oblige him to persevere to the very end. It is, in the cure, the founding moment of transference and the idealization of the analyst.

In its first moment, ethics rejects shame—and metaphysical thought remains at this level. Shame is the passion that holds fast in a sacrificial position the *object* offered to desire, and to the judgment of the other as subject. It inhibits and paralyzes action. The ethical act calls into question the traditional standards of the social world, and it would appear necessary to have to stand up to the shame that the other would like to inflict. But ethical individuality avoids all shame. Thanks to his virtue of *moderation* or *temperance*— "a virtuous man," says Aristotle, "never feels shame, if it is true that shame is born of base actions"[13]—and the prudence that it implies and that leads him not to go beyond the bounds of common opinion.

With existence and the unconscious, it is necessary, on the contrary, to enter into the trial of shame. What does it reveal? First of all, that of which we are ashamed. The linguistic ambiguity is significant: What we are ashamed of is both what we are and what an other is because shame is tied to identification and, specifically, to the fundamental symbolic identification with the father, constituent of the entry into social existence and partial sublimation. Shame of the father, of the sexual, and of being held in the primal scene of which one is also the refuse [*déchet*]—that of Noah for his sons. Next, that before which we are ashamed. Beyond the misleading evidence of social shame and because finitude and sexuality apply to all human beings, shame, at bottom, is not shame before the other *subject* but before the absolute *Other*, before God, first traversal of the fantasm and of the duality of object and subject toward the Other. This fixation of universal shame frees from individual shame as passion able to arise unpredictably, lifts inhibition and produces what could be called "exteriorization."

Traversing the trial of shame thus appears to be that which acts—Kierkegaard's idea, shared by other thinkers of existence. For him, the death of God on the cross is the essential event in history because it is *par excellence* that which brings shame to mankind, reminding even those, who divert it onto the victim through sacrifice, of their shame. An act by supreme Passion. The same is true in the ethic of tragedy where Antigone, for example, having assumed Polyneices' shame [*honte*] and replacing him as the sacrificial victim, shames Creon in his desire for a sacrifice. The same is true, finally, in psychoanalysis, the analyst having supposedly undergone, as patient, the relation of shame in the transference, and who incarnates on a social level sexual shame and refuse [*déchet*]. "Psychoanalysis teaches us that we are ashamed of being alive. . . . If there are in your presence reasons that are not quite ignoble, they may be just enough, I hope, for me, at times, to make you feel ashamed," said Lacan to his audience.

But with psychoanalysis, ethics in the end requires that shame be rejected. What ethical work discovers, beyond idealization in the transference, is that the absolute Other, disengaged through the trial of shame, does not exist beforehand but is produced by desire. To adhere to shame would lead in fact to *masochism*, not to the freedom necessary for a true relation with God, but to the maintenance of idealization in the relation with the other subject. Lacan echoes Kierkegaard when he says that one is held in "a never avowed knot that ties the father to transgression," to counter the danger of masochistic idealization, allow us to put forward the ethical assertion that *it is necessary not to refrain from vengeance*—which is not to set one's sights on resentment but to refuse to efface the pure negative of the shame inflicted by the other (Freud, for example, with the paternal humiliation of the hat thrown in the gutter).

Ethics next involves traversing the trial of *fear*. If one must act against passion and enter into total sublimation, one in effect comes up against the ascent of the death drive through which one is offered as sacrificial victim, whence the fear of the violence of the other, the moment, during the cure, when, refusing the seduction of the transference, the analyst leaves room for the development of the patient's desire.

At first, ethics, with metaphysical thought, rejects fear. It is passion that embraces the *subject before the other,* like a fetish-*object,* and brings about the fading of the subject. Descartes, after noting that fear is a "coldness," "a disturbance and astonishment of the soul which deprives it of the power to resist the evils which it thinks lie close at hand,"[14] stresses that fear has no usefulness. It would seem that one cannot avoid it and that one even provokes it from the moment one challenges a relation of domination. But through his virtue of *courage* and his resistance to the drive for pleasure, the ethical individual pushes aside fear; through the nobility of the aims that it implies, he guards himself against provocation.

If we affirm existence or the unconscious, it is, on the contrary, necessary to enter into the trial of fear. Of what are we afraid? Death and destruction as subject that fear anticipates. But before which other? At the outset, it is eminently before the fetish-*object* of fantasm, before the Oedipean rival, the father inasmuch as he possesses and forbids the mother, and threatens punishment. At bottom, before the maternal Thing and its effacement as absolute object, before the truth of desire—and the lure of rivalry protecting it, second traversal of the fantasm, no longer toward the Other as his beyond, but toward the Thing as his within. Heidegger opposes fear, inessential because before entities within-the-world, and anxiety, which is decisive, before being-in-the-world itself.[15] Along with the thoughts of existence, this is to remain with the obvious fact of the Other. The unconscious, making it necessary to go beyond, gives fear all of its significance. Freud as well makes something more of anxiety because it would be a reaction to an internal danger, rather than an external one. But although the Thing first appears to be exterior to the subject, it is indeed what is innermost—to discover fear a fear before the Thing makes it possible finally to disregard fear as a passion that surges forth, and in this way to feel afraid no longer. This event is called "interiorization."

Traversing the trial of fear thus appears to be an act. So it is for Nietzsche. To Kierkegaard's making-ashamed and to the negation of life, he opposes affirmation and making-afraid. If contemporary nihilism results from the fact that Christianity has made human beings feel ashamed of their instincts, it will only be overcome by those who know how to arouse fear because they themselves have traversed the trial, once again a reference to the ethic of tragedy, to the love of fate, and to the will to repetition of life as the Thing involving death. Lacan notes that at the end of the play Creon is moved by fear before Antigone and that this is what brings about his ruin. The same is true of psychoanalysis that introduces this terrifying Good that is the Thing amongst the comfort and concerns of shared social existence.

But with psychoanalysis, ethics finally requires that fear be rejected. Traversing the trial of fear is to take up the position of always having to sublimate more and thus to maintain idealization. This leads necessarily to *sadism* that desires to search for and encounter the agency of the Thing in everything. One sees this in Nietzsche's morality and in his praise of an affirmative life involving cruelty. Against sadistic idealization, the ethical assertion is that *it is necessary to resist the hatred of the beautiful*—for it is from the beautiful, and especially from woman, that man's call to greater sublimation appears to come, and it is he whom the impossibility of infinite sublimation constitutes as a cruel superego, and that, in its turn, is made to suffer.

The ethical act must be performed by passion because of impassable finitude (whence the trial of shame), but also against passion because it is absolutely free (whence the trial of fear). Unsolvable for the thought of existence, this antinomy is resolved with the unconscious and psychoanalysis. That which makes one traverse, beyond shame and fear, on the one hand, the trial of anxiety, as passion implied in the act against passion—but at this level where perversion in the other is met, the thought of the unconscious does not yet break with the thought of existence—on the other hand, the trial of guilt, as ethical passion proper implied by the act and the encounter with neurosis in the other—with psychoanalysis, it can then be assumed in an absolutely free act, a solution that presupposes the antinomy of *freedom resolved.* Can there be ethics when freedom is not essentially finite and doomed to evil? But does the ethical act not require absolute freedom? Dissimulated in anxiety, which is the trial of finite freedom appearing to come from the outside, it is posited and resolved with guilt, where finitude is assumed by freedom that considers itself absolute and that can effectively be so from the moment that what is transgression for man is, at bottom, repetition of the original creative act. A *comic* moment, if one may say so, of ethics, for even when the effort of total sublimation is successful, it must be recognized that it is inseparable from partial sublimation and the sexual. This is marked in discourse as *humor.*

Ethics involves traversing the trial of *anxiety*, as soon as starting from total sublimation is exposed the irreducible [*l'irréductible*] of partial sublimation and nonmeaning, of being gripped in fantasm and fascination, is exposed— the ultimate essence of all passion, an encounter with the sexual, for Kierkegaard the "dizziness of freedom" when, looking "down into its own possibility" it lays "hold of finiteness to support itself," or again "feminine weakness in which freedom faints."[16] The traversal of anxiety corresponds to this moment, in the cure, when the fundamental fantasm is reconstructed around the analyst, who "in a reversed hypnosis himself plays the hypnotized." The end of analysis on the side of the patient.

At first, ethics, with metaphysical thought, rejects anxiety. It is the passion endured when one is identified with the *Other* of sublimation, insofar as the opacity of the Thing remains, the trial of the limits of knowledge, apparently inevitable when accepted knowledge and the world order are put in question. Yet ethical individuality opposes this virtue that one calls *wisdom* with Plato (renewed doubt redirected to another knowledge), *magnanimity* with Aristotle, and even more precisely *generosity* with Descartes, the generous person recognizing in himself the gap between knowledge and volition, and being ready to give ethical meaning, by means of the will, there where the trial, fatal for mankind, of nonknowledge would be encountered.

With existence and the unconscious, ethics requires, on the contrary, entry into the trial of anxiety. That which causes anxiety is nonknowledge, the "real," the Thing insofar as it recedes. That which causes anxiety is, first of all, also the *Thing*—and Heidegger emphasized this identity—but it is, at bottom, the *object*, this nonsignifying remainder [*reste*] that separates from the subject in the fantasm and supports its identity over time. Anxiety is not fear that crops up in real time and stays there, calling forth invention and ostentation; it abstracts itself from all determined situations, leads [*entraîne*] into imaginary time, and the particular being that provokes it is only a pretext and is worth only what in it, like in everything, is the object and recalls the destiny of nonmeaning, no longer traversing the social fantasm, but "experiencing the fundamental fantasm," which creates the possibility of escaping from the sudden unforeseeable appearance of anxiety because it fixes the object from which no love can protect. No longer either exteriorization or interiorization, rather existence on the rift [*faille*], at the limit, one could say.

Traversing the trial of anxiety appears then to be an act. Among the thinkers of existence, this is the thesis of Heidegger. To Nietzsche's will to power, taken as an incessant revival of the confrontation with the Thing and interpreted as the will to will, he opposes the only thing that can let one access a new figure of the world, a true will [*volonté*] of not willing [*vouloir*]—effacement of subjectivity before the presence in itself of Being, trial of the finitude onto which it opens. The serenity or *Gelassenheit* that results from it characterizes the master, he who can become fetish-object for others, and thus abandons, lets himself go, because he has taken upon himself anxiety and its object. It is the image without gaze, peacefully fascinating, in the ball scene of the *The Ravishing of Lol Stein*.[17] And it is a question of an identical mastery emerging through analysis, when one has often enough encountered the limit of all sublimation, traversed anxiety, and fixed the analyst as object in the fundamental fantasm.

Yet, with psychoanalysis, ethics in the end requires the rejection of anxiety. For establishing oneself in the trial of anxiety means to desire the Other, and thus, on the one hand, to idealize once again, and, on the other hand, to presuppose the presence of the Thing posing the Other, that of the analyst for the patient. This leads to *hysteria*, where anxiety of the relation with the object and of the passage beyond social recognition is but a lure given to be seen [*donné à voir*] in the Thing to obtain recognition as the Other, the problem of all thought that, like Heidegger's, puts uppermost questioning and want of knowledge, whence its uncertain relation to politics. Against hysterical idealization, the ethical assertion is that *it is necessary to know how to wait for recognition*, that is, to endure the lack and thus enter into anxiety, but also to assume that one cannot escape the desire for recognition, beyond all anxiety.

Ethics, finally, involves traversing the trial of *guilt*. For there would be no ethics without an absolutely free act that poses partial sublimation and that holds in fascination and fantasm. If the ethical act is produced, it is, however, not through the trial of guilt, but rather inasmuch as it releases a level where transgression as entry into finitude is a completely positive act, the moment when the patient arrives at the place of the analyst's Thing and accepts being the cause of everything that is produced in the analytic relationship, of the finitude that is repeated and the anxiety that is felt.

In the first moment [*temps*], the moment where metaphysical thought holds itself, ethics rejects guilt. It is the passion of he who wishes [*vouloir*] to act in accordance with the Good and, not being able to rely on a law of the Other evident to everyone, must as *Thing* "make the law" [*faire la loi*].[18] Challenging the violent law of the relation of fascination, it would appear that ethics imposes the trial. But the ethical individual avoids it thanks to his virtue of *justice* because the law he incarnates in his particular person in all respects conforms to the pure law of the absolute Other.

With existence or the unconscious, on the contrary, it is necessary to enter into the trial of guilt. Of what is one guilty? Of one's transgressions, of the violence one inflicts, and more fundamentally of the desire that motivates one's actions. And before which other is one guilty? Not, as it at first appears, before the *Other* of the law, since it does not exist beforehand, but before the *subject*, the one who is subjected to the law and to the model of an impure desire. Guilt, not of the child before the parents who are supposed to incarnate the Other, but of the parents before the child, on whom they impose the weight of their own neurotic desire—this is the real basis of neurotic guilt. Instead of contenting oneself with pure desire and total sublimation, one has "given ground relative to one's desire," as Lacan says. What finally appears is that

beyond a particular transgression, one is caught up in the radical guilt of looking ceaselessly to "realize" the fundamental fantasm, of leading the other to
occupy the place of subject in it, to suffer from it, to be there as the sacrificial
victim (for example, *The Ravishing of Lol Stein*, commented upon by Lacan:
the scene at the edge of a rye field, the childhood friend as subject, the lover
as object of torment, the sadistic agent in fantasm, "cynical at having already
sacrificed her to the law of Lol,"[19] the one and the other dedicated "to realizing Lol's fantasm"),[20] a moment, neither of exteriorization or interiorization,
nor of existence in the fissure, but of insistence in destiny.

Traversing the trial of guilt thus appears to be what acts, among the
thinkers of existence, the position of Levinas. Against the Heideggerian ethic
of the confrontation with Being and its violence, for Levinas, we ourselves
must feel guilty for the violence suffered by the other and responsibility to the
point of substitution and renunciation of Being for his situation as victim.
Beyond the figure of the master [*maître*] appears that of the witness. "The true
knight of faith is a witness, never a master," notes Kierkegaard.[21] The witness
is he who, having renounced Being and the violent law, allows the pure law
of the Other to befall him and can respond to his persecution. Inspiration, says
Levinas. Lacan introduced the same idea under the name of the "passe."[22] For
the analyst who must occupy the place of the object, and of refuse [*déchet*], it
is indeed a question of testifying for psychoanalysis and for its law, for the
truth of knowledge in the Other.

Yet ethics with psychoanalysis is finally accomplished beyond guilt. For
to be established in guilt is always to idealize, to posit a view of infinite sublimation that, impossible for man even as a last resort, is however more like a
duty. This leads to *obsession*, a term that Levinas acknowledges and proclaims.
His "otherwise than Being" and his "obsession with the neighbour" that, aside
from all commitment and all choice, summons to an "unreserved sacrifice,"
responds to what Lacan says of the obsessional, "to be indebted not to exist."
Against obsessive idealization, and despite the truth it may have in the religious order, ethics comes back to this assertion that *it is necessary to choose
one's guilt*. An absolutely free choice, although made inevitable by guilt,
because it is brought about for the Good and rejoins the act of creation, that of
the divine Other (the Father of the Trinity) that posits the partial sublimation of
the creature, dooming it to obsession with the divine Other, Spirit [*Esprit*], total
sublimation posed as such. It reproduces original transgression that allows one
to break with the enchantment of the maternal orb and achieve a separate existence. It is act, to will transgression again, and itself transgression. Not realization, but "the enactment [*mise en acte*]" of the fantasm, no longer sacrifice
and, to protect oneself from the spiritual requirement of ethics, participation in
the religious illusion of madness in God (indifference of the Thing in a negative sense), but acceptance, for oneself and the other, of the situation of loss

[*déchet*], which is particular to all creation and all love (positive indifference). Thus when the founding act of creation is repeated, outside of any desire for rupture, the rupture that is history itself is accomplished.

—Translated by Denise Merkle

Translator's Notes

1. Dennis Porter chose to translate the polysemous *faute* by "transgression" in his translation of *The Ethics of Psychoanalysis*. His solution is particularly apt as the following argumentation clearly shows: "Lacan's word here, 'la faute,' is particularly difficult to put into English because of the great range of its potential equivalents— from wrong, error, mistake to blame, misconduct, and offense—and because the most obvious choice does not have the moral resonances of the French. 'The Attraction of the Fault' not only does not suggest anything, but even manages to sound like pidgin English. And the same is true of 'The Universe of the Fault'" (*Sé VII*, p. 1).

2. *Sé VII*, p. 319.

3. Ludwig Wittgenstein, *Tractatus Logico-Philosophicus* (London: Routledge and Kegan Paul, 1961), 6.421.

4. In his translation of this article [*Die Ethik mit der Psychoanalyse*], Hans-Dieter Gondek argues that to translate *faire acte* as "to become an act" [*zum Akt werden*] stresses the "act" and maintains a relation with the "ethical act." The use of the future construction gives the idea of transformation into the ethical act. Gondek believes is a reflection of Lacan's use of *faire acte* in his writings. Here we use the conventional translation of *faire acte* "to act, to take action."

5. *Plato: The Collected Dialogues*, edited by Edith Hamilton and Huntington Cairns (Princeton: Princeton University Press, 1961; reprint 1989), p. 361.

6. René Descartes, *The Passions of the Soul* in *The Philosophical Writings of Descartes*, vol. 1, translated by John Cottingham, Robert Stoothoff, and Dugald Murdoch (Cambridge: Cambridge University Press, 1985), p. 350.

7. Ibid., p. 384.

8. Soren Kierkegaard, *Fear and Trembling/Repetition*, edited and translated by Howard V. Hong and Edna H. Hong (Princeton: Princeton University Press, 1983).

9. Walter Kaufman uses this term in his translation of Friedrich Nietzsche's *The Will to Power* (New York: Vintage Books, 1967, p. 330). Although the concept *Retour éternel* is sometimes translated as eternal return, we have decided to retain "eternal recurrence," since this translation places the emphasis on recurring actions, or on the philosophical notion that "everything recurs."

10. In his translation of *The Four Fundamental Concepts of Psycho-Analysis*, Sheridan explains his decision to translate the French *instance* by "agency" in English,

after clearly defining the term. His arguments justify the decision to use "agency" in this translation. "Lacan's use of the term *'instance'* goes well beyond Freud's *'Instanz.'* It represents, one might say, an exploitation of the lingusitic possibilities of the French equivalent of Freud's German term. In the absence of any exact equivalent of Lacan's French term, one is thrown back to the term used by Freud's English translators, 'agency.' In Freud, the reference is most often to the three 'agencies' of the id, ego, and superego. In Lacan, one must bear in mind the idea of an 'acting upon' even 'insistence,' as in the title of the essay, 'L'instance de la lettre' (*Sé XI*, pp. 277–78).

11. Lacan expounds on the meaning he gives to the term, *das Ding*, the Thing, often left in the German, in *The Ethics of Psychoanalysis*. See especially pp. 52 and 68.

12. Allusion to the title of a book by Hesnard.

13. A more literal translation of *actions perverses*, in the cited French translation of Aristotle, would be perverse actions.

14. René Descartes, *The Passions of the Soul*, p. 392.

15. Martin Heidegger, *Being and Time*, translated by John Macquarrie and Edward Robinson (Oxford: Basil Blackwell, 1961), pp. 230–31.

16. Soren Kierkegaard, *The Concept of Anxiety*, edited and translated by Reider Thomte in collaboration with Albert B. Anderson (Princeton: Princeton University Press, 1980), p. 61.

17. Jacques Lacan, "Homage to Marguerite Duras, on *Le ravissement de Lol V. Stein*," translated by Peter Connor in Marguerite Duras, *Marguerite Duras* (San Francisco: City Lights Books, 1987), pp. 122–29. The first footnote explains that *Le ravissement de Lol V. Stein* was published in America by Grove Press (1966), under the title *The Ravishing of Lol Stein*.

18. Also means "to command."

19. Jacques Lacan, "Homage to Maguerite Duras," p. 126.

20. Ibid., p. 127.

21. Kierkegaard, *Fear and Trembling*.

22. An explanation of this term can be found in Alain Juranville, *Lacan et la Philosophie* (Paris: PUF « Philosophie d'aujourd'hui », 1984).

Chapter 7

Rethinking the Beyond of the Real

Drucilla Cornell

Introduction

It is commonplace to note that Sigmund Freud "discovered" another reality. This reality is the reality of the psychic life. The meaning of its unconscious underpinnings surfaces in the other world of dreams and in the slips of the tongue that indicate a beyond to the day-to-day life given to us by conventions of our form of life. Certainly Freud always returns us to the problematic of *Jenseits*, the other side, the beyond of the unconscious, which leaves its traces and marks on so-called "real objects," but which can never be simplistically identified with them. An obvious example of this mistake is the conflation of the penis with the phallus. Another is the identification of the unconscious fantasy object, the Phallic Mother, with actual mothers. Indeed, the ferocity of the debates between different schools of psychoanalysis can, at least in part, be attributed to the idea that unless one remains "true" to the unconscious as the beyond to "reality," there is no psychoanalysis at all, only the crude fix-it therapy that invests in the "world" of purportedly real familial objects, as if these objects should serve as the basis for analysis. Simply put, psychoanalysis begins with the differentiation of unconscious from conscious objects.

In recent times, there may have been no more fierce and persistent thinker of the analytic significance of the *Jenseits* in Freud than Jacques Lacan. It is this problematic in Freud that is frequently ignored by many analysts, precisely because it appears as poetic, mythological or, worse yet, a product of old-fashioned irrational mysticism. More specifically, Lacan's "return to Freud" involved the attempt to rethink the beyond to the pleasure principle, what Lacan himself called the real. To my mind, if there is a lasting contribution of Lacan it lies precisely in his insistence on the relationship between psychoanalysis and the problematic of the beyond, *Jenseits*, and the other side of the *Unheimlich*.[1] Furthermore, Lacan, in characteristically provocative fashion, connects this problematic not only with the real (which for him is the absolute Other to the web of significance given by the symbolic order), but also with the rethinking of the Kantian analysis of the transcendental conditions of morality and of the moral will. For Lacan, the very project of psychoanalysis should be understood as a preliminary to moral action. Thus, for him, ethics is not a side issue for analysts in the practice of their profession. Instead, psychoanalysis must be understood as moral practice in the very specific sense that I will both discuss and critique in the course of this paper. I applaud Lacan for his insistence that, for psychoanalysis, ethics is the very heart of the matter.

I want, then, to give this project of rethinking the relationship between radical alterity, what Lacan refers to as the real, the limit of the symbolic, and what I call the ethical relationship its due. Of course, the very use of the phrase "ethical relationship," which I borrow from Emmanuel Levinas, signals my central disagreement with Lacan and his concern with an explanation of how the moral law is established. In Levinas, my responsibility to the Other demands that I guard her alterity against appropriation by any system of cognition, including a system of morality when it is established as moral law. As we will see, both Lacan and Levinas argue, if for very different reasons, that the ontological elaboration of the Sovereign Good that classical ethics attempted is philosophically unjustifiable, even *unethical*. This rejection turns Lacan to his "Freudian" rereading of the inevitability of the imposition of the moral law because of the very impossibility of there being a Law of law in the sense of an actualized sovereign Good. Levinas, on the other hand, rejects any identification of the ethical relationship and the moral law, whether understood as the Ten Commandments or as the Kantian categorical imperative, two examples of the establishment of the moral law that Lacan discusses in his seminar on the ethics of psychoanalysis. For Levinas, the Good that provides the sanctity for the Other can never be reduced to a set of commandments because the Other calls me only as herself. Since her call is unique to her how to heed it cannot be known in advance nor simply through her identification with me as another moral subject. To reduce her to a set of definable categories would violate her alterity. This is a simple way of explaining why Levinas connects the respect for the alterity of the Other, and even more strongly put, the recognition of the Other, as the radical alterity that Lacan associates with the real, with the infinite responsibility imposed by the ethical relationship.[2] My responsibility is infinite because the Other is unique; therefore, I cannot know her through any in-place system of cognition in advance of my encounter with her. It is precisely because the Good is the good of the Other that it cannot be fully actualized. It is then *as The Other* that the Sovereign Good is always beyond any of our conventional systems of morality.

But it should now be becoming apparent that not only do Levinas and Lacan reach very different conclusions about the ethical significance of the unrealizability of the Sovereign Good, they do so because of different philosophical positionings concering radical alterity or what Lacan calls the real. The purpose of this essay is to return to the problematic of the *Jenseits*, through a challenge to Lacan's understanding of the real, as the real in turn establishes the moral law through its very foreclosure by the symbolic order that sloughs it off through the necessary erection of the barrier that guards the world of meaning and sense.

Lacanians frequently attest to the failure of "post–structuralists" to adequately grapple with the real.[3] I put "post–structuralism" in quotation marks because to my mind it is a code word that overwrites important philosophical disputes. Is Levinas's "Jewish humanism" adequately described as "post–structuralism"? Indeed, the damage done to even grasping what and, perhaps more aptly, who is at stake in the debate over how to heed the radical alterity of the real is itself a warning against facile stereotyping of subtle and important theoretical differences. Indeed, once we have revisited the dispute between the "post–structuralists," and the target here is primarily Jacques Derrida, the table can and should be turned on the Lacanians. It will be my contention that Derrida continuously grapples with the real as *radical alterity*. His deconstruction of metaphysics, including his engagement with the Heidegger after "the turn," has at its heart the "matter" of the real.[4] Ironically, Derrida's own deconstruction of Lacan is that Lacan does not fully apprehend the otherness of the real as "truly" beyond the symbolic.[5] We will return to that deconstruction shortly and its relationship to Levinas's philosophy of alterity. My own purpose is not simply to set the record straight on Derrida and the matter of the real. My emphasis will be on the relationship between the radical alterity of the real and the ethical relationship as opposed to Lacan's attempt to found the moral law through the other of the real.

My argument proceeds as follows: First I will summarize Lacan's understanding of the relationship between the pleasure principle and the beyond of the real. My focus will be on how Lacan's elaboration of this relationship could only make sense within his conceptualization of the radical foreclosure of the "positive" symbolization of the feminine within sexual difference. As we will see, Lacan conceptualizes the beyond of the real through the logic of castration. Accordingly, to Lacan, it is the logic of castration and the foreclosure it demands that establishes the law. In this section, we turn our attention to Lacan's discussion of the Kantian categorical imperative and the Ten Commandments as examples of how the moral law always demands a prior foreclosure, even if it is nowhere explicitly mentioned. Simply put, for Lacan, the moral law grounds itself through an always, already established foreclosure of Woman. This is my reading of the ethical significance given to the *le point de capition* by Lacan in his seminar on the ethics of psycho-analysis. Thus I will argue that the debate over how to adequately address the real, which is how I would understand the debate between Derrida and Lacan, necessarily has ethical significance, beyond the obvious implications for those of us marked as women within gender hierarchy.

As a result, the second move in my argument sets the stage for rethink-ing the relationship between the real and the limit of the symbolic conceived without the moral implications of foreclosure. I will return, then, to Derrida's deconstruction of the status of the phallus as the transcendental signifier. What is often missed in Derrida's deconstruction is how it proceeds through the deconstruction of the distinction between *Sinn/Beudeutung*, upon which Husserl relied to justify the very concept of a transcendental signifier. In psy-choanalytic terms, the result of this deconstruction is that the phallus is rede-fined as a partial object and thus returned to the chain of signification and metonymic deferral. Simply put, if the phallus cannot be maintained in the position of the transcendental signifier, its meaning can always be reinter-preted. It is only within the context of the establishment of the phallus as the transcendental signifier that we can understand how Lacan can justify con-ceptualizing the limit of the symbolic as a foreclosure necessitated by the very "nature" of the symbolic itself.

A further result of this logic is that the real can only be grasped as lack. Thus I will argue that the conclusion we can reach once we understand the sig-nificance of Derrida's deconstruction of the status given to the phallus within Lacan's logic is that Lacan fails to adequately address the alterity of the real. Lacan, in other words, ultimately roots the real in the meaning of the sym-bolic. I will argue that with this failure to adequately address the real comes the unjustifiable notion of destination, which guarantees the masculine sym-bolic against the intrusion of the feared feminine Other. It is this notion of des-tination, which keeps the feminine Thing in its place, "out there," that is the basis for Lacan's confusion of a positive conception of what is *impossible* with a quasitranscendental analysis of the significance of the limit of any pos-sible symbolic order. Lacan, in my own terminology, mistakenly conflates the "impossible" with "impossibility."

In conclusion, I will turn to how the limit understood as impossibility demands that we rethink the very notion of impossibility, as it in turn operates to always remind us of the fallibility of any moral law that seeks to establish itself as a barrier to continual challenge and change. Of course, the classic example of such a barrier is the erection of the phallus as a transcendental sig-nifier that forever blocks the symbolization and reimagining of feminine sexual difference. With the term *impossibility*, I mean to remind us of the ethical significance of the insight that the quasitranscendental conditions that establish any system as a system always imply a beyond to it. No system can turn in on itself to completely encompass its outside. Derrida has shown us again and again that the very attempt to enframe a system[6] and, therefore, define it as a system necessarily generates a supplement as it delimits itself. As we will see, the promise of fidelity to what remains other to the system informs Derrida's writing whenever he addresses Levinas's philosophy of alterity. Indeed, for Derrida, the promise of fidelity to what remains Other, what Lacan would call the real, is inseparable from the ethical relationship if the ethical is not to fall prey to sentimental figurations. But the impossibility of the full inscription of the real into any system of meaning does not yield the inevitability of the Lacanian law of destination; rather, it opens up the endless transformative possibility that attempts to eradicate injustice demands. In this sense, the end of conceptual knowledge in the strong sense is forever the beginning of hope. Justice and the promise of fidelity to the Other demand nothing less than that we never say never.

What Is Lacking in Lacan

The Real, the Pleasure Principle, and the Feminine Other

Lacan's Dialectic of Desire. In this section, I will argue that *ultimately* Lacan can only grasp the meaning of the real by ironically signifying it as the imaginary feminine Other, the repressed maternal "thing." At least in Lacan's system,[7] the real cannot be known except as what is not there, *apart* from reality. But as *a part* of the symbolic reality, the lack in the real is represented as the Thing. This is a paradox Lacan's analysis of the real sets up. My argument is that he cannot resolve it. In other words, in his own terms, he cannot give the real the difference from the imaginary and the symbolic that he himself attests marks the real as an unreachable beyond. If the real is unimaginable and unknowable, why is what is not *there* for us signified as "nothing" but lack? Lacan continuously struggles to provide a satisfactory answer to this question. He answers it by linking the pleasure principle and the resulting inevitability of sublimation to the paradoxical representation of the Thing as "Nothing," and then defines Nothing as emptiness. To quote Lacan, "This Thing, all forms of which created by man belong to the sphere of sublimation, this Thing will always be represented by emptiness, precisely because it cannot be represented by anything else—or, more exactly, because it can only be represented by something else. But in every form of sublimation, emptiness is determinative" (*Sé VII*, 155/*S VII*, 129–30).

But how can emptiness be determinative unless "the Thing that suffers" in the real is inescapably associated with the logic of castration? And what is it that causes this association if not the symbolic order that cannot give significance to the feminine as Other than the lack, the horrifying gaping hole? Lacan's theoretical apparatus is ultimately not up to answering these questions without presupposing the very act of determination that he must explain if the real is not simply to be reduced to the meaning given by the symbolic and the images of the Woman produced by the physical fantasy of Woman. His reasoning turns in on itself because it cannot explain the determination without denying the alterity of the real, which is exactly the presupposition he is attempting to justify. But to see exactly why Lacan cannot let the real truly be Other, the beyond to the symbolic order, we must review in greater depth his attempt to resolve the dilemma of how a purportedly unknowable real is only and inevitably known as "Nothing."

As is well known, Lacan distinguishes the imaginary, the symbolic, and the real. In his early seminars, which presented his searing critique of ego psychology, his focus was primarily on the relationship between the imaginary and the symbolic, and the transition between the other and the Other.[8] For Lacan, the little other is the ego itself. Through an act of identification with the other who mirrors it, the ego sees himself as the "*a*." The ego, in other words, imagines the little other as itself so as to believe that the ego is "him."

The Other in Lacan is the symbolic order. This Other marks us as the speaking beings we are fated to become. I use the word "marks" deliberately, because human beings—or more precisely "man," for women cannot be *signified* as *human* in the sense that they can both be *human*, speaking beings, and "women" at the same time—do not create the symbolic order; it stamps us. For Lacan, what exists, our entire reality, is given to us by this symbolic order. But how and why are we mandated to subject ourselves to this Other? For Lacan, the answer lies in the most basic desire "to be" at all, to become an existent. In the unique sense of temporality that Lacan gives to the human "being," we only are as we have already been spoken for. The symbolic order and only the symbolic order provides the process in which we come to be spoken for. To quote Lacan, "The fundamental relation of man to this symbolic order is very precisely what founds the symbolic order itself—the relation of non-being to being. What insists on being satisfied can only be satisfied in recognition. The end of the symbolic process is that non-being come to be, because it has spoken" (*Sé II*, 354/*S II*, 308).

To deepen our understanding of why we subject ourselves to the symbolic, we need to analyze why and how for Lacan it gives us our only chance "to be." From a psychoanalytic perspective, we would still need to know why we invest in this order. Why do we invest in ourselves as speaking beings? Why do we endure the burden of the subjection imposed upon us by the symbolic, and what exactly is the form of that subjection? How does it save us from engulfment by non-being?

According to Lacan, the answer lies in his reinterpretation of the Oedi-pal complex. He assumes that we initially invest in the Other because of a pri-mary narcissistic wound. For Lacan, the genesis of linguistic consciousness and with it the inscription into the symbolic order occurs when the infant is forced to register that the Mother is separate from himself. She is not just "there" as the guarantor for his identity. The registration of the Mother's desire and separation from her are thus inseparable, and such registration is, of course, inevitable, since mothers are also actual women. Simply put, there can be no desiring "Mommy" in the imaginary infant/Mother dyad. Therefore, it is fated to be broken up by the third, the one the mother desires. But does this third necessarily have to be the Father, or if not the actual Father, what the Father symbolizes? An answer "true" to the Oedipal complex would have to be yes. To understand why Lacan would argue that the third will inevitably be unconsciously identified as the Father, we need to explore the effects of this primary and inevitable narcissistic wound.

This primordial moment of separation from the Mother is literally life threatening because of the absolute dependence of the infant on this Other. The terror of the threat that the Mother presents in her separateness initiates the struggle to overcome dependence of the need the infant has of her. The move from need to demand, "Give me," is in part the infant's expression of resistance to the vulnerability of his need.

This resistance will be against the Mother because it is her desire that is registered as robbing the infant of his security. Of course, this kind of absolute security is a fantasy. The condition of this fantasy is that the Mother not "be" sexed. Thus, it is inevitably associated with the pre-Oedipal phase, the time before the registration of the significance of sexual difference. The fantasy of absolute security then rests on the corresponding fantasy that the Mother is whole in herself and thus a "being" unscathed by the rending of desire. This fantasy figure on whom the infant is totally dependent in its need is the Phal-lic Mother. Once the fantasized mother/child dyad is shattered, the Phallic Mother "remains" in the imaginary as all powerful and threatening in her power to both bestow and take away life.

One result of the entry of the infant into the Oedipal phase marked by the infant's awakening to the Mother's desire is terror of the fantasized other-ness of this imaginary, all-powerful Mother. The terror of and yet the longing for a return to this imaginary Other accounts for the repression of this figure into the unconscious. This terror can also potentially explain the drive to enter into the symbolic realm to seek the fulfillment of desire that can no longer be guaranteed by the fantasy of the Phallic Mother, who is only "there" for the infant. Simply put, this desire is for the one other who can always and forever guarantee the fulfillment of my desire. Registered as separate from the infant, and as therefore incomplete, she comes to be abjected for her lack, which is inseparable in the unconscious from her failure "to be" the fantasy figure who can guarantee the fulfillment of the infant's desire.

But this primordial moment of separation is not experienced only as terror and the fear of loss, it is also the gaining of an identity separate from Her. The attempt to negotiate the ambivalence of a loss that is also the gaining of identity is beautifully demonstrated in the fort/da game of Freud's grandson Ernst. The game enacts the fantasy that the child is separate but still in control of the Mother/Other.

But this negotiation in turn demands an unconscious identification with the One who is at least imagined to be able to bring the mother back because He is the site of her desire. The narcissistically wounded infant thus turns toward the imaginary Father because the imaginary Father is he whom "Mommy" desires. But what is it that singles out the Imaginary Father? What makes him so special? What is it, in other words, that Daddy has that Mommy desires, that symbolizes what "Mommy" wants? The simple answer is the penis, but Lacanians would never put it so simply. The identification with the imaginary Father is inseparable from the projection of the power to control the Mother, to literally give her a name and in that sense guarantee that she and correspondingly the infant is spoken for. This Other that keeps the Mother as "his," in the specific sense of stamping her with his name, is imagined as the guarantor of identity that is established, but only precariously, so through the loss of the fantasized Mother/child dyad. The terror is that he who is not spoken for slips through the cracks of social life into figurative nonexistence. With the crumbling of the fantasy that the Mother is phallic, with recognition of separateness, comes the desire to turn to the third to guarantee the infant's identity since he can no longer count on the Mother to secure his being through unity with her.

Thus, it is the name of the Father and the symbolic register of his potency that is the basis for the identification with him and not the simple "fact" that he has the penis. The biological penis takes on the significance it does only through its identification with the Other that secures identity through the power to control the Mother/Other. This power cannot be separated from the symbolic register established by patrilineal lineage, which identifies the Father as the one who names and thus can secure identity, and, in this sense, the "being" of the infant. It is the symbolic power that is read back into the penis. But read back into the penis, it will be given the establishment of a symbolic register that is based on patrilineal lineage and thus, gives to the father and only the father the power to name. On this account, it is the symbol of the phallus and its reinforcement by the law of patrilineal lineage that accounts for the meaning given to the penis and the corresponding significance given to the initial "sighting" of sexual difference. Sexual difference, or more precisely, the registration of feminine sexual difference as lack, would then be the result of a prior *citation* in the unconscious. It would be this prior citation that would explain why it is *the lack in the mother* that has structural consequence for the castration complex (*FS*, 83).

This lack-in-having is both a threat and a nostalgia because it is the only way in which the primordial loss of the Phallic Mother can be signified. Thus the phallus stands in as a bar to the return to the phallic Mother. But as the representation of what is not there, the lack in both "sexes," the phallus can only play its role as veiled (*FS*, 82).

On this interpretation of how the phallus comes to be "cited" as the signifier of lack in both "sexes"—an interpretation consistent with Lacan's own understanding of why the phallus can only play its role as veiled—there would be no necessary basis for the identification of the phallus with the penis aside from the automatic reading of an already registered citation, and therefore, there would no reason for the phallus to be appropriated to the side of the masculine.[9] In other words, there would be no biological or even representational basis for the identification of the penis with the phallus. It would just be a matter of a reading, even if that reading would be so automatic that it would appear as inevitable. But Lacan certainly struggles to try to draw a more direct connection between the penis and the phallus in his attempt to explain why the phallus cannot be totally separated from its representation by the penis (*FS*, 82).

But even if one rejects the attempt to find a representational explanation for the inextricable association of the phallus with the penis, the unconscious identification of potency with the Imaginary Father will yield an automatic reading of the "sighting" of sexual difference. Thus, even if the phallus represents the lack that triggers desire in both "sexes," the two "sexes" will be differentially positioned before this bar, precisely because of the identification of the penis with the phallus.

The significance of this differential positioning engenders each one of us as "man" or "woman." Recall Lacan's famous example of how the symbolic will inevitability generate the differentiation between the men's and the women's room. The consequences of this engendering of "man" is that it provides a fantasy of masculinity that can compensate for the primordial loss of the Phallic Mother and the resulting inevitability of symbolic castration. In fantasy, the condition of phallic deprivation gives rise to the necessity for phallic restoration. This fantasy arises in the psychic life of both "sexes." The one with the penis, however, can engage in a projective identification with the Imaginary Father who has the power to bring the Mother back by satisfying her desire. But this identification strategy is an impossibility for the little girl because she does not have the penis. Its lack is identified as a secondary disempowerment that leans on the primary narcissistic one. Deprived of the penis, the little girl is also deprived of the fantasy that she has the "phallus."

She is left only with the masquerade of "being" it, which is not "to be" at all. The cut from the feminine imaginary imposed by the Name of the Father and the masculine symbolic renders Woman beyond expression. As we have already discussed, what cannot be expressed for Lacan does not exist. Hence, for Lacan, Woman does not exist. Ultimately, Woman as the castrated Other "is" only as the symptom of "man," the inevitable return of the truth that he is inevitably marked as the "lack-in-having." "Man" endures this symbolic castration "to be" at all in sense of having his identity as a speaking being secured by the Name of the Father against the ever-threatening, if Imaginary, Other. Ironically, woman is denied this very guarantee that secures "man." What then would be her investment in this symbolic? Needless to say, we will return to this question.

But then it is to Woman that Lacan is always returning as he would have to, since there is no way to escape her as his symptom at least as long as he is a "man." Indeed, Lacan seemed to be fated to revisit the question of why we must always return to Woman. Is it because Woman is the repressed imaginary figure that will forever be "out there" as the unknowable object of desire, precisely because of the inevitability of her repression if "man" is to exist and secure his existence through entry into the symbolic order? Or is the return to Woman a signal of a more fundamental lack, a "hole" in reality itself that is represented by Woman through the process of substitution? For me, at least, if there is "a turn" in Lacan it involves the shift in emphasis from the repressed imaginary Woman to Woman as the signifier of the cut—often indicated for Lacan by metaphors of the vulva[10]—of what is missing in the reality given to us by the symbolic.

Significance of das Ding *in Lacan's Reading of Freud.* From the beginning, Lacan's answers to the previously discussed questions revolved around his reading and rereading of Freud's own writing on *das Ding* and the functioning of the pleasure principle. This rereading can only be understood against "the dialectic of desire" Lacan staged and, more specifically, against the transcendental position Lacan attributes to the phallus as "the privileged signifier of that mark in which the part of the logos is joined with the advent of desire" (*FS*, 82). Against this background, we can now return to the paradox of why the unknowable real is represented for Lacan as the cut that marks what is missing, the Woman's "sex." We can also understand why the real must always remain beyond, given our subjection to the pleasure principle, and yet this real will operate to forever reestablish the moral law.

According to Lacan, "the true pleasure principle as it functions in Freud is the dominance of the signifier" (*Sé VII*, 161/*S VII*, 134). We have already seen that what marks us as human is the symbolic order. This symbolic order that defines us as human in the sense of speaking beings is what separates animals from "man" in Lacan. Consciousness must come to terms with the out-side world to meet the most basic needs. Consciousness and the drive to sym-bolization are, under Lacan's view, inseparable and uniquely "human" (*Sé VII*, 58/*S VII*, 45).

The "I" begins by splitting itself off from what is other. This splitting results from the intensity of need and the resistance of the outside world. But it also takes the form in "man" of giving birth to the world of experience through the words to make it "his." The splitting combined with the resistance and the effort to control the otherness of things also renders the outside strange, *Fremde*, or even hostile. To quote Lacan,

> The whole progress of the subject is then oriented around the *Ding* as *Fremde*, strange and even hostile on occasion, or in any case the first outside. It is clearly a probing form of progress that seeks points of ref-erence, but with relation to what?—with the world of desires. It demon-strates that something is there after all, and that to a certain extent it may be useful. Yet useful for what?—for nothing other than to serve as points of reference in relation to the world of wishes and expectations; it is turned toward that which helps on certain occasions to reach *das Ding*. That object will be there when in the end all conditions have been fulfilled—it is, of course, clear that what is supposed to be found can-not be found again. It is in its nature that the object as such is lost. It will never be found again. Something is there while one waits for something better, or worse, but which one wants. (*Sé VII*, 65/*S VII*, 52).

The need to control the outside cannot be separated from the attempt to see to it that the object returns to us as that which will always be *there*. That something which is there prior to and yet demanding our engagement with it is what drives us into the world of signification. Significance gives us the world of our reality, but since that reality is marked by our intervention, it can-not give us "the thing in itself." Lacan here is just repeating the Kantian insight that knowledge both gives us our world of experience and keeps us from reaching beyond it to what is just "there." The thing is lost as soon as we give it significance. But what is added is the psychoanalytic insight into what motivates us to keep up the search for the lost object and the inevitability of our continuing it. Again, to quote Lacan, "The world of our experience, the Freudian world, assumes that it is this object, *das Ding*, as the absolute Other of the subject, that one is supposed to find again. It is to be found at the most as something missed. One doesn't find it, but only its pleasurable associa-tions. It is in this state of wishing for it and waiting for it that, in the name of the pleasure principle, the optimum tension will be sought; below that there is neither perception nor effort" (*Sé VII*, 65/*S VII*, 52).

The desire to control, to find the object again, is connected not only to the desire to recover the original lost object but to stabilize reality to guarantee satisfaction. It is the pleasure principle that sets up the conditions of the search not in the least through this effort at stabilization. The very effort to develop a consistent relationship between the *Vorstellung* and that which makes us proceed from *Vorstellung* to *Vorstellung* on Lacan's reading of Freud is sustained by this drive to stabilization.

Since the drive for consistency stems from the pleasure principle what is sought is not an actual object that corresponds to the representation but a world that allows the subject to minimize displeasure. Truth, in the sense of correspondence, is besides the point. This explanation of the motivation to represent at all explains an everyday experience we have all had of the futility of trying to convince someone to change their viewpoint with "evidence" that purportedly flies in the face of their organization of their world. Instead of change, such an attempt leads to a defensive reaction and to an even deeper commitment to the world as the subject represents it. Any good lawyer knows that she has to "outpsyche" the other side, the jury, and the judge to present the evidence consistent with their respective worldviews. Any experienced feminist lawyer knows just how difficult it is to present evidence that challenges a world that has been invested in as "true" to reality.

The psychoanalytic explanation of the hold that a correspondence theory of truth has had on "men" returns us to the pleasure principle and the drive to stabilization. We seek correspondence because we desire stabilization. However, we establish correspondence in our minds not through actually finding an object that matches our representation, instead, the illusion of correspondence is created by the way in which our psychic systems of organization present us with "reality." A classic Lacanian example is how the psychical fantasy of Woman, which splits actual women into two kinds, asexual, good Mothers and evil, manipulative whores, presents men with a reality in which all women seem to correspond to one of the two types. The correspondence is a function of the fantasy, not of the "reality" that appears to correspond to it.

Put more strongly, a lack of correspondence is inevitable, since the ultimate object, *das Ding*, is an unconscious object. We find "it" only in its substitutions and through its displacements. For Lacan, topographical representations of "it" are the result of signifying chains produced either by metaphor or metonymy.[11] To confuse its substitutions and displacements and the signifying relations around it with actual objects is the mistake of Anglo-American objects relations theory. Lacan always insists on the beyond of *das Ding* that in turn cannot not be separated from the "stranger within" of the unconscious: "Simply by writing it on the board and putting *das Ding* at the center, with the subjective world of the unconscious organized in a series of signifying relations around it, you can see the difficulty of topographical representation. The reason is that *das Ding* is at the center only in the sense that it is excluded. That is to say, in reality *das Ding* has to be posited as exterior, as the prehistoric Other that it is impossible to forget—the Other whose primacy of position Freud affirms in the form of something *entfremdet*, something strange to me, although it is at the heart of me, something that on the level of the unconscious only a representation can represent" (*Sé VII*, 87/*S VII*, 71).

For Lacan, this understanding of the relationship between so-called knowledge and the world of perception is Freud's addition to Kant's transcendental analysis of the conditions of experience. Lacan's explanation of not only why but how through the functioning of the pleasure principle we are cut off from *das Ding* accounts for why it is so difficult for rational men "to see" the world in the same way. There is a hallucinatory element in the very condition of representation, since it fills in what is absent. This hallucinatory dimension is inseparable from what is represented in the form of a representation.

It is the connection drawn between Kant and Freud that provides Lacan with his unique understanding of the beyond of the real and the Thing that suffers in it. But we can only understand the relationship between the real as the ground of law and the foreclosure of Woman if we return to Lacan's dialectic of desire, resting as it does on the abjection of the phallic Mother and the resulting turn toward the One who in fantasy has the phallus. Even if we agree with Lacan, and I do, that *das Ding* is "on the level of the unconscious something only a representation can represent," (*Sé VII*, 87/*S VII*, 71) why would that representation mimic the characteristics of the creature stamped by the masculine symbolic as the castrated Other? Why, in other words, in all our sublimations, would lack or emptiness be determinative?

The Law of the Hole. To begin our discussion, we should remember that the Thing in Lacan is not simply identical with the real. The Thing is that which "suffers in the real from the signifier," (*Sé VII*, 142/*S VII*, 118) suffers in the sense that "it" is fated to be subjected to representations that cannot be faithful to it. The use of the word "suffers" clearly has ethical overtones, and not surprisingly, since for Lacan there is an inevitable connection between his emphasis on the Thing as an unconscious object and his insistence that psychoanalysis is inevitably an ethical practice. It is the "nature" of the Thing to be posited as exterior and precisely because of this positing to suffer as the ground upon which "man" must stand in order to be "man."

It is only through the trauma of the suffering of the Thing that we run up against the real. The real, in other words, has operational force precisely because of the trauma that "is," the Thing. Put in terms that reinforce the circularity of Lacan's argument, the Thing is the trauma mandated by the impossibility of inscription faithful to the Thing. Through this failure of symbolization, the lack of correspondence, we are brought up against the barrier of the real. How do we know the real is there? We only know the real through the barrier that enforces a return. We are always forced by the real to go back to the trauma that is the Thing we cannot escape. If the real is at all, it is only there for us as trauma—a trauma inseparable from our enforced entry into the symbolic. It is only if we grasp the real *as trauma* that we can understand how it is that the real enforces a return so "it" is always found again. This return that is enforced through the trauma of the Thing explains why Lacan can argue that "[t]he real, I have told you, is that which is always in the same place" (*Sé VII*, 85/*S VII*, 70). Only if we connect the Thing with the trauma of lack introduced by the symbolic can we understand Lacan's statement that there is nothing lacking in the real. More forcefully put, there can be nothing lacking in the real because the real for Lacan is what remains beyond the scar left by inscription into the symbolic. As Lacan explicitly argues, "the fashioning of the signifier and the introduction of a gap or a hole in the real is identical" (*Sé VII*, 147/*S VII*, 121). To differentiate, to cut, is the very process by which some-thing is there, because something exists only as it is given significance. What is not cut is by definition fullness in itself. But then it is not there for us. With "men" comes the inevitably of cutting through the real with the signifier.

The Thing in itself results from the cut that necessarily posits it as the beyond to knowledge and yet what spurs us to have knowledge at all. But it is also to the Thing to which our desire for return attaches precisely because the way in which the pleasure principle functions so as to foreclose the very Thing we seek. Thus, the drive to know is inseparable from the drive to cut, which is in turn inseparable from our enforced entry into the symbolic—a symbolic that grounds itself only through the cut form the other, the Phallic Mother.

On this analysis the unconscious connection between Woman and the Thing is the result of an unconscious identification. If the Thing is what is cut out by man's knowledge of it and if Woman must be cut out from the symbolic for there to be knowledge at all, then through unconscious identification Woman comes to be imagined as the representation of the cut that can function to represent the Thing, which by definition can only be known through its substitutions. For Lacan, this explains why Woman can be placed in the position of an original domain of creation, *ex nihilo*. For one unfamiliar with how the masculine symbolic functions as a bar to the symbolization of the reproductive power of the feminine "sex," this association would not be a surprise given that it was a while in human history before the male role in reproduction was given its "due." Women could thus continue to be unconsciously identified as those who give birth out of "no where." But to imagine Woman in this way is still to imagine her and signify her power and that it is precisely what cannot be done if the phallus comes to be identified as the sole symbol of reproductive power. It is only because Woman through substitution stands in for the Thing that Lacan can explain to his own satisfaction "the incredible idea" that man places in "this beyond a creature such as woman" (*Sé VII*, 253/*S VII*, 214). Lacan is aware that the very phrase "incredible idea" might seem to be a judgment based on the attribution to her of "positive" if not affirmative characteristics. Thus, Lacan continues, "Rest assured that I am in no way passing a derogatory judgment on such beings. In our cultural context, one isn't exposed to any danger by being situated as absolute object in the beyond of the pleasure principle. Let them go back to their own problems, which are homogenous with our own, that is to say, just as difficult. That's not the issue. . . . If the incredible idea of situating woman in the place of being managed to surface, that has nothing to do with her as a woman, but as an object of desire" (*Sé VII*, 253–54/*S VII*, 214).

More precisely, there is *nothing* in actual women to desire. Indeed, the exact opposite is the case. If I may be allowed an aside here, as one who is not reassured about the lack of danger in the identification of oneself as an "object of desire beyond the pleasure principle"—which may explain "why getting back to our problems" involves getting out of that position—Lacan himself offers us the best possible explanation for why that position carries within it a serious danger. Lacan continuously reminds us that courtly love poetry is the classic example of men confusing their object of desire with an actual woman and therefore designating it as a woman with an actual name. A more insightful poet knows just how terrifying it is to face a Woman in the only form she may take as a signifier. Again, to quote Lacan, "By the way this is what explains the extraordinary series of ten line stanzas by the poet Arnaud Daniel that I read to you. One finds there the response of the shepherdess to her shepherd, for the woman responds for once from her place, and instead of playing along, at the extreme point of his invocation to the signifier, she warns the poet of the form she may take as signifier. I am, she tells him, nothing more than the emptiness to be found in my own internal cesspit, not to say anything worse. Just blow in that for a while and see if your sublimation holds up" (*Sé VII*, 254/*S VII*, 215).

What terrible action cannot be justified if it is only directed toward an "internal cesspool"? But putting my own incredulity toward Lacan's "reassurance" to those of us destined to take the form of "internal cesspools" aside, it should be noted that Lacan does not seem to be able to stop himself from filling in the emptiness with a "positive" description of Woman. Needless to say, an "internal cesspool" is hardly empty. It would be more consistent with Lacan's own "logic" to refuse the description of Woman as refuse. If woman stands in only as the substitute for the cut, the trauma which "is" the Thing, then her non-being cannot be described as Other than non-being. In other words, Woman cannot be described at all, not even as the refuse of the "internal cesspool." Lacan seems unable to avoid the temptation to contradict himself.

We would at least have to ask why he cannot avoid that temptation. Is the temptation separable from his logic? And perhaps more important, in spite of Lacan's specific assertions to the contrary, is the attribution to women of "positive characteristics" separable from her historical and fleshy reality, at least as "man" imagines it? To even begin to answer these questions we need to return to the question of whether the so-called real can ever be separated from the masculine imaginary and its embodiment in a masculine symbolic, particularly since Lacanians insist that it is the status they give to the real that separates them from the post–structuralists.

The Unconscious Identification between Woman and the Thing. At least on its surface, Lacan's analysis of the Imaginary Phallic Mother and Her abjection could explain why it is that women as the substitutes for this unconscious and abjected object are identified as "internal cesspools." What is always already abjected is, indeed, identified in the conscious mind as "yucky," and this "yuckiness" would have nothing to do with actual women but with male fantasy. But if the real is already emptiness "prior to" to the abjection of the imaginary Woman, why and how can this be the case? "Because the real just is that way" cannot be the answer since, as we have seen, it is the symbolic through the trauma of the Thing that marks the real as a lack.

If it is not the abjection of the Imaginary mother, what then explains "man's" drive to imagine the real and the Thing as lack, and to mark both with the form of Woman as emptiness? Lacan's insistence that it is not as women, even as fantasized objects of the flesh, that gives them the form of the signifier of emptiness would at first glance seem consistent with the so-called "turn" in Lacan from an emphasis on the Imaginary to an emphasis on the real. It is the Thing as trauma that returns us to the hole, the lack, that can never be filled in, that is the real. It is on this analysis the horror of the lack in the real that *causes* the abhorrence of Woman, and not vice versa, our projection of our terror of women on to the real. For me, this reversal is inseparable from "the turn" of the later Lacan. But is this reversal truly a reversal?

Before attempting an answer to that question we need to at least spell out the logic for the "later" Lacan of how Woman comes to take the form of the signifier of emptiness, even if through a different process of substitution not based in the first order on the abjection of the Phallic Mother.

This other logic would argue as follows: Women as the castrated Other can take the form of the object beyond the pleasure principle because they share with the Thing the impossibility of being known. "Man" is driven by the pleasure principle to signify the Thing. He looks around and finds woman, but why Woman? Lacan's only answer can be that Woman has the form of this signifier of emptiness precisely because they cannot *signify* as creatures of the flesh. Thus, his rhetorical stance of incredulity! How can a creature that cannot *signify* as a creature of the flesh take the form of the signifier of emptiness? How can a creature that cannot "be" at all as herself and as feminine stand in as the *ex nihilo*, as the Big Bang, the absolute beginning, and the ground of being? More important, why would "man" signify woman as *ex nihilo*, since it is "man" and "man" alone who introduces the signifier into the world? Why give the feminine this kind of significance, since it is men who are doing it? The answer to the paradox for Lacan is in "the lack" in our reality of Woman. Woman stands in for the Thing because she cannot signify as Woman, just as the Thing cannot signify as The Thing. Lack of significance is thus shared and can function as the basis of an unconscious identification.

This lack of significance of Woman as an actual creature of the flesh turns her into the signifier of emptiness or the hole. For Lacan, the very idea of the *ex nihilo*, which is that we can create something out of nothing, turns on an apparent contradiction that can be ironed out if we understand that Woman signifies the hole from out of "which" man can fashion his world. Lacan reinterprets Heidegger's fable of the vase to help us see his point. For Heidegger, the vase unites the celestial and terrestrial powers around it, as the signifier of the way in which emptiness and fullness are linked. In Lacan, fullness drops from sight as it must since what is full of itself, the very form of the Real, cannot be known. The vase for Lacan can only be filled because it is empty. It is this emptiness that determines the filling; therefore, there is no difference between emptiness and fullness. Thus, unlike in Heidegger, the vase is no longer pregnant with the meaning of the togetherness of emptiness and fullness. To quote Lacan, "This nothing in particular that characterizes it in its signifying function is that which in its incarnated form characterizes the vase as such. It creates the void and thereby introduces the possibility of filling it. Emptiness and fullness are introduced into a world that by itself knows not of them. It is on the basis of this fabricated signifier, this vase, that emptiness and fullness as such enter the world, neither more nor less, and with the same sense" (*Sé VII*, 145/*S VII*, 120). Like the vase, Woman signifies the hole out of which man can fill in his world. As the hole, she can represent "the existence of the emptiness at the center of the real that is called the Thing" (*Sé VII*, 147/*S VII*, 121).

But we would still need to ask, does the form of Woman as a signifier of the hole have nothing, as Lacan asserts, to do with the "fleshy and historical reality" of woman? If the answer is that Woman takes this form on the basis of an unconscious identification and therefore, one which is not a historical identification in any simplistic sense, there would still have to be an analysis of why this identification happens, and indeed, why it cannot be dislocated.

As we will see in the next section of this essay, my own argument will be that this unconscious identification turns on the engraving of a particular path of repression mandated by a symbolic order established by the positioning of the phallus as the transcendental signifier. For now we need to note Lacan's own attempt to reverse the order of the relationship between the abjection of woman and the definition of the real as lack. This reversal, as I have argued, is inseparable from Lacan's rereading of the Thing and the function of the pleasure principle in "man's" quest for knowledge of the real.

What I have just offered is clearly an attempt to render the relationship between the masculine symbolic, the Thing and the real, coherent, an effort no doubt inspired by a woman's desire to give meaning to the whole. But I would strongly argue that it is the interpretation of Lacan that remains true to his insistence that a faithful rereading of Freud, combined with a correct understanding of the real, will take us back to Kant's ethics. With this rereading to guide us, we can now turn to the way in which the real grounds the law, in Lacan, and how this law is inseparable from the foreclosure of the significance of Woman as a being with historical reality.

How Freud Turns the Foundation of the Moral Law on Its Head. For Lacan, the real grounds moral action because we are fated to "bang our heads against the wall." The real is the barrier that guarantees the Thing as the beyond to the pleasure principle, for Lacan ethics was historically grounded in the search for what always returns to the same place. This search is primordially attached to ethics, because ethics involves the establishment of order. Lacan repeats Lévi-Strauss's insight, that order itself is based on elementary structures of kinship as well as on elementary structures of exchange of goods and property. Lévi-Strauss gives to the exchange of women a central role in the establishment of these primordial ethical structures.

According to Lacan, these structures allow for the arising of human culture, a culture based on speech and on the ability of man to turn himself into the sign of the creator of significance. As we have already discussed, this reproduction of man as a speaking being is inseparable from the pleasure principle. The pleasure principle is what drives us into the search for the impossible object. For Lacan, it was Kant's world historical insight to make of ethics itself an impossible object, a pure and simple object, at the same time that ethics is also an application of a universal maxim. In Kant, the moral law demands that we rid ourselves of all of our petty desires as phenomenal beings. If we do good because we desire to do good we have not acted solely according to the dictates of the categorical imperative itself, the categorical imperative demands that we be able to universalize the basis of our moral action. The words "be able" are crucial here because they point us toward the problem of moral motivation. In Kant, the possibility of moral action and of a free moral will can be explained because of the divide he draws between the phenomenal and the noumenal world. Lacan is certainly right that Kant strove to maintain "man's" moral freedom against the deterministic worldview of Newtonian physics (*Sé VII,* 92/*S VII,* 76). It is only if we understand that experience itself is founded in the divide between the noumenal and the phenomenal world that we can explain why free moral action remains possible in spite of the Newtonian revolution.

Lacan's argument is that psychoanalysis makes a crucial contribution to Kant's insight by explaining why we are forced to turn ethics into an impossible object, one that is forever sought but never achieved. The Freudian answer for Lacan turns on the way the functioning of the pleasure principle operates to foreclose the object of *joussiance*. It is this foreclosure that makes the moral law possible, because it separates the law absolutely from the Good. The antimonic structure between law and desire that is the very basis of Kantian ethics, then, can be traced back to the functioning of the pleasure principle. It is because the outer extremity of pleasure is unbearable to us that the brakes will always be applied to prevent us from reaching the ultimate object of desire. The ultimate law organizes our inaccessibility to the ultimate object of *joussiance*, the Thing. It is this law that we cannot transgress precisely, because we are destined to be castrated from that ultimate object. Thus, ironically, the purportedly greatest transgressor of the moral laws that govern sexuality, the Marquis de Sade, is for Lacan a "true" Kantian. Sade always returns us to the law that forecloses our *jouissance*. This cut, this barrier to happiness, is what we are continuously returned to in Sade. For Lacan, no one more forcefully demonstrated the antinomic structure of law and desire than did Sade in his so-called "anti-morality" (*Sé VII,* 97/*S VII,* 80).

It is also not a coincidence that Lacan chooses an author whose attention to anti-morality is inspired by a call to sexual transgression. For Lacan, if we look at any moral code, we will be returned either directly or indirectly to questions of sexuality and the lack around which the law organizes itself. But the attention to sexuality is also inevitable at the secondary level of actual law and codes, because "men" become signs themselves only by entering the symbolic which has as its basis the enforced regulation of sexual difference or more precisely its lack. "Men" become "men" against the feminine object. They show that they are "men" through the regulation of this object which in turn, as we have seen, takes on significance as a substitution for the Thing. Thus when men regulate women and their relations to this object, they are always expressing in different forms the fundamental foreclosure that is the basis for the law itself.

Indeed Lacan gives an analysis of several of the Ten Commandments to prove his point that any moral code will be built around the fundamental law of the unconscious, the foreclosure of the Thing, and with it our enforced entry into the symbolic. For Lacan, the second commandment succinctly summarizes this law: "It is nevertheless the case that the second commandment, the one that formally excludes not only every cult, but also every image, every representation of what is in heaven, on earth, or in the void, seems to me to show that what is involved is in a very special relationship to human feeling as a whole. In a nutshell, the elimination of the function of the imaginary presents itself to my mind, and, I think, to yours, as the principle of the relation to the symbolic, in the meaning we give that term here; that is to say, to speech. Its principle condition is there" (*Sé VII*, 98/*S VII*, 81.)

But it is in his discussion of the commandment that addresses itself to the property of one's neighbor that Lacan most directly spells out his understanding of Woman, the Thing, and the Law. The commandment reads as follows: "Thou shalt not covet the neighbor's house, thou shalt not covet thy neighbor's wife, neither his man servant, nor his maid servant, neither his ox, nor his ass, nor anything that belongs to thy neighbor" (*Sé VII*, 100/*S VII*, 82). Lacan's focus is on the part of the commandment that forbids the coveting of the neighbor's wife. For Lacan, it is this part of the commandment that is central. The covetousness that is forbidden is "Not addressed to anything that I might desire but to a thing that is my neighbor's Thing." This is why this commandment is the most basic commandment for Lacan. It expresses the distance we must keep from the Thing given expression as the neighbor's wife. The Thing grasped for is, by definition, always over "there" with the neighbor and so we must leave it. Yet precisely because it is "over there," we *must* desire it. Desire flares up precisely because of the law that marks the Thing as Other and therefore as what is most desirable. But if we were to have "it," we would not be "men"—speaking beings. The commandment thus expresses for Lacan the condition in which we become "men"; that condition must be *established* distant from the Thing. Yet because it is absolutely forbidden, it is the only "Thing" truly worth having. The law enforces our desire for it precisely as it enforces its otherness. To quote Lacan,

> It is to the extent that the commandment in question preserves the distance from the Thing as founded by speech itself that it assumes its value. Is the Law the Thing? Certainly not. Yet I can only know the Thing by means of the Law. In effect, I would not have had the idea to covet if the Law hadn't said: "Thou shalt not covet it." But the thing finds a way by producing in me all kinds of covetousness thanks to the commandment, for without the law the Thing is dead." But even without the Law, I was once alive. But when the commandment appeared, the Thing flared up, returned once again, I met my death. And for me,

the commandment that was supposed to lead to life turned out to lead to death, for the Thing found a way and thanks to the commandment seduced me; through it I came to desire death. (*Sé VII,* 101/*S VII,* 83).

Lacan is deliberately mimicking the famous speech of St. Paul, in which he is speaking of the evil Thing called sexual intercourse, that which was supposed to lead to life and instead led to death, syphilis. This bad experience seemingly led St. Paul to equate the quest for eternal life with celibacy. Sin results from the seduction by the Thing in the guise of Woman, who seduces us through the fantasy that we can have her again. Keep the women out and you have a chance "to be."

I take very seriously Lacan's praise of St. Paul as having the Lacanian dialectic of desire "down," although since I have never found St. Paul very good company, I would try to avoid him on vacations (*Sé VII,* 101/*S VII,* 83). To summarize: The elimination of the imaginary is inseparable from the abjection of the Phallic Mother, the Other marked by the law as the Thing. It is only through her abjection that "man" can "be" at all. Thus we are returned to the very fundamental idea in Lacan, that castration is the price "man" pays for being. To be tempted by Woman is the temptation of the death of "man" as a speaking being, of psychosis. The Oedipal Complex not only abjects Woman, it gives us our image of God, Lacan's "Great Fucker" (*Sé VII,* 335/*S VII,* 304) in the sky who can eternally "do it" (*Sé VII,* 355/*S VII,* 307). It is the image of the one who can eternally "do it" that gives us our only embodiment of eternity. As the fundamental command then we are forced to turn away from the Mother, accept our castration from Her, our only real object of desire. As we do so, we find "life" through the Imaginary Father. St. Paul gives us Lacanism in a nutshell!

The use of Paul to summarize Lacanism can help us understand how Lacan understands the fundamental ethical message of psychoanalysis. That lesson is that there can be no Sovereign Good. The dominance of the signifier forever cuts us off from the Good. But for Lacan, psychoanalysis tells us why and how we are cut off from the good by the Oedipal complex. As Lacan explains, "Well now, the step taken by Freud at the level of the pleasure principle is to show us that there is no Sovereign Good—that the Sovereign Good, which is *das Ding*, which is the mother, is also the object of incest, is a forbidden good, and that there is no other good. Such is the foundation of the moral law as turned on its head by Freud" (*Sé VII,* 85/*S VII,* 70).

Psychoanalysis As Moral Practice. This foundation of the moral law gives us the battlefield of our experience built as it is around a fundamental lack, the hole that is always at the center of desire. Given the foundation of the moral law, we cannot help but be forever returned to the "impossible" sexual relationship, because Woman cannot take the form of the signifier except as emptiness. Very simply put, no "man" can have a "relationship" to this "nothing." Man cannot not "relate" to what is beyond the pleasure principle, although he is fated to encounter "it" precisely as what cannot be known. His "existence" as a speaking being, which as we have seen is for Lacan the only kind of existence that "man" can have, depends on his cut from the Thing, the object of *joussiance*. Thus those who attempt to thrust Her in man's face threaten him with the loss of sanity. The temptation is always there, precisely because she is what we are cut from, and yet the barrier *must* be maintained. Who better to tell us about the power of that temptation than Paul? That *must* is the moral law imposed by the name of the Father, which is why Lacan argues that psychoanalysis is inherently moral. Psychoanalysis illuminates the moral law and how we must exist if we are to be "men."

But on Lacan's own analysis of Freud, "men" are given to be "men" only by being damaged, damaged by their very castration. Thus, according to Lacan, the question of the impossible sexual relation, and how one lives with this "it" as impossible, has always been at the center of ethics. For Lacan, courtly love and its poets present us with a profound ethical code, precisely in the sense that this practice was an attempt to regulate the "damage" of inevitable castration to live with the absolute otherness of the Thing. On this complex understanding of the battlefield of men's moral experience, psychoanalysis has a crucial role to play, precisely because it must—again in the sense of a command—if it to be true to itself, and more particularly to its founder—return ethics to the hole that is at the center of moral life, the lack of love and of the sexual relation. Again, to quote Lacan, "Freud placed in the forefront of ethical inquiry the simple relationship between man and woman. Strangely enough, things haven't been able to move beyond that point. The question of *das Ding* is still attached to whatever is open, lacking, or gaping at the center of our desire. I would say—you will forgive the play on words— that we need to know what we can do to transform this dam-age into our 'dame' in the archaic French sense, our lady" (*Sé VII*, 102/*S VII*, 84).

What Remains to be Done. Lacanian analysis is driven then by the drive to transform this "damage," this "damn age," which given the analysis would have to involve a transformation. But is there not something contradictory in Lacan's suggestion of what must be accomplished in the transformation? On Lacan's own analysis, this transformation cannot truly be accomplished precisely because of the effects of the sublimation demanded by the project itself. Did not the poets of courtly love try to overcome this damage precisely by turning that horrific "yucky" Thing into "Our Lady"? Did not Paul's church? Isn't "Our Lady" just the Other side of the "damage," an other side that is always indicated in The Thing that cannot be reached?

Leaving aside for a moment how undesirable a feminist might find it to be transformed into any "body's" lady, we would still have to ask whether or not this attempt at regulation is doomed to failure by its own terms. And was it not Lacan that taught us that lesson? Is our damage the only thing that remains after the analysis? What remains for us to do, if we are to escape this law imposed on us as it is—at least according to Lacan—if we are to be "men"?

The debate between the post–structuralists and the feminists, as I now want to recast it, turns around the question of what *remains* to be done if we do not think that our "damn age" can be transformed by turning our "damage" into Our Lady. Lacan always reminds us that we cannot think at all beyond the conditions imposed by the law of the real. But is the battlefield of experience he so profoundly analyzes truly our fate? Or is there a beyond that operates precisely as the reminder of the limit of our experience? Must the real ground the law, or does it instead forever operate to disintegrate its basis? Before turning to the different configuration of the real, the law of the symbolic, an impossibility that I will spin out for the sole purpose of giving us another answer to the question of what remains to be done, we need to address why Lacan necessarily fails on his own terms to faithfully address the real.

Lacan's Infidelity to the Beyond of the Real. As we have seen for Lacan, it is only the symbolic that scars the real as lack. It is this symbolic that in turn signifies the Woman as the castrated Other. Even if this connection is an unconscious identification between the Thing and Woman based on a primordial lack that marks "man's" desire, the very significance given to lack cannot be separated from the symbolic. The real *appears* in Lacan, it is given form. That form is Woman and other embodiments of the emptiness she is the signifier for, like the vase. It is the appearance of the real, its identification with its representation as lack, that Lacan analyzes. Lacan's infidelity to his own argument lies here: he takes the appearance of the real *mandated* by this drive to representation as the real. But on the terms of his own argument there would be no basis for knowing what the real in *it-self* mandated.

Kant never thought that the real mandated any law in and of itself. It was the conditions of knowledge that gave us the laws of thought. The transcendental conditions of experience account for the possibility of objectivity and the laws that purportedly establish our world as shared. We know these laws through a transcendental deduction. But we do not know anything directly about the real in itself. Simply put, Kant is consistent in the terms of his own argument; he tells us only about the transcendental conditions that are the laws that establish our experience as shared, not about the real or what the real mandates.

The structure of Lacan's argument and his very rhetoric is, as we have

seen, Kantian. On this reading, Lacan is arguing about how the symbolic operates as law to give us the reality of our sexual difference, which in turn is read
back into the real itself because of the functioning of the pleasure principle.
That would be the law that could account for why emptiness is determinative
of all of our sublimations. But that would be an account of the law of the symbolic that inscribes the real as lack, not an account of what the real mandates.
Lacan recognizes that the signifier of the form of emptiness is introduced by
man, because all signifiers are introduced by man: "The fact is man fashions
this signifier and introduces it into the world—in other words, we need to
know what he does when he fashions it in the image of the Thing, whereas the
Thing is characterized by the fact that it is impossible for us to imagine it. The
problem of sublimation is located on this level" (*Sé VII*, 150/*S VII*, 125).

To know why man is driven to imagine the invisible in a particular way
is exactly that; an explanation about why "man" is driven to imagine "it" in
that way. Without an explanation of the unconscious identification between
Woman and lack through the elimination of the feminine imaginary, there is
no analytical basis for this identification. The analytic basis for Lacan is how
the Oedipal complex operates through the Name of the Father to foreclose the
symbolization of the mother and through her lineage the significance of feminine sexual difference. Before we turn to whether or not his foreclosure is
guaranteed by the symbolic, we have to focus on the contradiction in his own
thought that Lacan leaves us with, at least in terms of his claim to give a status beyond the symbolic to the real. If we cannot imagine the real in itself,
then we cannot imagine "it." What we have is an explanation of why "men"
imagine it in the way they do. Lacanian analysis on this reading would give
us an explanation of why for "men" emptiness is determinative of all their
sublimations. Appearance can be justifiably equated with what is "there" as
imagined.

Thus, what *remains* after Lacan is his very project of rethinking what
remains beyond the symbolic, and with it the question of whether the symbolic is guaranteed by its own law to endlessly reestablish itself as a system.
Given that the Lacanian law of the symbolic is inseparable from the foreclosure of Woman, to answer these questions we will once again find ourselves
returned to Woman and to the name of the Other, Woman.

The Post–structuralist Release of the Real

The Deconstruction of the Status of the Phallus

As we have seen for Lacan, the symbolic is guaranteed against the feminine Thing, which threatens his very existence as a speaking being, by the
establishment of the phallus as the transcendental signifier. This transcenden-

tal signifier cannot be known in and of itself; "it" can only be known through its displacement. For Derrida, in Lacan's seminar on Poe's story, "The Purloined Letter," the story is used to demonstrate the decisive orientation that the subject receives from the itinerary of a signifier. It is the itinerary of the signifier that allows us to reconfirm the status of the phallus since we cannot know it directly. It is the truth of the itinerary that is the economy of the fiction, in this case, Poe's story.[12] Thus Derrida interprets Lacan's statement that "truth inhabits fiction": "Truth inhabits fiction" cannot be understood in the somewhat perverse sense of a fiction more powerful than the truth which inhabits it, the truth that fiction inscribes within itself. In truth, the truth inhabits fiction as the master of the house, as the law of the house, as the economy of fiction. The truth executes the economy of fiction, directs, organizes, and makes possible fiction: 'It is that truth, let us note, which makes the very existence of fiction possible'"(*PC,* 436).

Ironically, Derrida's interpretation is "true" to Lacan's insight, that "man" is the creature of fictions in the more general sense that his reality is given by a symbolic order. This reality is inevitably encoded in a chain of significance inseparable from metaphoric substitution and metonymic deferral. Who better understood that than Lacan! Yes there is a dispute between Derrida and Lacan about the status of literature and the way it is used as "proof" of psychoanalytic insight, but the underlying disagreement behind that dispute is over how the itinerary of the signifier is established as truth. How is the itinerary of the signifier guaranteed so that the letter necessarily will return to its proper place? How can we *know in advance* that the letter will always return to its place? Indeed, how did Lacan come to give the letter the significance he gives to it as the truth of the itinerary of the signifier that points back to the phallus as the transcendental signifier?

The Lacanian answer is that the phallus as the transcendental signifier is always in its place by definition, and thus the truth of the Being of nonbeing will always be unveiled as a Woman. In terms of my own argument in the previous section, the Thing is that to which man is always returned and that Thing can only be figured as a hole. But the key word here, as I discussed, is figured. That the Thing must be figured is exactly what Derrida argues is the basis for the deconstruction of Lacan's truth claim about inevitable destination that allows us to know in advance the itinerary of the signifier. For Lacan, as we have seen, it does not shake his claim to truth that the Thing must be figured because that figure will *necessarily* be Woman. There can be no other figure. That is the law of foreclosure of the resymbolization of the feminine within sexual difference. It is solely on the basis of a guarantee that the figure of non-being has to be Woman and that she will remain the *only* object of substitution and displacement for the truth of the real that Lacan's claims about how truth inhabits fiction can stand up. Why is this the case?

Because it is a fiction, in the sense of representation, that Woman "is" the Thing. We "see" woman this way because she is designated *a priori* as the castrated Other, as the site of the lack of the penis. To quote Derrida,

> This proper place, known to Dupin, and to the psychoanalyst, who in oscillating fashion, as we shall see, occupies Dupin's position, is the place of castration: woman as the unveiled site of the lack of a penis, as the truth of the phallus, that is of castration. The truth of the purloined letter is the truth, its meaning is meaning, its law is the law, the contract of truth with itself in logos. Beneath this notion of the pact (and therefore of adequation), the notion of veiling/unveiling attunes the entire Seminar to the Heideggerian discourse on truth. Veiling/unveiling here concerns a hole, a non-being: the truth of Being as non-being. The truth is "woman" as veiled/unveiled castration (*PC,* 439).

Not only is Woman the substitution of the hole, this hole can be known and indeed described, so that the entire itinerary of the subject is organized around it. Without this knowledge of the contours of the hole there could be no accurate description of the economy of desire that could be analyzed as a regulated circulation that will necessarily replace the letter in its proper place. Again, to quote Derrida, *"The proper place, first of all.* The letter has a place of emission and of destination. This is not a subject, but a hole, the lack on the basis of which the subject is constituted. The contour of this whole is determinable, and it magnetizes the entire itinerary of the detour which leads from hole to hole, from the hole to itself, and which therefore has a *circular* form. In question is indeed a regulated *circulation* which organizes a return from the detour toward the hole" (*PC,* 437).

As we saw in the last section, even if the "later" Lacan reverses the order of how Woman comes to represent the lack in the real—the real is not imagined as lack because of the abjection of the Mother; instead Woman is the substitution for the always, already there hole in the real, The Thing—her form as a signifier still turns on an unconscious identification of Woman as emptiness, as *ex nihilo*. As I also argued, this unconscious identification can in the end not be separated from a particular trajectory of repression that is inseparable from the foreclosure of the sexual difference in the symbolic order. It is this foreclosure and the unconscious identification that designates Woman as lack that purportedly allows us to know the contours of the hole. This foreclosure is the law, but how is this law guaranteed? Without the law we cannot even know what the proper place of the letter is, let alone that it will return there.

When Lacan says that the letter has no proper meaning of its own, as Woman has no meaning in herself, he is still counting on another meaning by which he can know that; that is, know that the letter has no meaning of its own. To know that Woman has no proper meaning in herself is to know her as the sign of Truth, if not as Woman. How can Lacan count on this meaning?

This knowledge can only be guaranteed by a transcendental semantics, that as I previously argued has to be transcendental in the strong sense that it can analyze exactly how the cut in reality will take place. Knowing just how the real will be cut is what gives us knowledge of the contours of the hole. If we did not know how the real will necessarily be cut, we could not know why the letter is put into circulation in the first place. The place of woman, of the hole that is Woman, as "it" is always designated as what is missing in its place, is also the lack that is never missing from it. To quote Derrida,

> This is where the signifier (its inadequation with the signified) gets underway, this is the site of the signifier, the letter. But this is also where the trial begins, the promise of reappropriation, of return, of readequation: "the search for and restitution of the object". . . . The singular *unity* of the letter is the site of the contract of the truth with itself. This is why the letter *comes back to, amounts to* [*revient à*] woman (at least in the extent to which she wishes to save the pact and, therefore, that which is the King's, the phallus that is in her guardianship); this is why, as Lacan says elsewhere, the letter amounts to, comes back to Being, [*la lettre revient à l'être*], that is to the nothing that would opening itself as the hole between woman's legs. Such is the proper place in which the letter is found, where its meaning is found, where the minister believes it to be in the shadows and where it is, in its very hiding place, the most exposed (*PC,* 439).

The "Place" of the Phallus. Thus this place that is not "there" in reality is not "there" because it is a transcendental "place" deduced from a reading of a particular path of repression that always leads back to the object we set out to find, The Thing. It also is important to remember here that for Lacan it is the impossibility that is the real which keeps the Thing in its place. We will return to that conceptualization of the real shortly. For now we need to understand that Derrida's deconstruction of Lacan's concept of destination is itself put into circulation by Lacan's insight into how Woman's "place" as veiled/unveiled of castration gets the signifier underway. The destination of the letter is only guaranteed if the status of the phallus is that of the transcendental signifier, and this status, too, can be clearly established. Lacan himself always insists on the materiality of the signifier, even if he never gives any explanation of why this is the case. Derrida has already argued the letter as the letter can only return to its place if it is indivisible, if it is one. This very idea of oneness can only be guaranteed by a transcendental semantics that stamps the phallus as an ideal object. Only as an ideal object can the phallus be one, the barrier that guarantees the circular logic of castration. Thus, before we even get to Derrida's own rethinking of the beyond of the real, his deconstruction of Lacan shows in its first movement that the phallus can only operate to guarantee the law of the foreclosure of Woman if it is justified as an ideal object. To give this status to the phallus negates Lacan's insistence on the materiality of the signifier. A signifier marked by materiality can always be fragmented, and this fragmentation would open up alternative trajectories for the letter itself. Thus the law of the hole can only be established through a system of meaning guaranteed by an ideal object in Husserl's sense. It is his necessary commitment to ideality that opens up Lacan's phallic logic to Derrida's deconstruction.

This determination of the proper, of the law of the proper, of *economy*, therefore leads back to castration as truth, to the figure of woman as the figure of castration *and* of truth. Of castration as truth. Which above all does not mean, as one might tend to believe, to truth as essential dislocation and irreducible fragmentation. Castration-truth, on the contrary, is that which contracts itself (stricture of the ring) in order to bring the phallus, the signifier, the letter, or the fetish back into their *oikos*, their familiar dwelling, their proper place. In this sense castration-truth is the opposite of fragmentation, the very antidote for fragmentation: that which is missing from its place has in castration a fixed, central place, freed from all substitution. . . . The phallus thanks to castration, always remains in its place, in the transcendental topology of which we were speaking above. And this is why the motivated, never demonstrated presupposition of the materiality of the letter as *indivisibility* is indispensable for this restricted economy, this circulation of the proper. (*PC,* 441)

It is the phallus as the indivisible one that cuts the real to not only provide us with knowledge of the contours of the hole, but also to foreclose the possibility that Woman as a substitution can in turn be substituted and ultimately returned to the chain of significance and metonymic displacement. If she could be so returned, the letter would not necessarily be returned to its proper place. There would be no guarantee. But if the logic of the signifier has always already been castrated by the phallus that establishes its logic, then Woman will always be returned to her place as the truth of "the never had it." That return results from the circular logic of castration. Only on the basis of such reasoning can Lacan avoid the danger that if Woman stands in for the Thing she could always be represented. If the phallus cannot be kept in the position of the transcendental signifier, there *can be* no firm boundaries that would fix the hole's exact contours. Without the "stricture of the ring" there can be no guarantee that the signifier would not continue to slide.

Of course, if the meaning of the phallus by definition cannot slide, then Lacan would not have a problem with Woman. However, there is a further difficulty associated with the very idea of the phallus as a transcendental signifier. Transcendental signifiers can only be known deductively through their representations, precisely because they are transcendental. In the masculine imaginary the penis stands in for the phallus but as the stand-in, the penis is not it. Indeed, the penis marks the failure to be "it" because "it" only "is" a stand-in. What is marked in both "sexes" by the absent phallus, known only as a bar, is castration. Lacan's appeal to the turgidity of the penis in reproduction as the basis for the unconscious identification of the penis with the phallus is rather weak, because, let's face it, that turgidity "comes and goes." Indeed, it is precisely the "coming and going" of this turgidity that marks the penis itself as the mark of the failure of the "man" to have "it," the ever-erect phallus of the "great fucker" in the sky. Why then if the penis is only the stand-in for castration couldn't "it" be the signifier of what is forever lacking? If there is no firm connection between the phallus and the penis, if it, too, could represent castration as the very failure to achieve the imaginary but "eternal" turgidity of the Great Father in the sky, then there would be no rigid divide between the "sexes," since both would be viewed as having "sex" organs that marked their castration, and of course on the contrary, the woman and her body could be resignified as the One with the imaginary phallus. Judith Butler has brilliantly argued that on this reasoning the lesbian phallus is not only possible, it could disrupt the very logic of castration by dislocating the association of Woman alone, as the castrated Other. The very status of the phallus as an ideal object means that it cannot be protected from contamination by its representations. This contamination makes it inevitable that it be fragmented in the sense of given "body." This "body," as we have seen, is an imaginary identification of the penis with the phallus, but the underlying unconscious truth belies this fantasy, undermines this identification. The unconscious registration that no "no-body" has phallus means that the penis can be dislocated from this identificatory structure and that other possibilities besides Woman can stand in for the figure of castration. These possibilities would in turn mean that the letter would not necessarily be returned to its proper place because some figure besides Woman could be "it," and the "it" itself could be resignified as the phallic lesbian. It should be noted that these possibilities are based on the significance given to the phallus itself as the "lack-in-having" that marks desire in both "sexes" and therefore can never be actually identified with the penis.

But there is a more general philosophical point that Derrida makes. The phallus as a transcendental signifier cannot escape the deconstruction of the divide between *Sinn and Bedeutaung*, a divide that must be maintained in any transcendental semantics. A transcendental signifier must be true to its own form. But since we cannot know it directly but only in its expression and representations, it cannot achieve that purity. The very project of purifying the concept of form gets bogged down by the very productivity of language in which it must be carried out and explained. It would only be possible to achieve the goal of a transcendental semantics if expression and representation did nothing more than transport a constituted sense to the exterior, and by so doing merely reissue a noematic sense by providing access to conceptual form. This is why Derrida states that "Form 'Is' its Ellipsis."[13] The phallus can only be maintained in its position if it can escape the ellipsis inevitably associated with linguistic expression and representation. But how could "it" and "it" alone be uniquely salvaged from the fate of the transcendental signifier? Lacan's only answer has to be an appeal to the ideality of meaning in the *unity of speech* (*PC,* 465).

But what guarantees the unity of speech, or more precisely, in Lacanian terms, the unity of the symbolic order? The answer of course is the phallus. And what guarantees the phallus? The unity of speech. As we have seen, it is the itinerary of the letter's destination that supposedly allows us to trace our way back to the status the phallus must have for this logic to be maintained. The reasoning, as Derrida demonstrates, is circular. A circular logic does not and cannot fit with the rigor of a transcendental deduction.

Lacan's Fallback Position. There would seem to be a fallback position for Lacan that would attempt to explain why it is that the phallus continues to be reinstated in the position of the lack for both "sexes" but in such a way as to guarantee that Woman will remain in her proper place as the representation of the hole. That position would rely on the circularity of the argument itself to guarantee that the "effects," the establishment of the law of the Father and with it the appropriation for the phallus to the side of the masculine, would forever reinstate the "cause," the phallus as the "signifier of all signifiers." This is the retroactive performativity that Slavoj Žižek attributes to Lacan, which would free Lacan's argument from the need to rely on a transcendental deduction. In accordance with Lacan's argument about the role of the pleasure principle in the drive toward significance itself, the lost object would be produced by the search for it. The *cause* of the object then would be the search itself, which is why the effects of the search could become the cause. Žižek describes the paradox of retroactive performativity as follows: "First we have the paradox of a signifier which is part of the representation of reality (filling out a void, a hole in it). Then we have an inverse paradox of an object which must be included in the signifying texture."[14]

But this solution does not salvage Lacan's logic for the following reason. Even if we accepted the idea that the effects produced the object to be sought which then became the cause of the effects through the process of the search itself we would still have to ask why that object takes the form it does, why it is one particular search and only one possible object as the "result." In Lacan's words, we would still have to know why it is "emptiness that is determinative of all of our sublimations." Why, in other words, is it a particular signifier that fills out the hole in reality? The point of the seminar on "The Purloined Letter," and, as we have seen, of Lacan's teaching more generally, is that it will be Woman that figures castration and will stand in for the Thing which is sought. But we can only know that this substitution will take place, and therefore that the letter will be put into a regulated circulation, if the phallus is already in the position of the transcendental signifier to guarantee the unity of speech and the foreclosure of Woman. The response that desire produces an "object a" does not answer the question, because the question addresses the inevitability of the *form* of the object that will be produced. The question does not address whether there will be an "object a," a residue that will be produced by desire.

Any "Derridean," and dare I say "post–structuralist" feminist, would be more than happy to agree with that proposition. We need to have a specific answer about how the feminine object gets marked as it is for Lacan "the letter" and how it circulates in a regulated manner. Of course, Žižek's answer following Lacan is that it is the real that guarantees the designation and the destination of the letter. But this real as an inevitable trauma for Žižek "must be constructed afterward so that we can account for the distortions of the symbolic structure."[15] A real defined in this manner, as I argued in the last section, is deduced from the symbolic. As such, it fails to adequately address the real and as a result turns us back to why the "distortions in the symbolic" are structured in a particular fashion.

Thus even if we give Lacan his fallback position, we are still returned to the question of how the establishment of the phallus can be firmly established and the structures of its effects sedimented as reality. Even if the argument were presented that the citation of the phallus in the unconscious will determine how the "sighting" of the Mother's difference will be viewed—this is the interpretation I would give to Lacan's description of the circuit as a machine—this would still be a reading based on a past reading. Such past readings, as any good lawyer knows, can always be undone. Thus, there is an irony in the very idea of retroactive performativity. It is precisely the inevitability that language will "perform" on its objects that makes it impossible to guarantee the distinction between *Sinn* and *Bedeutaung* and with it the closed circuit that will always return the "effects" to their "cause," as Žižek suggests. The very temporality of the Lacanian symbolic depends on the phallus always already being in place as the transcendental signifier. But it is precisely that position that cannot be maintained because of the very conditions in which an ideal object must be "presented." As Derrida shows us, the very idea of a conceptually generalizable form gives way to the fragmentation of its expression. The phallus as a purportedly indivisible, and thus, ideal object cannot be spared this contamination. As a result, there can be no security against this fragmentation and with it the possibility of a multiplicity of meanings given to the phallus, Woman and sexual difference. As a fragmented object, the phallus is returned to the chain of meaning and more specifically of metonymic displacement and deferral. If the ultimate meaning is deferred then we will never be able to know for sure the pathway by which "the object a" is constructed, and, therefore, we will not be able to determine the destination by retroactively giving the "effects" a "cause." In place of the ideal, ever-rigid phallus there is only the dissemination of its meaning that overruns the neatly contoured "hole."

The only guarantee against the dissemination of the meaning of the phallus and with it the law of the hole, is the obedience of Woman, or in the case of the Purloined Letter, the Queen to the law. As Derrida reminds us,

The letter—[the] place of the signifier—is found in the place where Dupin and the psychoanalyst expect to find it: on the immense body of a woman, between the "legs" of the fireplace. Such is its proper place, the terminus of its circular itinerary. It is returned to the sender, who is not the signer of the note, but the place where it began to *detach* itself from its possessor or feminine legatee. The Queen seeking to reappropriate for herself that which, by virtue of the pact which subjects her to the King, that is by virtue of the Law, guaranteed her the disposition of a phallus of which she would otherwise be deprived, of which she has taken the risk of depriving herself, that she has taken the risk of dividing, that is of multiplying,—the Queen then, undertakes to reform, to reclose the circle of the restricted economy, the circulatory pact. (*PC*, 440)

On this reading, the circuit is a "pact" that depends on Woman. And what guarantees her compliance? Her compliance to the law is only the result of her fear of being detached from the only position in which she could dispose of the phallus, the position of the King's wife. The risk she takes if she does not comply is of that position. But what makes this the only position by which she can dispose of the phallus? The answer is the system in which Woman can only be as lack. If that system cannot be guaranteed, if there are other positions in which Woman can dispose of the phallus, then there would not be the same risk of noncompliance with the law. Queens could start to reinterpret what it means to be queens.[16] If the whole edifice turns on Woman's compliance with the law to secure the pact, then the true foes of

Lacanism are the feminists and deconstructionists. But they are foes because they undermine the law, not because they deny the real.

To summarize, if the symbolic cannot be secured against the slippage of the signifier, then we cannot replace knowledge of the real with knowledge of the law of the cut established by the barrier of the phallus. As a result, the distortions of the symbolic cannot be read back into a definition of the real, so the real becomes the impossibility of escaping those distortions. In other words, the distortions of the symbolic cannot be read as the inevitable trauma of castration. For Lacan, this trauma is our destiny. That is the ultimate meaning of truth in Lacan: "man" is destined to be "man," thus castrated. Derrida's deconstruction of Lacan's transcendental semantics shows us that that truth cannot hold up as the law that establishes the unity of the symbolic. As Derrida himself succinctly summarizes his difference with Lacan, "The difference which interests me here is that—a formula to be understood as one will—the lack does not have its place in dissemination" (*PC,* 441).

The Neographism of Differance

The previously mentioned quote could be interpreted to prove the "truth" of the criticism that Derrida denies the real. On this reading of "dissemination" there is nothing other to this endless process by which meaning slips away from itself in the sliding of the signifier. By returning everything that is to the field of the signifier, Derrida purportedly denies the beyond of the real. But for Derrida, on the contrary, the dissemination of the order of the symbolic is mandated by the attempt to be "just" to the alterity of that which remains Other to all conceptual systems. "Deconstruction is justice" in precisely this sense; deconstruction gets underway as an address to the Other that proceeds though the promise of fidelity to the remains.[17] As we have seen in Derrida's deconstruction of Lacan, what slips away from itself in the effort to maintain the phallus in the position of the transcendental signifier is the ultimate meaning of the logic of castration. Dissemination disperses the unity of speech that is the symbolic order. It is the ordering of the Real through the logic of castration that is deconstructed. What is left after that deconstruction is precisely what is left over, beyond any symbolic system. In Derrida, too, the limit of all symbolic systems is that to which we are always returned as the impossibility of the full inscription of the otherness of what Lacan calls the real.

But this "real," this ~~Being~~, operates against the attempts of man to ensnare alterity and secure himself against it. It is not just the nonidentity of what matters with its current designations that calls for the deconstruction of identity logical thinking, it is the very conditions of presentation of what comes to be that defers any static definition of the real.[18] The real, or in the

Heideggerian terminology adopted by Derrida ~~Being~~ as it is presented, as beings, as objects, is Other to these forms. This is Heidegger's distinction between the ontic and the ontological. But Derrida radicalizes the very idea of the *es gibt* through the introduction of temporization. It is, then, not just the difference between beings that keeps ~~Being~~ other to reality. The very presentation of being in time introduces a fundamental multiplicity and complexity that displaces any lingering stasis inherent in a notion of a beyond that "is," even as it disappears in what "is."

For Derrida, we encounter the real through the operational force of *differance*. This "real," however, as a *force*, has none of the traditional properties associated with the real defined as it has been in Western metaphysics, including in Lacan, as a substance, subject only to limited divisibility. The law of this limited divisibility of the one substance was thought to be knowable and, therefore, limited divisibility would not lead to the multiplicity and complexity that would demand a new explanation of the real. The great scientific revolution of Galileo introduced a pictorial representation of cause and effect to guide scientific experimentation. But this pictorial representation rested on the idea that there were substantive objects definitively located in time and space to guide scientific experimentation. This view still relied on the idea that there were objects "out there" with knowable properties and predictable reactions separable from the observer, their temporalization, and their entanglement in a web of relations. This view of classical physics, including the pictorial representation of cause and effect and more specifically Newton's understanding of the law of inertia, not only informs but is the basis of Lacan's understanding of the real.

The debate, then, between Derrida and Lacan is how to adequately address the real and about how one "knows" its operational force, including the effects of sublimation. Once the debate is redefined in this manner we can reexamine its ethical significance. Indeed, we are called to return to the ethical precisely because we cannot separate the ethical from competing modes of address to the real. Lacan was certainly right to insist that there is an ineradicable connection between the competing conceptions of reality and ethics. If we think in terms of fidelity to the *Jenseits*, which for Lacan was the very heart of the matter of psychoanalysis, Derrida's promise to the real and to the ethical is always a promise to what remains beyond to any of our current systems of symbolization.

Differance *as a Disordering, Ordering "Principle."* Before we return to the ethical we need to examine the disordering ordering "principle" that disrupts any conception of the Law of law including that introduced by Lacan's phallo-logocentrism. Derrida heeds this disordering, ordering "principle" as *differance*, which is not a principle in any strong philosophical sense. For Derrida, by definition one cannot know the real by conceptualizing it because what would be known would only be the concept, not the real. Thus, he insists that *differance*, at least in the traditional philosophical sense, is "literally neither a word nor a concept" (*M*, 3). If there could be a concept in the strong sense of the underlying principle of reality, it would reintroduce a notion of the Law of law.

For Derrida, the Law of law that could establish the law of limited divisibility is undermined by the inherent temporalization of Being. Being, what is, only presents itself in intervals. As Derrida explains, "An interval must separate the present from what is not in order for the present to be itself, but this interval that constitutes it as present must, by the same token, divide the present in and of itself, thereby also dividing, along with the present, everything that is thought on the basis of the present, that is in our metaphysical language, every being, and singularly substance or the subject" (*M*, 13).

The Deconstruction of the Traditional Representation of Cause and Effect. Differance cannot be separated from the becoming time of space and the becoming space of time. This becoming space of time and the becoming time of space is always already underway, as soon as anything "is." Thus there cannot be an adequate pictorial representation of a "before" this presentation of what is, because what "is" is already, always temporalized. The idea of temporalization undermines the pictorial representation of an empty space as "nothing" in which something comes to be in that space that is already "there." As a result, the traditional notion of the separation of time and space is philosophically undermined, with the idea of a "prior" nothing, as is only too evident, Lacan's metaphors of the "Nothing," as the Other, indeed, even as the origin clearly partakes of an older worldview in which there is a "there of nothing" before the symbolic world of things. It is that Nothing that remains real in Lacan, which is precisely why we know "it" as Woman.

But if Being is always already in intervals, and thus temporalized, there can be no absolute past that was just there "before," even as Nothing. Such past would not be presentable because as things are presented they are always, already in time, or more precisely things only are through time. Again, to quote Derrida, "In constituting itself, in dividing itself dynamically, this interval is what might be called spacing, the becoming—space of time or the becoming time of space (*temporization*). And it is this constitution of the present, as an "originary" and irreducibly non-simple (and therefore, *stricto sensu* nonoriginary) synthesis of marks, or traces of retentions and protentions (to reproduce analogically and provisionally a phenomenological and transcendental language that will soon reveal itself to be inadequate) that I propose call archi-writing, archi-trace, of *differance*. Which is (simultaneously) spacing (and) temporization" (*M*, 13).

This "simultaneity," which denies in any simple sense a past and present, motivated me to use the phrase through time rather than in time. The phrase in time still indicates an object there "before" that then enters time and indeed the whole structure of scientific investigation. It is precisely this "before" and "after," and with it a sense of deterministic relationship, that is inherent in the traditional pictorial representation of cause and effect.

But is *differance* as "the non-full, non-simple, structured, and differentiating origin of differences" (*M*, 11) itself just another conception of the Law of law as an originary causality that causes things to be a certain way, or, more precisely, gives us another law of limited divisibility? My own interpretation of *differance* would answer that question as follows. *Differance* is not a Law of law in the strong sense of an original causality because the line between the "before" and "after," active and passive, cannot be maintained. A differentiating origin of differences cannot be known as an origin that is "there." What is always already differentiated and in a web of relationships that is constitutive of the things themselves undermines the traditional notion of an original law of causality. For example, we cannot know in any rigid sense then how and why the law of the ontic/ontological is maintained. Objects are not caused to be differentiated by *something other*, so we can know exactly how they will be differentiated. They are as differentiated and in a web of relationships in which what was the cause and what was the effect can be read differently because "nothing" can be taken out of the knot of reality and put absolutely in the prior position of the cause. As a result, there would not be a neat line that could distinguish cause and effect because what was there would be the relationality of what Derrida calls the "sheaf." For Derrida, the word "sheaf" seems to mark more appropriately that the "assemblage to be proposed has the complex structure of a weaving, an interlacing which permits the different threads and different lines of meaning—or of force—to go off again in different directions, just as it is always ready to tie itself up with others" (*M*, 3).

This idea of a sheaf of differentiations, which are knotted and reknotted, but not in accordance with any prior law, goes beyond the idea of limited divisibility to introduce multiplicity and complexity into the very heart of the real itself. Once one has introduced the idea of multiplicity and complexity into the very heart of the real there can be no way to predict absolutely, according to Law of law, how things will next be cut. In Derrida's language there will be "retentional traces and protentional openings" (*M*, 21) rather than any simple pictorial representation of cause and effect. Any strong notion of determinism depends on that picture. *A* causes *B* as the effect. Such deterministic reasoning assumes that there is *A* that can be designated separate from the sheaf. Given the complexity and multiplicity of the figure of the sheaf, we cannot reassure ourselves if there are those of us who would find it reassuring by appealing to the inevitability of any order. The real cannot, as

Lacan would like to maintain, be "there" as the inevitability of order. Instead, as Derrida reminds us, "Not only is there no kingdom of *differance*, but *differance* instigates the subversion of every kingdom. Which makes it obviously threatening and infallibly dreaded by everything within us that desires a kingdom, the past or future presence of a kingdom" (*M,* 22).

Derrida's "Beyond" to the Pleasure Principle

"Cinders There Are." It is precisely because Derrida "knows" that he cannot know that; the truth of Woman, that allows him to theoretically *open up* a possibility of a "real" *beyond* the automaton of the Lacanian pleasure principle. That opening that cannot be closed is inseparable from the real, if a real given to us by *difference*. The difference between an opening and a gap is that one cannot know what awaits on the other side, what "is" over there. In other words, "man" cannot know the contours of the opening or into what he will fall. This suspicion of Lacan's truth is inseparable from Derrida's profound awareness of how the unity of masculine symbolic has marked the tradition of Western metaphysics. Thus Derrida is earnest when he questions whether or not one can even think the *es gibt* "before" sexual difference, since the form of being has been inseparable from the metaphors of Woman. In his insistence that Western metaphysics is phallologocentric, the question of woman is elevated to philosophical status in a very traditional sense. We need to know how and why these metaphors of Woman have shaped the very conditions of knowledge and our most basic experience of what is. Thus, the deconstruction of phallologocentrism also always returns us to Woman, and more important, to the limit of her meaning as imposed by a masculine symbolic. It is precisely this emphasis on the limit of the meaning of Woman that has been misunderstood in Derrida as one more attempt to put her in the place of the mysterious, unknowable Other. But it is only if we dislocate the meaning imposed upon Woman that we can even begin to recapture a feminine imaginary. This, however, is my project.[19] For Derrida, the question of Woman is associated with the question of how to adequately address the "real" alterity of the Other, an alterity that is by definition beyond the masculine symbolic. But both projects depend on the disruption of the economy of desire described by Lacan.

Let me turn then to the question of how for Derrida there can be a beyond to the automaton of the pleasure principle, particularly as this automaton guarantees that emptiness will be determinative of all of our sublimations. The first step is to rethink the law of the pleasure principle. To do so we are once again returned to the operational force of *differance* and more specifically to the way the deferral of *differance* disrupts the specific itinerary of the destination of desire given to us by Lacan.

For Derrida, as we have seen, objects, all objects, are constituted through a temporalization that disrupts the very idea of a "past," even one that is only there as the automatism of repetition (*M,* 18).

It is the deferral of the ultimate meaning of any of the principles, since they can only be understood through *differance,* that keeps Freud's work from being turned into the ultimate theoretical justification of a restricted economy of desire. The detour of Derrida ascribes to *differance* could be the detour of the more traditional understanding of what the pleasure principle demands. Do we have to save ourselves only by cutting ourselves off from our pleasure? Is the choice between calculated pleasure and death? For Derrida the other to the pleasure principle with its restricted economy is only death if we already accept that we are fated to be in that economy. The either or in other words, is created by the way in which the pleasure principle and the reality principle are read together in traditional readings of Freud, including even Lacan's, rather than read through their difference from one another to leave open the possibility of a risk of oneself to the other that would not just be an unconscious investment in absolute loss. Indeed, the very idea that advance calculation is safe depends on the idea that there is a reality just there that will ultimately ensure that there will be a payoff for the expenditure of energy. The either/or of presence or absence is displaced by the operational force of differance.

For the economic character of *differance* in no way implies that the deferred presence can always be found again, that we have here only an investment that provisionally and calculatedly delays the perception of its profit or the profit of its perception. Contrary to the metaphysical, dialectical, "Hegelian" interpretation of the economic movement of *differance,* we must conceive of a play in which whoever loses wins, and in which one loses and wins on every turn. If this displaced presentation remains definitively and implacably postponed, it is not that a certain present remains absent or hidden. Rather, *differance* maintains our relationship with that which we necessarily misconstrue, and which exceeds the alternative of presence and absence. (*M,* 20)

For Derrida, the unconscious should be understood as exemplary of the excess of the dichotomy of either present or absent. It is other to consciousness, neither there as lost or as found. Thus in Derrida, unlike in Lacan, there is no such "thing" as an absolutely lost object that can be known in its very loss. Psychoanalysis proceeds down the path of aftereffects, which are "the traces of unconscious traces" (*M,* 21). It is precisely the deferral that leaves only aftereffects that disrupts the very idea of the retroactive reconstruction of the unconscious *cause* as "The Thing" that is lost. The irony is that in Lacan's attempt to know the unconscious Thing, even as what is lacking, he once again reinstates an identity between the unconscious and a present entity. A hole known in its contours is *something present*. Thus through his analysis of the Thing, Lacan is "untrue" to his own insistence on the otherness of the unconscious. Retroactive performativity still renders what is absent present to present us with the Thing as *cause*. It is only through this presentation that Lacan can establish the Real as an inevitable trauma that guarantees the restricted economy of the psyche Lacan describes as the destination of the letter. It is this restricted economy that is an expression of the law that we are forbidden access to the object of our desire that is lost always, already. The *law of the detour* of *differance* replaces the law of inertia of Lacan's automatism. *Differance* endlessly defers the law that makes the "sexual relationship impossible." The impossibility of knowing absolutely what "sex" is or what it cannot be, which is a knowledge dependent on knowing what "sex" is, does not foreclose possibility, including the possibility of "hetero" sexual love. But a love for the *hetros* demands that the other remain other beyond the knowledge of gender. This is why for Derrida homosexuality and heterosexuality are dichotomous opposites, dependent on the gender hierarchy. To challenge the restricted economy of gender also then necessarily implies a challenge to the rigid line between homosexuality and heterosexuality.

The Impossibility that Gives Possibility

Love for the Other as the *heteros*, as other begins where any system of knowledge that attempts to capture the Other leaves off. Lacanians "know" that "Woman" is the symptom of man. If Derrida knows anything at all he knows that he cannot know that that representation of Woman is her truth. The renunciation of that knowledge is not an attempt to transgress the law. If it is based in anything it is based in the knowledge that there is ultimately "nothing" out there that we can know in its contours. Therefore, there need not be the Sadian choice between destruction or subjection before the law that forbids *joussiance*. The knowledge that one cannot know the truth of "sex" is not a moral law in that it prescribes anything like a rule we can follow. But this lack of knowledge that inevitably refuses lack is a crucial moment in the ethical relation that lets the other remain beyond as Other. Thus the impossibility of full inscription of the reality of the Other, and yes as the Other, Woman does not function as a foreclosure in Derrida. Indeed, impossibility if one is consistent with the very idea of impossibility cannot function as a foreclosure. Put differently, love is the possibility kept open by the impossibility of knowing the reality of the "sex" of the Other or, indeed, knowing the other at all.

No literature with this, not with you my love. Sometimes I tell myself that you are my love: then it is only my love, I tell myself interpellating myself thus. And then you no longer exist, you are dead, like the dead woman in my game, and my literature becomes possible. But I also know—and for me, moreover, this morning, this is the definition of knowledge, I should publish it—that you are well beyond what I repeat as "my love," living, living, living, and I want it so, but then I have to renounce everything, I mean that love would come back to me, that turned toward me you let me even hear what I am saying when I say, say to you or say to myself my love. (*PC,* 29)

The paradox of this renunciation is that it makes pleasure possible. The search for the lost object is still a secure investment of energy as long as one can determine that the object will remain lost. But the renunciation of knowledge is also to give up the guarantee that one will not find her again (*PC,* 29).

If she remains other, she remains. The other that remains Other is the beyond to the pleasure principle, at least as it is defined as an automatism that always secures the destination of the letter. This Other that remains cannot be even retroactively analyzed as the cause that makes "emptiness determinative of all of "man's" sublimations. The effect of the loss of "my love " is evoked differently by Derrida, not as emptiness but as the secret of what was there and is still, the Cinder.

Who is Cinder? Where is she? Where did she run off to at this hour? If the homophony withholds the singular name within the common noun, it was surely "there," *là*; someone vanished but something preserved her trace and at the same time lost it, the cinder. There the cinder is: that which preserves in order no longer to preserve, dooming the remnant to dissolution. And it is no longer the one who has disappeared who leaves cinders "there"; it is only her still unreadable name. And nothing prevents us from thinking that this may also be the nickname of the so-called signatory. Cinders there are, the phrase thus says what it does, what it is. It immediately incinerates itself, in front of your eyes: an impossible mission (but I do not like this verb, "to incinerate"; I find in it no affinity with the vulnerable tenderness, with the patience of a cinder. The verb is active, acute, incisive).[20]

The "real" other remains a secret. She can only be evoked as what has been given, recalled through another memory that does not reduce her to what I remember of Her. The name figures but only to remind of the inadequacy of any representation of the Other: "It is obviously a figure, although no face lets itself be seen. The name 'cinder' figures and, because there is no cinder here (nothing to touch, no color, no body, only words), but above all because these words, which through the name are supposed to name not the word but the thing, they are what names one thing in the place of another, metonomy when the cinder is separated, one thing while figuring another from which nothing remains."[21]

The vulnerable tenderness of the Cinder can be heeded as the trace that points beyond itself. It is in this trace of otherness that always remains beyond that calls us to the ethical relationship. In his engagement with Levinas, Derrida argues that the alterity of the Other cannot be separated from her being and thus Levinas rejects Heidegger too quickly. As Derrida explains: "If to understand being is to be able to let be (that is, to respect Being in essence and existence, and to be responsible for one's respect), then the understanding of being always concerns alterity, and par excellance the alterity of the Other in all its originality: one can have to let be only that which one is not. If Being is always to let be, the Being is indeed the other of thought."[22]

This respect for the being of the other then cannot be separated from the promise of fidelity to what remains other. This respect for being, this aspiration to fidelity to the remains is inherently ethical, which is why it shares an affinity with Levinas's ethical philosophy of alterity. For Derrida, Levinas's suspicion that any reference to the being of the Other is reducible to ontology misses the fundamental point that it is precisely the "thereness" of the Other that keeps her as other. It is this "thereness" that remains that must be respected in the ethical relationship. And it is precisely because the otherness of the Other makes her irreducible to a relationship with me that makes this respect ethical and not moral. My responsibility to her cannot be reduced to a set of commandments based on our identity as "rational" men. We cannot know in advance what we should do and when we have met our moral duty because our responsibility is to this unique other. It is to her call that we must respond. It is her "thereness" that makes her unique, absolutely singular, and therefore beyond the law that would limit our responsibility by generalizing, by setting the parameters of what is owed to her on the basis of a set of generalizations.

But the specific evocation of the "thereness" of the Other as Cinder makes another contribution to Levinas's ethical relation. The figure of responsibility upon which Levinas frequently relies is the pregnant Woman who completely gives her body over to the son. This sentimentality expresses what Lacan calls the physical fantasy of Woman. The feminine is evoked as the figure of the ethical relation but only as the good mother. But this is hardly to evoke the otherness of the Other but to once again imagine her within the structure of masculine fantasy. The identification of the Cinder as the feminine *"là"* marks the unconscious association of the feminine as Other but only through the impossibility of embodying her. The paradoxical figure of the Cinder marks the otherness of the Other as beyond any of her fantasy embodiments. In this manner, Derrida's rereading of the beyond of the pleasure principle makes a significant contribution to rethinking the how, the "thereness," of the other, and more specifically, of the Other Woman, what marks the other as the *heteros*. But this "thereness" of the Other also demands the recognition of the singularity of her being. It is her uniqueness, her singularity, her being that constitutes her alterity that calls us to justice. It is the Lacanian law that woman must be denied the otherness of her being for man "to be" man. Deconstruction is justice precisely as it enacts the deconstruction of the Lacanian law that ultimately denies the beyond of the "real" Other.

Notes

1. It is important to note that Lacan himself rarely if ever writes of the *Unheimlich* in spite of how seriously he takes the problem of the *Jenseits*.

2. See Emmanuel Levinas, *Tel* and *AE*.

3. See Slavoj Žižek, *The Sublime Object of Ideology* (London: Verso, 1980), p. 153.

4. See Jacques Derrida, "Differance," in *Margins of Philosophy*, translated by Alan Bass (Chicago: The University of Chicago Press, 1982), pp. 3–27. Subsequent references to this text will be cited as *M*.

5. Ibid. Also see Jacques Derrida, "Le Facteur de La Verite," in *The Post Card: From Socrates to Freud and Beyond*, translated by Alan Bass (Chicago: The University of Chicago Press, 1982), pp. 413–96; and "Outwork" in *Dissemination*, translated by Barbara Johnson (Chicago: The University of Chicago Press, 1981), pp. 1–59. Subsequent references to the former text will be cited as *PC*.

6. See Drucilla Cornell, *The Philosophy of the Limit* (New York: Routledge, 1992), pp. 116–54.

7. I am using "system" in the specific sense given to that term in the work of Niklas Luhmann. I have argued that the gender hierarchy as elaborated in the work of Lacan should be understood as a system as Luhmann defines it. See Drucilla Cornell, "The Philosophy of the Limit, Systems Theory, and the Ethical Relationship," in *Deconstruction and The Possibility of Justice*, eds. Drucilla Cornell, David Gray Carlson, and Michel Rosenfeld (New York: Routledge, Chapman & Hall, 1992), pp. 68–91.

8. See *Sé II*, 275–88/*S II*, 215–47.

9. Judith Butler has brilliantly argued for this conclusion based on Lacan's own understanding of how the phallus comes to signify lack in both sexes. See Judith Butler, *Bodies That Matter* (New York: Routledge, 1993).

10. Lacan openly speculates about the use of slang expressions associated with the term *vulva*, as these also indicate castration. See *Sé VII*, 168–69.

11. For a detailed discussion of Lacan's unique understanding of the centrality of metaphor and metonomy in the constitution of topographical representations of the unconscious object, *das Ding,* see Drucilla Cornell, "What Place in the Dark," in *Transformations* (New York: Routledge, Chapman & Hall, 1993), pp. 170–94.

12. See Drucilla Cornell, *Beyond Accommodation: Ethical Feminism, Deconstruction, and the Law* (New York: Routledge, 1991), pp. 79–118.

13. See Jacques Derrida, "Ellipsis," in *Writing and Difference*, translated by Alan Bass (Chicago: The University of Chicago Press, 1978).

14. Žižek, *The Sublime Object of Ideology,* p. 161.

15. Žižek, *The Sublime Object of Ideology,* p. 162.

16. For an excellent analysis of why queens taking themselves seriously as "queens" would disrupt the law of gender hierarchy, see Judith Butler, *Gender Trouble* (New York: Routledge, 1990).

17. I have figured Derrida as the ultimate chiffoner to bring into focus the ethical relation that is promised to the remains by deconstruction. See Drucilla Cornell, "The Ethical Significance of the Chiffoner," in *The Philosophy of the Limit*, pp. 62–90.

18. Thus although there are clearly important affinities with Theodor Adorno's negative dialectic, there also are important points of divergence in the philosophical positions of the two thinkers. For a more lengthy discussion of the differences between Adorno and Derrida, see Drucilla Cornell, "The Ethical Message of Negative Dialectics," and the conclusion, "The Ethical, Political, and Juridical Significance of the End of Man," in *The Philosophy of the Limit*, pp. 13–38, 170–83.

19. See Drucilla Cornell, "The Feminist Alliance with Deconstruction," in *Beyond Accommodation*, pp. 9–118.

20. Jacques Derrida, *Cinders*, translated by Ned Lukacher (Lincoln and London: University of Nebraska Press, 1991), pp. 33–35.

21. Ibid., p. 71.

22. Derrida, *Writing and Difference*, p. 141.

Chapter 8

Dis-possessed:
How to Remain Silent "after" Levinas

Rudi Visker

As we look back today to that obscure but for none of us insignificant period of (post)structuralism, it would seem that none of the slogans which at that time were intended to sweeten its message can still claim any credibility.[1] Far from being dead and buried, like some purloined letter, the 'author' seems to have been with us all along, barely hidden by the folds of those quotations marks from where he was laughing behind our backs.[2] And far from taking over the place of the subject, 'structure' has, so to speak, only displaced it: much to our surprise, the 'eccentric' subject is still a subject—it is precisely its dependence on something that it did not itself institute or constitute that has prevented it from dying a peaceful death. Forcing the subject to abdicate from the center did not entail the subject's destruction.[3] Quite to the contrary, this decentering has managed to revitalize the subject, and the unexpected result of its rejuvenation is simply that its accusers are now themselves accused: relieved of the heavy burden of a center where it stood constantly accused of falling short in its every endeavor, the subject seems to be thoroughly enjoying its new freedom to linger wherever it pleases, as long as it is not in the center, and to exploit its elusiveness to harass whoever came in its place with new, apparently insoluble, questions and problems.[4] Granted, discourse functions without a meaning—giving subject underlying all knowledge; but then what could it mean that *I* know? And, of course, knowledge evolves according to rules I have not made, and which continually escape me; but why would I not attempt to break into that archive and show the complex genealogy by which those rules came to be? To be sure, I go through life with a certain name—the name of my father, the name of my people—which precedes me and which obligates me; but is it not normal for me to try and know what this obligation asks of me and, failing to get an answer, can I be blamed for attempting to determine what this debt consists in?

Instead of sounding the death knell of the subject, decentering seems to have resulted in a new and different kind of subject, one that would like to know why it was not allowed to die and what the nature of its debt could be; a subject that must try to find its own way, having been denied a center that would provide all of the answers. An explosive situation no doubt, for what could be more dangerous than a debt that is determined by the debtor himself? Is it not the echo of such explosions that recently gave cause for alarm: one need only think of the recent upsurge of nationalism. The difficulty seems to be that the subject is far from content with the ambivalent situation in which it finds itself after being decentered: what it cannot tolerate is not so much that it is excluded from the center, but that it cannot do away with that center, to which it is nonetheless denied access. Now that it has given up its claims, it fails to understand why it cannot die in peace. It fails to understand that whatever dispossessed it after all still obligates it. It thought it could disappear—we all remember "a face in the sand . . ."—but now that it has sobered up, it discovers that the scenario for its voluntary retirement was really just an excuse to make it work even harder. In its old age, the subject finds itself forced into discharging a debt it has nothing to do with, a debt to a center that it thought it had turned its back on and left behind. . . .

Decentering the subject, then, aimed at more than a mere change of position: at stake was an asymmetry in which the subject is obligated by "something"[5] without ever having given its consent and without even being consulted in the matter. The position from which it finds itself being put under obligation is not a position it could possibly occupy in its turn. The addressor and the addressee of 'obligation' belong to nonsubstitutable and nonsimultaneous positions: the reason why the subject cannot disappear—and perhaps one must define the subject today as a "not-able-to-disappear"—is to be found precisely in its decentering. The subject did not just happen to arrive too late to take up its place in the center; it is itself the effect of this originary delay. It is that which cannot be where it would like to be. It is not without a center, but caught in the unbreakable spell of something from which it derives its singularity. Accordingly, what is most 'proper' to the subject, what lies at the basis of its irreplaceability, of its noninterchangeable singularity—in short of its being "itself"—has nothing to do with some secret property or some hidden capacity, but results from a lack of resources on its part, from its ineliminable poverty, its incapacity: the subject is something that has missed an appointment, and it would have never even existed without that break, rent, or gap through which it gains, rather than loses, its intimacy, or without that non-simultaneousness or that 'retardation' *vis-à-vis* itself through which, if we are to believe Levinas, it can fall into time and be 'related' to the Other without being absorbed into them.[6] Even before it is able, the subject is a "not-able," and whatever it can do, it can only do on the basis of and within the horizon opened by the "not-able."

No doubt this is why, instead of seeing in the subject an active principle, contemporary philosophy prefers to emphasize the receptivity that must precede this activity. The subject is no longer thought of as an auto-affection, but as an affectedness by the other. And contemporary thought seems to expect a kind of salvation from this passivity or passibility (Lyotard) which, as the expression goes, precedes all opposition between activity and passivity. The anesthesia of a completely technical world in which there is a system that controls not only its own output but also its own input,[7] this nightmare which, since Heidegger, has emerged on our horizon, could only have its inexorable advance arrested by a renewed attention for this affectedness or this "anesthesia" that involves the subject in a past that is absolute and irrevocable: a past that has never been present nor ever will be present; a past that, precisely by withdrawing, leaves behind a being who must find salvation in his helplessness.

One might wonder if such commonplaces bring us any further. They are, no doubt, too suggestive to be precise. But perhaps for that very reason they are able to invoke something of our strange climate of thought that might best be defined by a certain impatience with all of those (supposed) attempts to eliminate the subject, and by the desire to know how things stand with it and what will come after it, assuming its place has been vacated. Questions that seem of utmost importance, and that have led—or misled, as some would argue—such a notable philosopher as Habermas to the conclusion that what is at stake in the attempt to find a way out of the philosophy of the subject is the heritage of modernity itself. But the paradigm shift that Habermas represents—a turning from subjectivity to intersubjectivity[8]—has, to put it mildly, not been greeted with universal enthusiasm. And since the opposition that is marshalled in the name of a certain postmodernity seems to be concerned precisely with this emphasis on the receptivity of a subject who finds himself in an irrevocably asymmetric position, I thought it not unwise to drop anchor for a moment in these murky waters to which the pilots of modernity and postmodernity have towed the Kantian ship, or into which, Levinas will suggest, that ship has towed them. This suggestion seems to me to merit consideration: it ought to allow us to appreciate the uncompromising position that Levinas occupies in the contemporary crisis of post–Kantian ethics. This is more or less the program for my first half: an attempt, let us say, to not underestimate the 'opponent.' And what an opponent! For how could one even begin to think about the problems under consideration here without first having spent some time—and perhaps a very long time[9]—wandering through the incredibly rich heritage Levinas has bequeathed us? Was he not one of the first to have insisted on the absoluteness of a past that is too much past to ever become present, and to have linked this absoluteness with all of those themes so dear to us, and for which we use his own words: asymmetry, hetero-affection, passivity older than every opposition between activity and passivity? Was it not Levinas who taught us to define the subject as something that does not have the choice of disappearing, and who related the subject to an outside that is so much outside that it can allow itself to go to the very heart of the subject without running the risk of becoming a part of it or being absorbed by it? Are we not quoting Levinas when we speak of the 'other in the self,' and do we not share his *own* suspicion when we attempt to think of the subject on the basis of a "dispossession" that would be more originary than every form of possession? All of this is undoubtedly true and we should be grateful. But Levinas, whose entire philosophy attempts to dispel even the tiniest hint of ek-stasis, would surely agree that gratitude should be coolheaded and should maintain an awareness of the distance separating the one who teaches from the one who is taught. Keeping this distance is the program for my second half: as we shall see, it is a matter of a single, but not insignificant, word. It is, for Levinas, the first word, a word that passes our lips, nowadays, none too easily, a word that we tend to mention rather than use, which is why the significance and function of this word in Levinas fascinate me, and why I would like to know what happens when this word is dropped, or rather—since it is a word that we have wanted to drop for a long time—I would be interested to know how much damage resulted from leaving this word behind. Perhaps I should apologize for such curiosity. It will take up much of our time, but that is just the time needed to answer the question that this article was meant to address: the question whether "subjectivity implies a certain closedness that seems difficult to reconcile with the desire for openness and receptivity so prevalent these days."[10] There is, in my opinion, nothing to be said about this closedness as long as one avoids confronting this first word of Levinas. I have not yet said *what* word, but it will not keep us waiting long—for it is only by introducing the word 'God'[11] that Levinas can avoid being drawn into the maelstrom where Habermas and Lyotard attempt to keep their boats afloat. But not to panic: we will maintain, as mentioned already, a safe distance.

Levinas in the Crisis of Post–Kantian Ethics

I

It is well known that, for Kant, practical reason is both legislation and efficient causality. To bring autonomy into ethics, Kant had to show that reason contains within itself both a *principium diiudicationis bonitatis* and a *principium executionis bonitatis.*[12] Reason should be capable of showing us what has to be done, without having recourse to any considerations other than those that follow from the structure of reason itself (first principle). Yet reason also should have the power to execute the actions that are proposed because they comply with reason (second principle). The first principle led Kant to the discovery of the categorical imperative, while the second led— much later—to what became known as the doctrine of the "fact of reason." Only by bringing these two principles together could Kant reach the conclusion that the law is obligatory *because* it is universal, where, as Lyotard has shown,[13] the "because" operates like an "iff." Accordingly, Kant's first formulation of the categorical imperative lends itself to a double reading: not only "if the norm of such-and-such an action is a universally obligatory norm, then you must perform this action," but also "if you must accomplish such-and-such an action, then the maxim of your will is a universally obligatory norm." Both "if p then q" (if reason then will), and "if q then p" (if will then reason, i.e., universality); in other words, "p if q."

In support of his claim that the underlying transformation of an obligation into a norm is valid, Kant had to introduce an extremely elaborate conceptual architectonics. Since it is precisely this architectonics that was so vigorously assailed by Kant's immediate followers,[14] it should come as no surprise that it is on this exact point that contemporary Continental philosophy appears to have become deadlocked. Take, for instance, Habermas's attempt to reformulate the categorical imperative, giving it the intersubjective spin of a discursive ethics organized around the so-called "D-principle": "only those norms may claim to be valid that could meet with the consent of all affected in their role as participants in a practical discourse."[15] As a consequence, the categorical imperative would be freed from its bondage to a "monologic" reason and readapted to function as a rule of argumentation in practical discourses: "for a norm to be valid, the consequences and side effects of its general observance for the satisfaction of each person's particular interests must be acceptable to all" (ibid.). But Habermas's critics reply that this only holds for the logic of norms and, moreover, already presupposes what is to be shown: that the transition from obligations to norms is unproblematic. Thus, Lyotard's objection that the whole question of the lawfulness of the law—of its obligatory character—is not even raised here. Lyotard insists that one cannot understand why an ethical law holds if one remains caught in this alternative: either *convincing* (hence reasonable) or else *constraining* (hence unreasonable).[16] For a law does not hold because it convinces, nor because it constrains, but because it *obligates*. It takes the form of a prescription that places the addressee in the asymmetric position of a "Thou" to whom the prescription is directed. Such a prescription obligates whether or not the addressee is convinced of its correctness. Its prescriptive force does not depend on such a deliberation; indeed, to make it so depend would mean abandoning the logic of obligation and transforming the law into a commentary on the law, thus replacing *prescription* with *description*. And, of course, for Lyotard, who has made it his task to 'testify to the Differend,' this is an unjustified move. The prescriptive clause "it is an order that p" is transformed into the descriptive clause "someone has said that p must be done (by me)." And it is precisely this transformation that Habermas carries out to determine what "valid norms" are: the maxim that says that p must be done will only be a valid norm if, in Habermas's formulation, it can count on the agreement of all of those concerned. But this whole procedure necessarily presupposes that instead of remaining in the asymmetric position of one who is obligated by a prescription, each participant in such a practical discourse can freely occupy the position from which the prescription is addressed. A norm is valid only if the addressees of the prescription could "at the same time" regard themselves, without coercion, as its addressors, which is to say that a norm is valid only if it could *convince* all of those concerned. But of course, like Kant, Habermas also wants to make the reverse claim: if one is convinced by a (moral) validity claim, then one is committed to defending it, and the result of such a defense must be such that it satisfies the conditions for a valid norm.[17] Just as with Kant, "p if and only if q."

Both Lyotard and Levinas would protest here, though not for the same reasons. I will come back to this point later. For the moment, let us concentrate on their rather curious alliance against humanism, or at least against a certain version of humanism.[18] For both Lyotard and Levinas, it is a humanism that still believes in the possibility of doing away with an *Unmündigkeit* (the famous "immaturity" in Kant's "What Is Enlightenment?") that one owes only to oneself. And yet, Lyotard wonders,[19] might there not be a different *Unmündigkeit* than the one Habermas has in mind, and is *this Unmündigkeit* not excluded *a priori* whenever one substitutes the logic of norms ("either convincing or else constraining") for the logic of obligation? Is there not in obligation another, more deeply buried *Unmündigkeit*, an inability to speak and—*a fortiori*—to argue, an "in-fantia" that one cannot and should not render communicatively transparent, for to do so would mean destroying 'something' (something that Lyotard calls "the inhuman") that belongs to the very condition of our humanity? An 'inhuman' that, far from being a simple denial of our humanity, constitutes its very tissue, to the point that Lyotard can even refer to it as our "soul": that other in me to whom I owe a vague debt, but which is precisely *in*human because it left me this debt without telling me what I must do to pay it off. The result of this emphasis on the passivity (or "passibility") of the subject is that the human subject's humanity is tied to a "mancipium"[20] from which it cannot e-mancipate itself. There is some "Thing" that obligates it without it ever being able to abandon the position it is forced to take as a result of this (quasi) obligation. The subject is de-centered, not because it lacks a center but because, in its singularity, it gravitates around a center it can neither have access to nor simply leave behind. Given this position, one can well imagine why Lyotard remains skeptical about the hopes that Habermas has invested in the operative power of practical discourse. For in terms of the aforementioned discussion, it seems that the Habermasian transformation of values into valid norms would require participants who not only argue *from* a center that has them in its grasp (the values "have" them), but who also have managed to break *into* that center and exercise argumentative control over it (they "have" the values). Failing such ideal participants, practical discourse could not consist only of those reactions to validity claims allowed by Habermas's model: affirmation ("yes"), negation ("no"), or suspension (a future "yes" or "no").[21] If one of the participants were to say, for example, "and yet these are my values; I have them simply because I have them," then *according to this model* the discussion would only come to a temporary end, since the reason given is actually not a reason at all. There is only an incapacity for argument, an "in-fantia" which, for Habermas, is only the temporary absence of something still to come (or which should have already come). Such a subject—in opposition to Lyotard and Levinas—is only temporarily *unmündig*. Its lack of *Mündigkeit* would not point to its decentering but would need to be seen as deriving from its being only stalled halfway in its attempt to break into a center to which it already had right of access, and the ensuing dissociation between the participants would need to be regarded as a *dissensus* that emerges against the background of a possible *consensus*. Not that Habermas would go so far as to say that one could (or should) in principle reach a consensus; his point is only that, if one enters into argument, then one is already committed to a possible "yes" or "no," and the "no" which claims that things are like this simply because things are like this is not really a "no." It is rather a kind of silence that derives its status from the order it has withdrawn from. That it could derive this status from an order opposed to the argumentative order that Habermas has in mind; that it could point to an obligation that obligates without the addressee knowing the reasons for the obligation; that it could be a silence that concerns something more and something other than simply the factual absence of future speech; the silence of a dissensus that cannot be forced into an argumentative "yes" or "no"—this possibility is ruled out from the start by the assumptions from which Habermas explicitly begins: there is no 'silence' that does not already point to an imminent 'yes' or 'no.' In the end, 'validity' will rule over 'meaning.' Consequently, the dispute over the possibility of what Lyotard calls the "differend" is itself at the root of the "differend" separating Habermas and Lyotard.[22] The hiatus between prescription ("you must") and description ("something obligates me to do this or that") cannot be traversed by argument, for that would presuppose that one has access to the "something" that oblig-ates, and that one could assent to its reasons for obligating—which means that the hiatus must already have been bridged before it can be bridged.

But, of course, if one denies Kant or his followers the transition from prescription to description, then one replaces autonomy with heteronomy. As a consequence, the law is no longer obligatory because (iff) it is universal; it is now obligatory because it is obligatory.[23] In doing this, however, one would seem to have thrown away Kant's first principle (*diiudicatio bonitatis*) and thus to have surrendered ethics to what Lyotard calls "the anxiety of idi-olect."[24] For if it is only the fact of obligation that allows me to recognize the ethical law, and if I am the only one who finds himself in the asymmetric posi-tion of the law's addressee (hence *idio*-lect), and if there is no possibility of trading or even comparing my responsibility with that of others (cf. 'is my maxim universalizable?'), then how can I ever know if the appeal that oblig-ates me is an *ethical* one? How will I even know that there is an appeal? Both Abraham and President Schreber heard the voice of God, and they each heard a voice that spoke only to them (i.e., *idiolect*). Did they *both* hear the voice of God? And did they both hear the voice *of God*? Can a voice that commands me to kill my own son be the voice of God? Did I not just imagine hearing a voice, when in fact it was only my own infanticidal urges? Does it even really matter which voice I heard, as long as there is obligation? Instead of trying to escape these problems, Lyotard seems satisfied with simply acknowledging them. Suggesting a *rapprochement* with Levinas, he seems content to sum-marize them in the statement that "obligation should be described as a scan-dal for the one who is obligated" (*D* nr. 170). And on this point the alliance falls apart. Levinas's position may not be modern, but neither is it postmod-ern.[25] As we shall see, it is—and I use the term in a neutral sense—anti-mod-ern.[26]

II

Although Levinas would side with Lyotard in stressing the importance of the asymmetric position of the one obligated by the ethical law, he also would want to protest against Lyotard's pagan appropriation of some of his major concepts. Their disagreement has to do with the identity of what Lyotard calls the "addressor." Contrary to Lyotard, Levinas is not content to characterize the ethical law solely by the fact that whoever is put under oblig-ation finds himself "placed in the position of addressee for a prescription" (*D* nr. 163) and then to simply call this a scandal. Levinas would like to say a word about the addressor as well. Though he will emphasize that responsibil-ity "precedes freedom" (*OB,* 197 n 27) and that values "'weigh' on the sub-ject," thus pointing to a fundamental passivity "which cannot assume what it receives, but which, in spite of itself, becomes responsible for it" (*OB*, 198 n 28), what he wants to emphasize above all else is that this "antecedence of responsibility to freedom" signifies "the *Goodness of the Good*: the necessity that *the Good* choose me first before I can be in a position to choose, that is, welcome its choice" (*OB*, 122). To be sure, ethics has to do with an absolute appeal, as Lyotard also admits, but this appeal is precisely an *ethical* appeal because its addressor is the Good. Neglecting this difference and mistaking what is only a necessary condition (obligation) for a sufficient one inevitably leads to the problems that Lyotard has signaled under the heading "anxiety of idiolect." But for Levinas, these problems are only a consequence of the pagan *quid pro quo* that makes values depend on drives, instead of *vice versa*. "From the Good to me there is assignation: a relation that survives the 'death of God.' The death of God perhaps signifies only the possibility to reduce every value arousing an impulse to an impulse arousing a value" (*OB*, 123). Accordingly, Lyotard's brand of postmodernism is for Levinas only the return of the sacred, a return that becomes inevitable when, along with the idea of the Good, the idea of the holy is lost as well. For the holy is not the sacred but the only thing that can prevent it from overwhelming us.

If one misses this distinction between the sacred and the holy, one will have missed the structure of Levinasian ethics. To be sure, ethics for Levinas is a matter of 'something' that "has chosen me before I have chosen it" (*OB*, 11) and he, too, will consider the ethical subject as carrying an 'other-in-himself' that he will explicitly designate as the "soul" (*OB*, 191 n 3). But what thus "penetrates" the subject "with its rays unbeknownst to itself [*á l'insu*]"[27] (*OB*, 11) is not simply that inhuman "Thing" around which we gravitate without ever reaching it, as Lyotard thinks in the wake of Lacan. It is not something that attracts us but that we can never reach, since the condition for its "fatal attraction"[28] is that we have always already lost it and that we derive our singularity from this loss, since it is only through this loss that we are who we are. To be sure, ethics for Levinas also is about an absolute past and refers back to a trauma that is too great to be taken up. But, unlike for Lacan[29] or Lyotard, the problem for Levinas is not that of a "tragic ethics," which says we should not "give way on our desire" and at the same time shows us the terrible consequences of not giving way on our desire. The problem is not how we should relate to the "Thing" that makes us noninterchangeable nor how, at the same time, that opaque attachment must be interrupted by another dimension (Lacan's "law of the signifier," Lyotard's "norms") so we can maintain enough distance from that point where we would, as it were, become so singular that we would suffocate in our own singularity. The Good for Levinas is not good because it attracts us, but because it interrupts such an attraction: "The fact that in its goodness the Good *declines the desire it arouses* while *inclining it* toward responsibility for the neighbor, *preserves difference* in the non-indifference of the Good, which chooses me before I welcome it" (*OB,* 123, my emphasis). One does not "gravitate" *around* the Good. The Good is only good because it breaks that sacred spell—that desire to touch what we have always already lost and which, by that very fact, attracts us—and reorients the course of the dynamic thus awakened, inclining it toward the others. This makes all of the difference between the heteronomy Lyotard supports and the special kind of heteronomy found in Levinas.

The Good would be no different from Lyotard's "inhuman" if it were only to place us in the position of an addressee of a (quasi)obligation, leaving us "disoriented" with regard to that "vague debt" we do not know how to deal with. It would obligate us without itself feeling the least obligation to us, thus surrendering us to the whims of that capricious and opaque "law without law" that Lacan calls "the Thing." There would be "something" in us that would, in Levinas's words, "reign *in its own way*" (*OB,* 194 n 2). A classical heteronomy, where the law is given by an authority outside the law, an "*Hors-la-loi*"[30] that also behaves as an outlaw. But such is not the heteronomy of Levinas; it is rather the sort of heteronomy one gets when the link between the absolute and the Good is severed, as Lacan and Freud have done[31]—a heritage that, as we have seen, Lyotard has no hesitation in accepting. But Levinas not only refuses to sever that link; he likewise refuses to see the Good as that authority which precedes the law and arrogates to itself the power to make the law, as is the case in an ordinary ethics of heteronomy. For Levinas, there can only be an ethical law because the Good renounces such a power, because it abdicates and *refuses to "reign"* (*OB,* 194 n 4): "an-archy" of the Good which "chooses" us, but refuses to subject us, thereby making us free. No one, says Levinas, "is enslaved to the Good" (*OB,* 11). We would have been condemned to slavery had the Good manifested itself to us in its full splendor, for then we would have had no chance to avert our gaze. But because the Good is good— that is, holy and not sacred, "not numinous" (*TI,* 77)—it has given us that chance. And, as is well known, Levinas 'deformalizes' this by pointing us to the trace of something that refuses to present itself, the trace of a transcendence that already "effaced" itself before it could be "assembled" (e.g., *OB,* 161; *TI,* 104). This trace is, of course, the face of the Other: an appeal directed to us, but which is defenseless against our refusal, lacking the means to exact what it asks. The face of the Other is not sacred; it is holy. It is not the object of a taboo, not something whose separation attracts me and, despite the prohibition, arouses in me the desire to touch it. The face is holy because it speaks, and speech for Levinas means establishing a distance. Speech is a prohibition of the contact that would bridge the distance thus established. According to Levinas, the one who speaks to me does not arouse in me the desire to touch him, but accuses me of that desire, transforming it into a desire to serve and give.

Yet the word of the Other would not have this force were it not the echo of a word that preceded it, were it not the descendant of that first word, "God." The Other can only deflect my urges and escape my attempts at appropriation because he is more than what I see of him. The face is not a phenomenon. In the words of Levinas, "the face breaks through the form that nevertheless delimits it" (*TI*, 198; *CP*, 96). The Other can only be other because he finds his light in himself, and bears his meaning within. He is, therefore, *kath'auto*: more than what I can know and comprehend—not unknown but unknowable. So the alterity of the Other is ab-solute and this absoluteness comes to me under the form of a prohibition, in the face: "Thou shalt not kill me." To kill the Other is to extinguish his light, to reduce him to his form—in other words, to make of him a phenomenon, to reduce his meaning to what I can see of him. And since the Other is not only face, but also form, not only a speaking *to* me, but also a spoken that I hear, the possibility to "kill" him, to reduce him to what I see and hear of him, will always remain open. Without this possibility, there would be neither ethics nor responsibility. Nor could there be ethics or responsibility if this choice I have to make would be indifferent, if it were not qualified. The Other must be not only outside me, but *above me*. To kill him must signify: his *murder*.[32] To reduce him to his form must signify: to commit an injustice, to rob him of his ethical dignity. *And the Other does not owe this ethical dignity to himself.* The Other is face, a *surplus* over his form; he is a face that is *too large* for his form, and the Other owes this infinity to the fact that he is in the trace of the Infinite. Consequently, the Other for Levinas, *pace* Sartre, is "not simply another freedom: to give me knowledge of injustice, his gaze must come to me from a dimension of the ideal. The Other must be closer to God than I" (*CP*, 55–56). This elevation of the Other that Levinas calls face would not have been possible without the abdication of the Good that lends his ethics a special sort of heteronomy. By coming in the trace of the Good—or of *the* Infinite, as Levinas so often calls it—the face of the Other is invested with a value that I must and at the same time do not have to respect. The appeal comes from above, but it is an order that implores. I am free to respond to it or not, but whatever I do, I cannot keep *silent*: "I cannot evade *by silence* the discourse which the epiphany that occurs as a face opens, as Thrasymachus, irritated, tries to do, in the first book of the *Republic*. . . . Before the hunger of men responsibility is measured only "objectively"; it is irrecusable. The face opens the primordial discourse whose *first word* is obligation, *which no "interiority" permits avoiding*. It is that discourse that obliges the entering into discourse, the commencement of discourse rationalism prays for, a "force" that convinces even "the people who do not wish to listen" and thus founds *the true universality of reason*" (*TI*, 201).

Hence the program for my second half: what to think of a philosophy that tells us that we cannot be silent, that grants us our interiority but then seems to make this interiority fully signifiable through ethics? What to think of an ethics that *precisely for that reason*—as I shall explain—has made sacrifice "the norm and criterion of the approach" of the Infinite?[33] What if it has come too late? What if, apart from this ethical dispossession (*TI*, 172) or decentering that Levinas speaks of, there is still another dispossession that he will not or cannot think, in order to be able to think as he does? At stake then, is but a word, but for Levinas it is the "first word": "monotheism, the word of the one and only God, is precisely the word that one cannot help but hear, and cannot help but answer. It is the word that obliges us to enter into discourse. It is because the monotheists have enabled the world to hear the word of the one and only God that Greek universalism can work in humanity and slowly unify that humanity" (*DF*, 178, translation corrected). The death of Parmenides?[34] Or ethical henology?

How to Keep Silent after Levinas

III

There would be no silence, then, that could evade "the discourse which the epiphany that occurs as a face opens" (*TI*, 201). Of course, Levinas is not denying the obvious here, as if, when confronted with the face of the Other, one would not be able to hold one's tongue and refuse to speak. He means that any refusal to respond to the appeal of the face, and thereby to enter "ethical discourse" should be seen as a silence that receives its meaning from that appeal and within that discourse: "silence" is already a falling short of what is demanded. Not only literal silence of course; every attempt to evade the appeal of the Other, every excuse made, is a kind of silence—even if it is announced out loud. For this "true universalism" there is no interiority that can avoid the ethical obligation. We can try to outwit God, like Jonah; we can hide from him, taking refuge in a ship's hold and falling asleep in the midst of a storm. But then we take to sleep the very thing we were trying to avoid,[35] thus affirming what we wanted to deny: it may be that there are some responsibilities that we cannot handle, but this does not mean that we do not have them, and once we have them, there can no longer be anything like the sleep of the innocent. *All* sleep is now a lack of wakefulness.

One might find this somewhat exaggerated, but in that case one must ask oneself just what it is about Levinas's ethics that leads to such exaggeration. Better still: one must ask why it is founded upon this exaggeration and cannot get around it. For according to Levinas, ethics begins by "penetrating"[36] the armor of my interiority. It is this interiority that is thrown into question by the face: the face does not accuse me of having neglected to do something, nor of doing something that I should not have done. Such is not the responsibility the face confronts me with. Rather, it blames me for something that was out of my hands, for a guilt without fault, or a 'fault' that I am not guilty of, but that I am nonetheless responsible for. This 'fault' is my existence itself: just by 'being there,' by taking up a place, by breathing and eating, by all those processes in which I arbitrarily appropriate things, I *inevitably* and unwittingly make a claim on something to which I have no right. And the fact that I have no right to it is not something that Levinas just postulates; he tries to find a phenomenological basis for it in his description of what exactly happens when I am confronted with the appeal of the Other. It is to this description that one must refer if one maintains that Levinas is doing a phenomenological ethics, or an ethical phenomenology—a characterization that should be kept separate from the role played by the notion of the 'face' in this ethics since, as we have seen, the face is not a phenomenon. Indeed, according to Levinas, it is precisely because the face is *not* a phenomenon—precisely because it does not *show* itself to me, but rather *addresses* me and *appeals* to me—that it manages to embarrass me. The appeal of the Other does something to me that no phenomenon could ever do: it disconcerts me and gives me a conscience that is primarily and necessarily a *bad* conscience, since it questions and casts in doubt something which, until then, I would not have been able to question: "What is most natural becomes the most problematic. Do I have the right to be? Is being in the world not taking the place of someone?"[37] "Does not my existence, in its peacefulness and with the good conscience of its *conatus*, mean that I let the other person die?" (*DQI*, 248). The Other puts my very existence in question: my place on this earth suddenly appears as a usurpation, for which I am ashamed. And this shame forms the phenomenological cornerstone on which Levinas's ethics rests. Place this in question, and one places all the rest in question.

Nevertheless it is a question that can hardly be avoided. For is it indeed the case that my reaction to the appeal of the Other is one of shame? Do I then suffer the bad conscience of one who realizes that he has no right to his rights nor even to his existence, and for whom that existence, formerly so evident, suddenly appears in all its "hatefulness" (*DQI*, 248), "imperialism" (*OB*, 110, 121) and "egoism" (*TrO*, 353)? Is it true that in the confrontation with the face of the Other, I not only see my naturalness put into question, but that in the same move I also experience it as something which, for me to keep it, will henceforth require me to make an unnatural (for ethically qualified) move? Levinas seems to think so, and it is perhaps unsurprising that in order to buttress this assertion—or this description—he resorts to a vocabulary deriving from Sartre: the ethical appeal, one reads in *Otherwise Than Being*, turns me into a *pour autrui* (*AE*, 81/*OB*, 64)). I cease to be *pour soi* (*AE*, 67/*OB*, 52)) and become a hostage of the Other without ever coinciding with him; I am "turned inside out," "denucleated," "dispossessed," "uprooted" and, strangely enough, it is this "abdication" that takes place "despite myself,"[38] this abandoning of my spontaneous naturalness that, for Levinas, frees me (*TI*, 88), humanizes me, and summons me to my "final essence" (*TI*, 179). In order to be, to be "there," to be "someone," being—as it were—had to be enclosed within my person, and not by choice but by necessity; the alternative would mean that I as a person would disappear in the anonymous night of what Levinas calls the *il y a*. And yet, it is exactly this *conatus*, this "closedness" (*TI*, 148) in Being that is thrown into "crisis" by the gaze of the Other (*DQI*, 248). A crisis that, for Levinas, summons this interiority "from the outside" (*OB*, 150) and exposes a level deeper than my "closedness" where I am first of all an "openness" (*OB*, 115), an inability to "remain in [my]self" (*CP*, 149), an "inability to shut myself up" (*CP*, 150), and yet a 'self' that is not interchangeable with that of others, because it is *this* self that is responsible for those others, and it has this responsibility to thank for the dispossession that singularizes it and makes it a self. It is with regard to this level that Levinas calls ethics a *religion*: *religare* that binds me *with others* (*noué, AE*, 96/*OB* 76) and devotes me to them (*voué, DQI*, 249) even before I am bound to myself. And it is from this point of view that henceforth *every* attempt—albeit only momentary—to escape this appeal, the *least* remainder of concern for myself, will be seen as a closure of a preexisting opening. It will be seen as a refusal of the orientation to which the Good has invited us, without compelling us since, as we have seen, the Good is only good because it does not take possession of us, because it "inspires" (*OB*, 140ff) us without becoming our master. And it is in order to safeguard this distinction between the holiness of the Good that liberates us and the *ecstatic* obsession of the sacred that strips us of our position, our *stasis*, that Levinas must simultaneously recognize and deny the possibility of keeping silent: "The will is free to assume this responsibility in whatever sense it likes; it is not free to refuse this responsibility itself; it is not free to ignore the meaningful world into which the face of the Other has introduced it" (*TI*, 218–19). To be able to keep silent means to be able to disregard the appeal, to not have to take it up. But, as Levinas will insist, this presupposes that it has already been heard: "The being that expresses itself imposes itself, but does so precisely by appealing to me with its destitution and nudity—its hunger—*without my being able to be deaf to that appeal*" (*TI*, 200). It is from this hearing before one has chosen to listen, from this "unconditioned 'Yes' of submission" (*OB*, 122), that Levinas will derive his "true universality"—a universality that has its origin in an asymmetry *and therefore* in a hierarchy between Good and Evil. For there can be little doubt that what is at stake here, for Levinas, is this hierarchy. From the moment there is an appeal, "silence," interiority, and closure have an *ethical* significance: it is the "claim" of *"Evil"* to be "the contemporary, the equal, the twin, of the Good" (*CP*, 138).

This is a strong thesis, but one which is, for Levinas, unavoidable. It is the idea that my naturalness, my spontaneous, and my involuntary self-concern cannot *appear* without thereby immediately losing this naturalness and becoming the object of my free choice. Ethics is the *complete* submission of nature to the order of good and evil that breaks into that nature *from without*. This is why Levinas says, and tirelessly repeats, that ethics is a *liberation*. The face of the Other liberates me because it confronts me with the possibility of choosing something that, left to myself, I could never have chosen. One only becomes human when one's existence is no longer *conatus*, no longer something working behind one's back, but choice, in other words, "morality": true humanization comes from the Other, that is, from the invitation to place, above my own existence, something else—the existence of the Other. Hence, for Levinas, what defines the humanity of man is his ability to sacrifice. Man is the sort of being who can reject his being, "reverse" his *conatus* (*OB 70*) and sacrifice himself: "To discover in the I such an orientation is to identify the I and morality" (*TrO*, 353).

Such an identification is only possible for Levinas if he can refer to something that would bring into the I, from the outside, this orientation against naturalness, against *conatus essendi*. And this outside which is so much outside that it can enter the I without becoming part of it—and which owes its *orientational power* precisely to this refusal to participate in the I or to let the I participate in it—this outside is the Good, or the idea of the Infinite, whose trace is the face of the Other. By being a trace of this idea, the face of the Other can make an appeal to me that I cannot take possession of (since the face overflows the form lying within my reach) but which *dispossesses* me, because I cannot not hear it and because, from the moment I have heard it, the naturalness of my being shows up only to immediately 'take its leave.' The face effects a phenomenological reduction that does not add a dimension to my being, but takes one away. The feeling of shame with which I react to the gaze of the Other does not concern the fact that, with this gaze, I receive a nature and with the purity of my *pour soi* lose the absoluteness of my freedom. According to Levinas, and contrary to Sartre,[39] I am ashamed not so much of the nature that I become, but of the nature that I was. The gaze of the Other does not enslave; it liberates. And it liberates because there is no way for me to transcend it without already submitting to it. Keeping silent is merely a refusal to speak. It is merely the expression of an *impassibility* that Levinas can only treat as a shortcoming, and hence as "egoism or Evil" (*CP,* 137)—but this link can only be made if one can rely on a universe that is also a *univers de discours* that has ascribed *all possible* discourse a place within it. And for Levinas, there is such a universe. For there is a word that "one cannot not hear, to which one cannot not answer" *(supra)*. It is through the operation of this word—'God'—that the ethical situation becomes, for Levinas, a religious situation: "a situation in which the subject finds it impossible to hide," "an exceptional situation in which one is always before the face of the Other" and, let us note, *"where there is nothing private."*[40] I would like for a moment to consider, in concluding, what would happen if one would put this word out of operation. I would even go so far as to start from one place—but it is a central one—where Levinas unexpectedly seems to have put this word out of operation himself, although apparently without realizing it and without drawing the necessary consequences. And it is perhaps not without importance that, at the very moment when he was offered the opportunity to free himself from Sartre, he let it pass.

IV

But why should Levinas have taken such an opportunity? Did he still need it? Have we not just seen that the simple introduction of an ethical factor had enabled Levinas to exorcise the entire Sartrean universe? For if the Other is not only outside me, but also above me, then is he not just "another freedom," irreconcilable with mine, who need only look at me to transcend my freedom and make me an object in the world, just as I, in turn, can make him an object in the world by looking at him and transcending his transcendence? This whole endless aporia that turns Sartre's description of intersubjective relations into that hell where 'love' boils down to a choice between sadism (the Other is an object) or masochism (I am an object for the Other) seems to fall apart from the moment one realizes that "the Other is not transcendent because he would be free as I am" (*TI*, 87), but that this transcendence points to a "superiority" (ibid.) which makes his gaze "incomparable" (*TI*, 86) to mine, allowing him to give me the "bad conscience" of a freedom that is not just transcended but qualified, a freedom that is ashamed of being still *too much* nature, the freedom of "a tree that grows without regard for everything it suppresses and breaks, grabbing all the nourishment, air and sun" (*DF*, 100). It is shame—shame for the "arbitrariness" and "injustice" of a freedom that was mere *conatus*—that chastens me, turns me into a moral being and, according to Levinas, gives me the possibility of carrying out that *metanoia* that, it is true, Sartre mentioned,[41] but conspicuously failed to articulate.

For this chastening to occur, there must be a "disproportion"[42] between the Other and me, a disproportion referred to by Levinas when he says that the Other is "closer to God than I" *(supra)*: "For me to feel myself to be unjust I must measure myself against the infinite" (*CP*, 58). But that infinite that provides me with a measure does not, as we know, show itself to me directly. It comes to me in the face of the Other that appeals to me, and it lends that face the force needed for an *"ethical* resistance"*: to ignore the imperative of that face means, as was pointed out earlier, to let oneself be judged by it. This is why it is crucial for Levinas to maintain a distinction between the face of the Other and what I can see of the Other. Only if the Other is *more* than this form that I see, only if there is something about him by which he finds his meaning in himself and can thus always question the meaning I give to him, can there be any talk of an ethical resistance and an injustice that I commit against him by reducing his face to its form. And in the course of making this crucial distinction, Levinas takes the *further* crucial decision to link that "surplus" of the face over its form—that "something extra" by which the face can break through the form that manifests it—with the idea of the infinite: "The idea of infinity, the infinitely more contained in the less, is concretely produced in the form of a relation with the face. And the idea of infinity alone maintains the exteriority of the other with respect to the same, despite this relation" (*TI*, 196). While, for Levinas, the form is only an exteriority that turns toward me, thereby becoming involved with my interiority, the exteriority of the face is, through the idea of infinity, ab-solute: "A face is the unique openness in which the signifyingness of the trans-cendent does not nullify the transcendence and make it enter into an immanent order" (*CP*, 103). To attain this status, then, the face must be *completely independent* of form; although it manifests itself in form, this form can in no way affect or "touch" it. Hence the face, even before entering into the form that manifests it, must already have withdrawn from it: a "supreme anachronism" that Levinas calls "trace," yet which he notes is not "simply a word" but "the proximity of God in the face of my neighbor."[43] Without this proximity of a "God who passed" (*CP*, 106), that is, without this "abdication" of the Good that has always already withdrawn from the desire which it awakens and which orients that desire toward my neighbor(s), the face would not be independent of form: "The supreme presence of a face is inseparable from this supreme and irreversible absence," which Levinas calls "God" or "He" or "*illeity* of the third person" (*CP*, 104). A "face, wholly open, can at the same time be in itself because it is in the trace of illeity" (*CP*, 106).

Without this independence of the face with respect to form—without this autarky—the otherness of the Other could not be ab-solute. And without this ab-solute foreignness that the face has by virtue of its being in the trace of the illeity of a God who passed, it could not impose its rights on me nor put up any (ethical) resistance against my attempt to brush aside its appeal. But *if the ethical value of the Other is to be situated in the face*, if, in other words, the face is not dependent on the 'form' or the 'context' in order to be what it 'is,' if it is "*signification without a context*" (*TI*, 23), manifestation "over and beyond form" (*TI*, 66), "*not disclosure but revelation*" (TI, 65–66), then how can Levinas at the same time call this autarky of the face, this "infinity of the Other," a "destitution" (*TI*, 213)? How can something that "is not of the world" (*TI*, 198), and that enters the world without ever becoming a part of it, at the same time *suffer* under "its absence from this world into which it enters" (*TI*, 75)? How can Levinas call this absence from form, which is also called supreme presence and the condition for the alterity of the Other, an "exiling" (ibid.)? How can this strangeness that guarantees the alterity of the Other be, at the same time, "strangeness-destitution," "his condition of being stranger, destitute or proletarian" (ibid.)? Why does the nakedness of the face—which is naked because it exceeds form and whose status requires independence from form—why does this *glorious* nakedness extend "into the nakedness of the body that is cold" (ibid.)? How can Levinas say that the face is naked because it "breaks into the order of the world," that it is without context because it is "wrested from the context of the world"[44] and, at the same time, call this nakedness "a distress" (*CP*, 96)? Does this mean that, contrary to what was suggested, the distress of the Other does have some 'relation' to the 'context' or the 'form' from which his face was supposed to be independent? But can we then keep situating the ethical dignity of the Other in his face? Could it be that it is less independent from form than the analysis of the face that Levinas himself has given us might have led us to suspect?

Levinas, of course, could easily make room for this objection by pointing out that it is precisely through form that this ethical dignity is *ethical*—a dignity that *makes an appeal to me*—because it is through form that the Other is vulnerable. To *keep* his dignity, the other is dependent on my help; after all, I retain the possibility of reducing his face to its form—I can murder him— and it is this possibility that makes the "ethical resistance" of his face an *ethical*, not a real resistance.[45] The *dignity* of the Other, then, has to do with his face, but because that face cannot circumvent the form, from which it is nevertheless independent, this dignity is, *in concreto*, an *ethical* dignity.

And yet, this answer is hardly satisfying and passes over the problem I want to pose. For if Levinas calls the face "naked" and sees in this nakedness the "destitution" of the Other—in other words, the fact that he is not only "above me" but also "beneath me," that he not only commands but supplicates—he is alluding not only to the fact that the Other, as a concrete person, remains vulnerable in that form from which his face becomes detached in the very moment the form shines forth (*CP*, 96). For Levinas, this nakedness also alludes to *a lack of form*: "Stripped of its very form, a face is frozen in its nudity. It is a distress" (ibid.).[46] The nakedness Levinas has in mind *here* is precisely what the word says: a lack of clothing, in other words, a need for 'form' or 'context.' But, once again, how can this face—which for Levinas is "living" because it "undoes the form" that would make it "adequate to the Same" and would "betray" and "alienate" its "exteriority" (*TI*, 66)—how can this face that is a "bareness *without any cultural ornament*" suffer because of the absence of something from which it *already* withdrew, even *before* entering? And yet this is what Levinas suggests when he sees the nakedness of the

Other as his destitution, calls the Other "fatherless," "stranger," "uprooted,"
and contrasts this lack of roots, home, and a fatherland with my own situation:
"To hear his destitution which cries out for justice is not to represent an image
to oneself [to know the 'form' of this destitution—R.V.], but is to posit oneself as responsible, *both as more and as less than the being that presents itself
in the face.* Less, for the face . . . judges me . . . [and] comes from a dimension of height. . . . More, for my position as *I* consists in being able to respond
to this essential destitution of the Other, finding resources for myself. The
Other who *dominates* me in his transcendence is thus the stranger . . . *to whom
I am obligated*" (*TI*, 215). To take up the appeal of that stranger, or even
already to receive that appeal (and, as we have seen, one cannot not hear it)
means to be ashamed of one's own wealth, to experience one's own existence
as a usurpation, to lose one's titles—in short, to be oneself uprooted and *dispossessed* by the appeal of the other who is uprooted, to cease being *pour soi*
and to become completely *pour l'autre*, for the "altruism" in question here is
"total."[47] One will no doubt recall "nothing private." "The I in relationship
with the infinite is an impossibility of stopping its forward march . . . it is, *literally*, not to have time to turn back. It is to be not able to escape responsibility, to not have a hiding place of interiority where one comes back into oneself, to march forward *without concern for oneself*" (*CP*, 98). Ethics is
"without calculation, *for going on to infinity*" (*CP*, 72). Sacrifice becomes the
norm and criterion for the approach of the Other.

A 'conclusion' that both presupposes and implies that for Levinas the
nature and definition of ethics does not *ultimately* depend upon the 'destitution' of the Other, but upon what Levinas calls his "height" (i.e., the infinity
of his face). The Other's destitution is infinite, thus asking an infinite sacrifice from me, *since this destitution comes from the face*—a face that Levinas
has defined as always already being stripped of a form it has no need of and
in which it cannot be at home precisely because of the infinity of being a face.
Strange as it may sound, it seems that, by its very definition, there is nothing
I can do to prevent such a face from being "frozen" for it lacks and will always
lack that clothing or context or form that I apparently possess. Which is why,
for Levinas, the essential uprootedness of the Other cannot but have my
uprootedness as a consequence. Since the Other (by definition) "lacks" roots,
in other words, something which, according to Levinas, I possess, he can
never become rooted like me. Rather, I will have to become like he is by giving up in an *infinite* sacrifice the roots he does not have. And in that process,
I will asymptotically approach my true humanity, for that ground to which I
am attached, that attachment itself is, for Levinas, only a sign of my naturalness. Humanity, after all, "is not a forest" and the individual "is not a tree"
(*DF*, 23). Being uprooted is a humanization, a leaving nature behind. True universality: community of the uprooted.[48]

But is one a stranger only when one has no roots? Is uprootedness always a 'lack' of roots?—this strange lack, which for Levinas, as we have seen, cannot really be a lack since it results from his definition of the face, which is infinite and therefore cannot really be in need of a form that is too small, too finite, to contain it. *But what if what Levinas insists on treating as a 'lack' of roots were really an 'excess'?* Might there not also be an uprootedness that comes from an excess of roots, an excess that is yet *not enough* to be rooted like a tree? Does the difference between a man and a tree lie in the absence or presence of roots, as Levinas suggests, *or in the nature of the rootedness itself?* What is the cold that makes the face freeze? What, finally, is the destitution of the Other?

Let me try to make these questions and this suggestion of an alternative somewhat more concrete by coming back to the opposition that regulates all of Levinas's thought and which, *in the final analysis*, amounts to an ethicization of Sartre's dualism. Levinas does not deny that the Other has a 'form' by which I can 'perceive' him, nor that I can encounter him in a context where he fulfills a certain role and is situated by this role, the context of a culture, for example. What he opposes is that the Other would be reduced to this form, context, or culture, for then he would lose his alterity and be swallowed up by something that I can know, which "appears" to me. If the Other is only "in a cultural whole and is illuminated by this whole, as a text by its context," then understanding the Other would be "a hermeneutics and an exegesis" (*CP,* 95). To avoid this, Levinas wants the Other *also* to have its "own meaning" that would not depend on "this meaning received from the world" (ibid.) but that would disrupt it. To avoid what he perceives as the danger of contextualism—whether in the guise of relativism or culturalism—the worldly (mundane) meaning of the Other must be thrown off balance by "another presence that is abstract (or, more exactly, absolute) and not integrated into the world" (ibid.). This other meaning—which, both for Sartre and Levinas, comes from "*au-delà du monde*," and which both call 'infinite'—is for Levinas the face, a face that he calls "ab-stract" because it "disturbs immanence without settling into the horizons of the world" (*CP,* 102). Because the face is *independent of* world, context, and culture, because it comes from an "elsewhere . . . into which it already withdraws" (ibid.) even before it arrives, Levinas sees in it a guarantee that the Other is more than a "cultural meaning" who approaches me from out of his cultural whole. Ethics, therefore, must *precede* culture: as face, the Other is an "*abstract* man," in the sense of someone "disengaged *from all culture*" (*CP,* 101).

But does not this ethics begin too late? Is there not something that precedes it, something that it wanted to suppress but that ultimately returns and disrupts its analysis? What seems to be taken for granted in this entire discussion is precisely the opposition between infinite and finite, face and form, transcendent and immanent, uprootedness and rootedness, an opposition that seems to undergo slippage when Levinas states that the face, "stripped of its form," and hence in all its nakedness, is "frozen" (*supra*). Has the shivering of this nakedness, this destitution, really been understood when one forces it into the aforementioned oppositions and clings to the alternative: "either swallowed up by context like a thing, or without context, hence a person"? In other words, either *en soi* or *pour soi*, either mundane or transcendent, either visible form or 'invisible' face—oppositions all of which Sartre made already and which, despite all of his criticism of Sartre, seem also to govern Levinas's definition of the Other. But does the Other's destitution allow itself to be forced into these oppositions? What if this destitution would consist of the Other being stuck with something that he can neither get free of nor dissolve into? Is that not, for example, the relation one has with one's 'ground,' in its literal or metaphorical sense—the ground, for instance, of one's history, or of one's culture or one's personal life? Was it not Levinas himself who said that "the great experiences of our life have properly speaking never been lived [*vécu*]" (*CP*, 68), and is it not exactly this inability to fully live these moments that gives them, for every one of us, a surplus of meaning? Is it not precisely this inability to work through moments that for others perhaps were insignificant, since they could work through them; is it not precisely this inability to forget, this recollection *despite ourselves*, that singularizes us? Is it not this, this unassimilable strangeness, that makes us different from trees and from things, but also from one another?

What I am suggesting, then, is that there is a nakedness that cannot be thought if one adheres to the opposition between face and form, finite and infinite. The nakedness of a being that is attached to 'something' that *it cannot do away with nor even less have access to*.[49] Such a being is naked in the double sense of having not enough 'form' to clothe itself in, and yet too much 'form' not to notice its nakedness. Of course, Levinas is correct when he draws our attention to the violence involved in fully clothing a person with that 'form' that he presents to us, and he deserves praise for warning us of the temptation to let the Other be absorbed and determined by the functional, everyday context in which we meet him. But in averting this danger, he seems to have made an overcorrection, one that consists in fully detaching the person's dignity from this 'form' or context and hence reducing his nakedness to only the first of the two senses previously mentioned. To make the dignity of the Other depend on this "visitation" or on this "revelation of the other . . . in the gaze of man aiming at a man precisely as abstract man, *disengaged from all culture*" (*CP*, 101) means perhaps that one ascribes, unwittingly and with the best of intentions, a dignity to the Other that ignores his true destitution, and the full extent of his nakedness. Might it not be that the true nakedness of the Other has less to do with his being disengaged from all culture, all context, all form, and more to do with his being engaged in it in such a way that the engagement never renders its secret to him? Is not the Other not only an Other to me, but also someone who owes his 'own' alterity to some 'Thing' that remains 'other' to him and yet singularizes him at the same time?

In other words, perhaps the Other is, *like myself*, primarily a "stranger," not because he is without those roots that I possess but because we are both attached to 'something' that is too close to leave us indifferent, but not close enough to be called our possession. Is it not this structure that makes us similar to one another at the very moment when it distinguishes us? But the Other would then be decentered *like me*. And yet he would be an Other precisely because that vague debt that he must discharge is still not 'vague' enough to let it coincide with mine. And is that not the reason he 'bears' a name—in the sense that connotes an *effort*—that is different from mine? Where is the Other more naked than in his name—a name that he does not possess, but has received; a name that he does not coincide with, but which can neither leave him indifferent; a name that summons him to life, but that also will survive him? In other words, what I am suggesting here, and will have to further develop elsewhere, is that one misconstrues the Other's ethical dignity when one thinks of it in terms of the opposition between a face that is a "living present" and a form that sucks the life out of that present and "congeals" it (*TI,* 66). The dignity and destitution of the Other do not have to be thought of on the basis of that face that speaks and in which "the revealer" "coincides" with "the revealed" (*TI,* 67). The destitution of the Other seems rather to reside in the fact that he is neither that presence of the face nor that absence of form, but someone caught in a tension between face and form that must be thought of in such a way that they *precede* this opposition—which, ultimately, is the opposition between exteriority and interiority, infinity and totality.

To work this out would require, among other things, a different ontology than the one with which Levinas is arguing, whose traces, despite all of the criticism, he still carries with him. And perhaps the problem of the name could point the way to this new ontology. For a being who bears a name cannot be grasped in the categories of *pour soi, en soi,* and *pour autrui* that Levinas provides with an ethical meaning. The name to which someone is attached *without the meaning of this attachment ever being clear to the person* might itself be an example of that tension that seems to precede the opposition between face and form. To have a name is to be-in-the-world by being, first and foremost, "present" to "something" in the world—a certain sound, a privileged signifier—which is nearby but, at the same time, at a distance. To have a name is, in this way, an example of all those forms of *en soi pour soi* where the subject is already attached to something even before it could have chosen it, and which, for that reason, precedes the opposition between *en soi* and *pour soi.*[50] But this is a privileged example because the name, like the

Good for Levinas, is not sacred but holy. There is something about the name which, like the Good, turns me away from itself and directs me toward others. And ethics must be about this turning away, this *metanoia*. Yet there is also something about the name that escapes this turning and cannot be consoled by it: that which escapes discourse, punctuating it with a silence that no word can break. I think it is not only a mistake to try and force that silence by naming it with a word that one cannot not hear and—an important qualification—by making that word do ethical work. I think it is also dangerous because one will then run the risk of closing off the only source from which we could draw in an attempt to extinguish the flames of that fire which is slowly but steadily burning away everything in us that points to the possibility of a common humanity that would not need to pay the price of universality to avoid the folly of blind particularity.

Notes

1. A first Dutch version of this text appeared in *Tijdschrift voor Filosofie* 57, no. 4 (1995). I wish to thank Dale Kidd for his help in translating this text. This work has been supported by the Belgian National Fund for Scientific Research.

2. This is an ironical reference to a Dutch book I published in 1990 on Foucault's use of quotation marks (such as in "human 'sciences'"), and which was recently translated as: *Michel Foucault: Genealogy as Critique* (London: Verso, 1995). On Heidegger's quotation marks, see Jacques Derrida, *De l'esprit: Heidegger et la question* (Paris: Éditions Galilée, 1987).

3. Cf. Jacques Lacan's intervention in the discussion following Foucault's "What is an Author?": "structuralism or not, it seems to me it is nowhere a question, in the field vaguely determined by that label, of the negation of the subject. It is a question of the dependence of the subject, which is quite different. . . ." (*Bulletin de la Société française de Philosophie* 64 (1969): 104).

4. For both of the following questions, which were inspired by Foucault's work, and which have to do with the transition from an 'archaeological' to a 'genealogical' approach, see my "Fascination with Foucault: Object and Desire of an Archaeology of Our Knowledge," *Angelaki* 1, no. 3 (1994): 113–18, in which I turn the idea of decentering elaborated here against a rather common fascination for Foucault's work

5. An expression that comes up regularly in Lyotard's more recent work. Cf. the references in my, "Dissensus Communis: How to Remain Silent after Lyotard,"in *Dissensus Communis: Between Ethics and Politics*, eds. Philippe Van Haute and Peg Birmingham (Kampen: Kok Pharos, 1995), pp. 7–30. (The considerations about 'silence' that follow are intended as a provisional development of the problematic presented there.)

6. For example, Emmanuel Levinas, *TA/TO* and *DE/EE*.

7. Jean-François, "Grundlagenkrise," *Neue Hefte für Philosophie* (1986): 1–33.

8. Cf. the title of the penultimate chapter of his controversial *The Philosophical Discourse of Modernity: Twelve Lectures*, translated by Frederick Lawrence (Cambridge: MIT, 1990): "An Alternative Way out of the Philosophy of the Subject: Communicative versus Subject-Centred Reason."

9. In any case, much longer than is possible here—a promissory note that, I hope, will incur the clemency of those who will object, with some irritation, that many of the important Levinasian themes (the *il y a*, the third person, justice, etc.) are not discussed here. One must begin somewhere.

10. I am citing the brochure for the symposium, "Interpretaties van subjectiviteit" ["Interpretations of Subjectivity"], where this text was first presented (University of Amsterdam, April 1995).

11. Levinas calls the word "God" the "first word" in, among other places, "Language and Proximity," *CP,* 125–26. All italics found in references to Levinas's texts are my own.

12. On this distinction, cf. Dieter Henrich's brilliant piece: "Ethik der Autonomie," *Selbstverhältnisse* (Stuttgart: Reclam, 1982,) p. 14 and *passim*.

13. Jean-François Lyotard, "Levinas' Logic," in *The Lyotard Reader*, edited by Andrew Benjamin (Oxford: Blackwell, 1989), p. 297.

14. For a perspicuous overview, cf. Dieter Henrich, *Selbstverhältnisse.*

15. Jürgen Habermas, "Morality and Ethical Life," in *Moral Consciousness and Communicative Action,* translated by C. Lenhardt and S.W. Nicholsen (Cambridge: MIT, 1990), p. 197 and cf. p. 66.

16. Jean-François Lyotard, *The Differend: Phrases in Dispute*, translated by Geroges Van Den Abbeele (Manchster: Manchester University Press, 1988), nr. 176 (I will henceforth refer to this work as *"D,"* followed by the number of the paragraph being cited). Habermas is not mentioned in this passage, but he is clearly the target.

17. Jürgen Habermas, *Moral Consciousness and Communicative Action,* pp. 197–98. Habermas sees here a possibility of working Kant's *Faktum der Vernunft* into communicative theory—clearly this implies a distancing from Kant that does not contradict the symmetry noted here, but qualifies it to a significant extent.

18. Cf. the very title of Levinas's collection *Humanisme de l'autre homme* (Paris: Fata Morgana, 1972); cf. also *OB,* 128 (ordinary humanism is "not human enough"). For his part, Lyotard discusses humanism in *The Inhuman: Reflections on Time*, translated by Geoffrey Bennington and Rachel Bowlby (Cambridge: Polity Press, 1991).

19. Besides the work just mentioned, cf. especially *Lectures d'enfance* (Paris: Éditions Galilée, 1991), specifically the exordium on the idea of "infancy," and *Moralités postmodernes* (Paris: Éditions Galilée, 1993).

20. Jean-François Lyotard, "The Grip," in *Political Writings*, translated by Bill Readings and Kevin Paul Geiman (Minneapolis: University of Minnesota Press, 1993), pp. 148–58. Lyotard refers here to the etymological origin of "mancipium": "*Manceps* is the person who takes hold, in the sense of possession or appropriation. And *mancipium* refers to this gesture of taking hold. . . . We are held by the grasp of others since childhood, yet our childhood does not cease to exercise its *mancipium* even when we imagine ourselves to be emancipated. . . . We are born before we are born to ourselves. And thus we are born of others, but also born to others . . . subjected to their *mancipium* which they themselves do not comprehend. For they are themselves children. . . ." (pp. 148–49 *partim*).

21. I have tried elsewhere to explain the price of this restriction and why, in this way, one makes it too easy on oneself, overlooking the real problem of the *so-called* relativism of Habermas' opponents (Foucault, Heidegger, etc.): "Habermas on Heidegger and Foucault: Meaning and Validity in *The Philosophical Discourse of Modernity*," *Radical Philosophy* 61 (1992): 15–22; "Transcultural Vibrations," *Ethical Perspectives* 1, no. 2 (1994): 89–100, esp. 94–95.

22. For Lyotard, a differend, as explained elsewhere ("Dissensus Communis," *supra* note 4), is a dispute between two parties that cannot be settled for lack of a common idiom or, I would add in light of Lyotard's recent writings, for lack of any idiom *at all*—a lack of which the assertion "it is like this because it is like this" seems to be a symptom.

23. Lyotard, "Levinas' Logic," *The Levinas Reader*, 307.

24. *D* nr. 206 (cf. nrs. 144, 145, 162, 164 . . .).

25. The characterization of Levinas's ethics as 'postmodern,' introduced by Marc-Alain Ouaknin in his rather facile *Méditations Erotiques. Essai sur Emmanuel Levinas* (Paris: Éditions Balland, 1992) and taken over by Z. Bauman in his *Postmodern Ethics* (Oxford, Blackwell, 1995), for example, 84 is, I believe, profoundly misleading. Surely one is doing an injustice by painting black perhaps the only cow that stands out in the night of our present time.

26. Levinas would have no problem with this qualification—cf. for instance *TI*, 210: "In positing the relation with the Other as ethical, one surmounts a difficulty that would be inevitable if, *contrary to Descartes*, philosophy started from a *cogito* that would posit itself absolutely independently of the Other. For the Cartesian *cogito* is discovered, at the end of the Third Meditation, to be supported on the certitude of the divine existence qua *infinite, by relation to which the finitude of the cogito, or the doubt, is posited and conceivable*. This finitude could not be determined without recourse to the infinite, *as is the case in the moderns*. . . ." Cf. also Derrida: "But by the force of a movement proper to Levinas, he accepts this extreme 'modern' audacity only to redirect it toward an infinitism that this audacity itself must suppose, according to himself; and the form of this infinitism is often quite classical, pre-Kantian rather than Hegelian" (*Writing and Difference*, translated by Alan Bass [Chicago: The University of Chicago Press, 1978], p. 104.

27. An expression that crops up regularly in *OB* and that, interestingly enough, also gives the title to a brief article in Lyotard's *Moralités postmodernes* (chapter 12).

28. Philippe Van Haute, "'Fatal Attraction': Jean Laplanche on Sexuality, Subjectivity, and Singularity in the Work of Sigmund Freud," in *Radical Philosophy* 73 (1995): 5–12, specifically nr. 73. In his conclusion, the author adopts the terminology from the article mentioned in note 4, and thus indirectly poses the problem of whether it is correct to consider his analysis as an ontic filling of an ontological base structure (e.g., note 20, earlier). But even if he would not object to his analyses being used as support for an ontological base structure *that Levinas never takes account of*, one might still expect Levinas to ask if every enigma refers back to the sexual/erotic enigma described by Van Haute, and if there is not an asymmetry between that register and the register of the Infinite that provokes metaphysical Desire.

29. In this and the following sentence, I refer to a number of ideas from Lacan's important seventh seminar: *L'ethique de la psychanalyse (1959–1960)*, especially 361—"tragique"—and *passim*). What Lacan means by *"ne pas céder sur son désir"* is explained, although with other (not insignificant) accents, in Rudolf Bernet, "Le sujet devant la loi (Lacan et Kant)," and Paul Moyaert, "Sur la sublimation chez Lacan: Quelques remarques," both in *La pensée de Jacques Lacan: Questions historiques, Problèmes théoriques*, eds. Steve G. Lofts and Paul Moyaert (Louvain/Paris: Editions Peeters), pp. 23–44, 125–146. In this seminar, Lacan repeatedly uses words such as *graviter* or *tourner autour de* ("gravitate around") to indicate our (decentered) position with respect to *das Ding* (*Sé VII*, 90/72, 93–94/77 . . .).

30. For this expression, see Jacob Rogozinski's excellent "Vers une éthique du différend," in *Enlightenments: Encounters between Critical Theory and Contemporary French Thought*, eds. H. Kunneman and H. De Vries (Kampen: Kok Pharos, 1993, pp. 92–119, especially p. 102.

31. For a lucid presentation of the way this link is severed in Lacan and Freud see Paul Moyaert, *Ethiek en sublimatie: Over de ethiek van de psychoanalyse van Jacques Lacan* (Kampen: SUN, 1993), pp. 92–119.

32. *TI*, 198: "The Other is the sole being I can wish to kill."

33. *CP*, 72: "To the idea of the infinite only an extravagant response is possible. There has to be a 'thought' that understands more than it understands . . . a 'thought' which, in this sense, could go beyond its death. . . . To go beyond one's death is to sacrifice oneself. The response to the enigma's summons is the generosity of sacrifice outside the known and the unknown, *without calculation, for going on to infinity. . . .* I approach the infinite *by sacrificing myself. Sacrifice is the norm and the criterion of the approach. . . .*"—a train of thought that is rigorously taken up in *OB* (1974) but, in light of the previous citation, in a way that is not completely foreign to the framework of *TI* (1961). But the readers of Levinas who see a *caesura* between *TI* and *OB* will, of course, disagree. They should, perhaps, reconsider.

34. It is the hesitation before this murder that, for Levinas, has hindered the development of a pluralistic ontology. But killing Parmenides means primarily the

overthrow of ontology as *prima philosophia*, and henceforth deriving it from ethics. This is the very project of *TI*, which thus can be read as "totality *or* infinity": Only the exteriority of infinity can bring a pluralism into being and prevent it from closing into the totality which, for Levinas, it would become if left to the devices of ontology. For this reason, one might use the following adage to describe Levinas's metaphysics: "*bonum et dispersum convertuntur*" (cf. e.g., "The social relation engenders this surplus of the Good over being, multiplicity over the One" (*TI*, 292).

35. *OB*, 128: "The impossibility of escaping God, the adventure of Jonas, indicates that God is at least here not a value among values. . . . The impossibility of escaping God lies in the depths of myself as a self, as an absolute passivity . . . [as] the impossibility of slipping away . . . the birth . . . of a 'being able to die' *subject to sacrifice.*" The reader will perhaps recall the quotation in note 33.

36. Ethics, for Levinas, is a penetration (*OB*, 49: "one-penetrated-by-the-other") but, according to his recurrent formula, "*before* eros" (e.g., *OB*, 192 n 27). A penetration, then, without the consolation nor even the fantasm of union, whose consequence is that the subject penetrated becomes an ever wider "opening" ("*ouverture*") that can never contain or encompass what is always already inside without being absorbed by it, an opening that seems rather to be a hole through which interiority continually discharges itself: "It is always to empty oneself anew of oneself, to absolve oneself, like in a hemophiliac's hemorrhage" (*OB*, 92)—a "hemorrhage" that already shows that Levinas, as we shall indicate later, is ethicizing the Sartrian universe all the while using Sartre's own concepts and metaphors.

37. Levinas, *EI*, 121.

38. These terms are standard vocabulary in *OB*. They can be found on almost any page.

39. Jean-Paul Sartre, *Being and Nothingness: An Essay on Phenomenological Ontology,* translated by Hazel E. Barnes (New York: Philosophical Library Inc., 1956), especially Part 3: "Being-for-Others."

40. Emmanuel Levinas, "Transcendance et Hauteur," *Bulletin de la Société Française de Philosophie* 54, no. 3 (1962): 110.

41. Sartre, *Being and Nothingness*, p. 412n: "These considerations do not exclude the possibility of an ethics of deliverance and salvation. But this can be achieved only after a radical conversion which we cannot discuss here." *OB* should be read as one long description of this process of conversion whose central—and never argued—premise would not have satisfied Sartre: the idea that the wound which the Other's appeal not so much brands me with, but burns me with again, has a chastening effect.

42. Emmanuel Levinas, "Signature," *DL*, 326. (This version of "Signature" is not included in *DF*.)

43. Emmauel Levinas, "Un Dieu Homme?" in *Entre Nous: Essais sur le penser-à l'autre* (Paris: Grasset, 1991), p. 73.

44. Ibid.

45. On the distinction between an ethical and a real resistance, see Emmanuel Levinas, "Freedom and Command," *CP,* 15–23; and *TI,* e.g., 199; *OB,* 198 n2.

46. Here I have altered the English translation that reads "paralyzed" for «*transi dans sa nudité*» (*Humanisme de l'autre homme,* 52). In preferring "frozen" to "paralyzed," I am following Adriaan Peperzak in his annotated Dutch translation of *Humanisme, Humanisme van de andere mens* (Kampen/Kapellen: Koko Agora/DNB/Pelckmans, 1990), 78, which paraphrases «*transi*» as "shivering with cold"). The change is not unimportant given the point I shall be making.

47. "Transcendance et Hauteur," *Bulletin de la Société Française de Philosophie,* 97.

48. Note that, according to Levinas, Christianity can for essential reasons only make an incomplete contribution to this universality: "If Europe had been spiritually uprooted by Christianity, as Simone Weil complains, the evil would not be great. And it is not always the idylls that have been destroyed by Europe's penetration of the world . . . *but is Europe's unhappiness not due to the fact that Christianity did not sufficiently uproot it?*" (*DF,* 137). Though I hope to have made it clear from which standpoint I am myself arguing—but is it not a surprising alliance?—in light of this quotation (which is in no sense a *hapax*) one can only wonder at the success with which Levinas's ethics has been assimilated by certain moral theologians from the *Catholic* world (for a noteworthy exception: U. Dhondt, "Ethics, History, Religion: The Limits of the Philosophy of Levinas," in *Eros and Eris: Contributions to a Hermeneutical Phenomenology,* Liber Amicorum for Adriaan Peperzak, eds. P. J. M. Van Tongeren *et al.* [Dordrecht: Kluwer, 1992], pp. 273–80).

49. Cf. the introduction to this article, where these two moments were used in defining the concept 'decentering.' As soon as one of these moments is relinquished, problems arise. Nationalism, for instance, rests on a misrecognition of this *double* structure of 'decentering' in that it claims to *have access to* that 'something' to which a nation is irrevocably 'attached.' In other words, the mistake is that it purports to be able to specify what I called in this article's introduction the 'vague' debt. Nationalism pretends to know what 'our' debt to the nation consists of. On the other hand, the stress on the *two* moments in decentering allows one, in principle, to steer away from an extreme cosmopolitan/universalistic correction to the mistake of nationalism/particularism, an overcorrection that consists of the claim that there is no singular attachment as such (and hence gives up decentering, 'in-fantia' as such). In other words, 'decentering' seems to point the way to an alternative position that is neither universalistic nor particularistic in the traditional sense. I shall leave it for another occasion to spell out the political consequences of this 'third' way.

50. The endo-ontology that Merleau-Ponty was working on in *The Visible and the Invisible* can provide scant inspiration here. It is insensitive to the problem of singularity that we have indicated in the preceding lines. The thought of the chiasm and the polymorphism of vertical Being ["*l'être brut*"] can explain why we do not live in

a *different* world, but seems able to conclude from this only that we live in the *same* world because it turns in the direction of an asubjective phenomenology, for which "the I-other problem is a *Western* problem." See *Maurice* Merleau-Ponty, *Le visible et l'invisible suivi de notes de travail* (Paris: Gallimard, 1964), p. 274. Cf. my article "The Untouchable: Merleau-Ponty's Last Subject," forthcoming.

Contributors

Paul-Laurent Assoun teaches philosophy in France. He is the director of the collection "Philosophie d'aujourd'hui" for Presses Universitaires de France. He has published many books and articles on psychoanalysis, social practice, and philosophy. Some of the titles include *Freud, la philosophie et les philosophes*; *Marx et la répétition historique*; *Le Entendement Freudian*; and *Freud et Wittgenstein*.

Donna Brody obtained her doctorate of philosophy at the University of Essex. Her interests include the philosophy of Emmauel Levinas, psychoanalytic thought, the problem of alterity, and the phenomenological tradition, especially Martin Heidegger. An essay entitled "Emmanuel Levinas: The Logic of Ethical Ambiguity," appeared in *Research in Phenomenology* in 1994.

Tina Chanter teaches philosophy at the University of Memphis. She has published many articles on Hegel, Heidegger and Levinas, and Irigaray and feminist philosophy. Her most recent publication is *The Ethics of Eros: Irigaray's Rewriting of the Philosopher's*.

Drucilla Cornell is a professor in the School of Law at Rutgers. She is the author of *Beyond Accommodation*; *The Philosophy of the Limit* and is co-editor of *Deconstruction and the Possibility of Justice* and *Hegel and Legal Theory*. She has, in addition, published numerous articles on philosophy, feminism, and legal theory.

Angela Esterhammer is Director of the Program in Comparative Literature at the University of Western Ontario. She has published *Creating States: Studies in the Performative Language of Minton & William Blake* (1994) and the first English translation of Ranier Maria Rilke's *Two Stories of Prague* (1994).

Hans-Dieter Gondek is a philosopher, psychologist, and sociologist in Germany. He is currently fellow of the German Society for the Advancement of Scientific Research and a lecturer in philosophy at the Universities of Bochum and Bremen. He is currently working on a monograph on the subject of "Ethics and Psychoanalysis: After Heidegger and Lacan." Translated titles of some of his most significant publications are *Anxiety—Imagination—Language: Freud Kant Lacan*, "Anxiety as 'that which does not falsify,'" "Responsibility for the Other and Justice for the Third Party," "Derrida's Right to Philosophy," and "Law, Justice, and Responsibility in Levinas." He also is co-editor of *Ethics and Psychoanalysis. From the Categorical Imperative to the Law of Desire: Kant and Lacan.*

Sarah Harasym has a Ph.D. in English literature from the University of Alberta (Canada) and is earning a Ph.D. in philosophy at Duquesne University. She has edited also Gayatri Chakravorty Spivak's *The Post-Colonial Critic: Interviews, Strategies, Dialogue.*

Dianah Leigh Jackson is completing her doctorate in French literature at the University of Minnesota. Ms. Jackson's research interests lie primarily in the eighteenth century, including representation of the body in medical and philosophical discourses.

Alain Juranville is an eminent French philosopher. He has published extensively on philosophy. *Lacan et la philosophie* (1984) and *Physique de Nietzsche* (1973) are two of his significant works. He currently teaches philosophy at the Universite de Rennes I.

Philippe Van Haute studied philosophy in Leuven, Strasbourg, and Paris. He earned his Ph.D. at the University of Leuven with a study on the influence of Heidegger and Kojève on the work of Jacques Lacan. He was awarded the first Van Helsdingen prize of the Foundation for Philosophy and Psychiatry (the Netherlands) for his book on *Philosophy and Psychoanalysis. The Imaginary and the Symbolic in the Work of Jacques Lacan* (Peeters, Leuven, 1990). He has published extensively on the relation between philosophy and psychoanalysis and on political philosophy. He is a member of the Belgian School for Psychoanalysis. Since 1994 he has been a professor of philosophical anthropology at the University of Nijmegen (the Netherlands).

Denise Merkle teaches translation into English and terminology at the Université de Moncton (Canada). She is completing her doctorate in French studies (Victorian translations of select novels of Flaubert and Zola) at Queen's University (Canada).

Rudi Visker is a senior researcher of the Belgian Fund for Scientific Research. He teaches phenomenology and contemporary philosophy at the Institute of Philosophy of the Catholic University of Leuven. He is the author of *Michel Foucault: Geneology as Critique* (Verso, 1995) and has written extensively on contemporary Continental philosophy.

Index

A

abjection, 154, 159
alienation, 25, 31–33, 40, 45, 46, 91
alterity, ix, xi, xii, 16, 57, 60, 66, 67, 70, 79–88, 90–92, 94–97, 141–43, 180, 199, 203
Antigone, xi, xii, 103, 113, 115
Antigone, 106, 111
anti-Semitism, 25, 26
aphanisis, 40
Aristotle, 74, 103, 124, 127, 130, 134
até, 114, 115
aufheben, 3, 70

B

the beautiful, xii, 102, 103, 105, 110, 115, 116
Being and Time, 7, 16, 63
being-in-the-world, 10
Bernasconi, Robert, 30
bien-dire, 117, 118
Blanchot, Maurice, 6, 24, 88, 89
body-image, 10–12
Borch-Jacobsen, Mikkel, 2
Brentano, 59
Butler, Judith, 180

C

Cartesian, 91
castration, 91
categorical imperative, 140–41, 156, 186
catharsis, 115, 116
cause, 5, 28
Chasseguet-Smirgel, Janine, 26
Cezanne, 117
contra-Hegelian, 88
cogito, x, 2, 5–8, 10, 12, 29–31, 34–36, 38, 41, 45, 88

D

Daniel, Arnaud, 153
death drive, 41, 108, 113
Derrida, xiii, 8, 9, 15, 18, 30, 141, 143, 163, 165–74, 176, 177
Descartes, x, 3–6, 10, 13, 15, 29, 31, 35, 36, 124, 132, 134
desire, ix–xii, 11, 25, 26, 33, 37, 39, 40, 43, 46, 75, 85–87, 90–93, 96, 97, 103, 106, 109, 113, 114, 116, 121, 122, 127, 132, 135, 145, 153, 159, 161, 164, 169
Dichtung, 117
differance, 172–175